HONDA

350-550cc FOURS • 1972-1978
SERVICE • REPAIR • PERFORMANCE

ERIC JORGENSEN
Editor

JEFF ROBINSON
Publisher

CLYMER PUBLICATIONS

World's largest publisher of books devoted exclusively to automobiles and motorcycles.

12860 MUSCATINE STREET • P.O. BOX 20 • ARLETA, CALIFORNIA 91331

FIRST EDITION
First Printing November, 1972
Second Printing April, 1973
Third Printing October, 1973
Fourth Printing June, 1974

SECOND EDITION
Revised to include 1973-1974 models
First Printing September, 1974

THIRD EDITION
Revised to include 1975-1976 models
First Printing July, 1976

FOURTH EDITION
Revised by Brick Price to include 1977 models
First Printing May, 1977
Second Printing September, 1977

FIFTH EDITION
Revised and expanded coverage
First Printing September, 1978

Printed in U.S.A.

ISBN: 0-89287-287-X

MOTORCYCLE INDUSTRY COUNCIL

Performance Improvement chapter by Chris Bunch

•

Cover photo by Mike Brown — Visual Imagery, Los Angeles, California

•

Technical assistance by Kolbe Honda Sales/ Service, Woodland Hills, California

CONTENTS

QUICK REFERENCE DATA

BREAKER POINTS

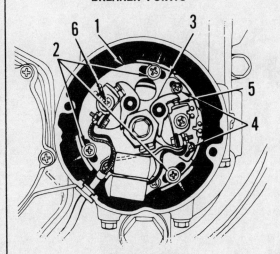

TIMING MARKS

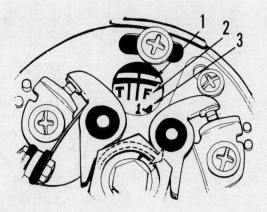

1. Contact breaker base plate
2. Base plate locking screws
3. Contact breaker right base plate
4. Right base plate locking screws
5. 2-3 cylinder breaker points
6. 1-4 cylinder breaker points

1. Index mark
2. "F" (fire) mark
3. Cylinder number
   1-4 cylinder shown; 2-3 180° opposite

TUNE-UP SPECIFICATIONS

	CB350/400	CB500/550
Valve clearance (cold)		
Intake	0.002 in. (0.05mm)	0.002 in. (0.05mm)
Exhaust	0.002 in. (0.05mm)	0.003 in. (0.08mm)
Spark plug type	NGK D8ESL	NGK D7ES
	ND X24ES	ND X22ES
	Bosch X290 T-17	Bosch X270 T-17
	Champion A8Y-MC	Champion A7Y-MC
Spark plug gap	0.024-0.028 in. (0.6-0.7mm)	0.024-0.028 in. (0.6-0.7mm)
Breaker point gap	0.012-0.016 in. (0.3-0.4mm)	0.012-0.016 in. (0.3-0.4mm)
Breaker point dwell	92-98° (2 cyl. scale) 46-49° (4 cyl. scale)	92-98° (2 cyl. scale) 46-49° (4 cyl. scale)
Ignition timing	Static—see text	Static—see text
Idle speed	1,200 rpm	1,000 rpm

RECOMMENDED FUEL AND LUBRICANTS

Item	Capacity	Type
Engine oil		
All temperatures	——	SAE 10W-40 or 20W-50, SE
Above 59°	——	SAE 30W, SE
32-59°	——	SAE 20W or 20W, SE
Below 32°	——	SAE 10W, SE
CB350/400	3.7 U.S. qt. (3.5 liters)	——
CB500/550	3.2 U.S. qt. (3.0 liters)	——
Fork oil (per tube)		
CB350	4.2 oz. (125cc)	ATF
CB400	5.6-5.8 oz. (160-165cc)	SAE 10W-30
CB500	5.4 oz. (155cc)	SAE 10W-30
CB550	6.5 oz. (190cc)	ATF
Swing arm bushing	As needed	Lithium grease
Drive chain	As needed	SAE 30W or special chain lube
Brake fluid	To "Full" mark	DOT-3 or J-1703
Fuel		
CB350	3.2 U.S. gal. (12 liters) total	86 octane (pump)
	0.5 U.S. gal. (2 liters) reserve	91 octane (research)
CB400	3.7 U.S. gal. (14 liters) total	86 octane (pump)
	0.8 U.S. gal. (3 liters) reserve	91 octane (research)
CB500/550	3.7 U.S. gal. (12 liters) total	86 octane (pump)
	1.1 U.S. gal. (4 liters) reserve	91 octane (research)

TIGHTENING TORQUES

Tightening Point	ft.-lb.	cm-kg
Steering stem nut	56-87	800-1,200
Fork top bridge to front forks	13-17	180-230
Handlebar holder	13-17	180-230
Front fork bottom bridge to front forks	13-17	180-230
Spokes		
Front wheel	1.9-2.2	25-30
Rear wheel	1.5-1.9	20-25
Swing arm pivot bolt	40-51	550-700
Front axle nut	33-40	450-550
Front fork axle holder	13-17	180-230
Engine hanger bolt	22-29	300-400
Rear axle nut	58-72	800-1,000
Final driven sprocket	29-36	400-500
Brake arm	6-7	80-100
Front and rear brake torque links	13-17	180-230
Rear shocks	22-29	300-400
Foot pegs	33-40	450-550
Gear change pedal and kick arm	6-7	80-100

ADJUSTMENTS

Clutch lever free play	0.4-0.8 in. (10-20mm)
Rear brake pedal free play	0.8-1.2 in. (20-30mm)
Front brake lever free play	0.6-1.2 in. (15-30mm)
Throttle grip free play	10-15° of grip rotation

ELECTRICAL SYSTEM

Battery	12 volt, 12 ah
Fuse	15 amp
Replacement bulbs*	
Headlight	12V-40W/50W
Tail/stoplight	A4828
Turn signal light	A4527
Indicator lights	A72

*These are Stanley numbers but General Electric has SAE bulbs which are exact replacements.

TIRES

Item/Model	CB350/CB400	CB500	CB550
Front pressure	26 psi	26 psi	28 psi
Rear pressure (one rider)	28 psi	28 psi	28 psi
Rear pressure (two riders)	32 psi	32 psi	32 psi
Size, front	3.00 x 18	3.25 x 19	3.25 x 19
Size, rear	3.50 x 18	3.50 x 18	3.75 x 18

HONDA

350-550cc FOURS • 1972-1978

SERVICE • REPAIR • PERFORMANCE

CHAPTER ONE

GENERAL INFORMATION

This book provides maintenance and repair information for all CB350/400 and CB500/550 4-cylinder motorcycles.

Procedures common to different models are combined to avoid duplication. Read the following service hints to make the work as easy and pleasant as possible. Performing your own work can be an enjoyable and rewarding experience.

MANUAL ORGANIZATION

All dimensions and capacities are expressed in inch units familiar to U.S. mechanics as well as in metric units.

This chapter provides general information and specifications. See **Table 1**, at the end of the chapter. It also discusses equipment and tools useful both for preventive maintenance and troubleshooting.

Chapter Two explains all periodic lubrication and routine maintenance necessary to keep your bike running well. Chapter Two also includes recommended tune-up procedures, eliminating the need to constantly consult chapters on the various subassemblies.

Chapter Three provides methods and suggestions for quick and accurate diagnosis and repair of problems. Troubleshooting procedures discuss typical symptoms and logical methods to pinpoint the trouble.

Subsequent chapters describe specific systems such as the engine, transmission, and electrical system. Each chapter provides disassembly, repair, and assembly procedures in simple step-by-step form. If a repair is impractical for a home mechanic, it is so indicated. It is usually faster and less expensive to take such repairs to a dealer or competent repair shop. Specifications concerning a particular system are included at the end of the appropriate chapter.

Some of the procedures in this manual specify special tools. In all cases, the tool is illustrated either in actual use or alone. A well-equipped mechanic may find he can substitute similar tools already on hand or can fabricate his own.

The terms NOTE, CAUTION, and WARNING have specific meanings in this manual. A NOTE provides additional information to make a step or procedure easier or clearer. Disregarding a NOTE could cause inconvenience, but would not cause damage or personal injury.

A CAUTION emphasizes areas where equipment damage could result. Disregarding a CAUTION could cause permanent mechanical damage; however, personal injury is unlikely.

A WARNING emphasizes areas where personal injury or even death could result from negligence. Mechanical damage may also occur. WARNINGS are to be taken seriously. In some cases serious injury or death has been caused by mechanics who have disregarded similar warnings.

Throughout this manual keep in mind two conventions. "Front" refers to the front of the bike. The front of any component such as the engine is that end which faces toward the front of the bike. The left and right sides refer to a person sitting on the bike facing forward. For example, the shift lever is on the left side. These rules are simple, but even experienced mechanics occasionally become disoriented.

SERVICE HINTS

Most of the service procedures covered are straightforward and can be performed by anyone reasonably handy with tools. It is suggested, however, that you consider your own capabilities carefully before attempting any operation involving major disassembly of the engine.

Some operations, for example, require the use of a press. It would be wiser to have these performed by a shop equipped for such work, rather than to try to do the job yourself with makeshift equipment. Other procedures require precision measurements. Unless you have the skills and equipment required, it would be better to have a qualified repair shop make the measurements for you.

Repairs go much faster and easier if the bike is clean before you begin work. There are special cleaners for washing the engine and related parts. Just brush or spray on the cleaning solution, let it stand, then rinse it away with a garden hose. Clean all oily or greasy parts with cleaning solvent as you remove them.

> WARNING
> *Never use gasoline as a cleaning agent.*
> *It presents an extreme fire hazard. Be*
> *sure to work in a well-ventilated area*
> *when using cleaning solvent. Keep a fire*
> *extinguisher, rated for gasoline fires,*
> *handy at all times.*

Special tools are required for some repair procedures. These may be purchased at a dealer (or borrowed if you're on good terms with the service department) or may be fabricated by a mechanic or machinist, often at considerable savings.

Much of the labor charge for repairs made by dealers is for the removal and disassembly of other parts to reach the defective unit. It is frequently possible to perform the preliminary operations yourself and then take only the defective unit to the dealer for repair at considerable savings.

Once you have decided to tackle the job yourself, read the entire section in this manual which pertains to it, making sure you have identified the proper one. Study the illustrations and text until you have a good idea of what is involved in completing the job satisfactorily. If special tools are required, make arrangements to get them before you start. It is frustrating and time-consuming to get partly into a job and then be unable to complete it.

Simple wiring checks are easily made at home, but knowledge of electronics is almost a necessity for performing tests with complicated electronic testing gear.

During disassembly of parts keep a few general cautions in mind. Force is rarely needed to get things apart. If parts are a tight fit, for example, a magneto on a crankshaft, there is usually a tool designed to separate them. Never use a screwdriver to pry apart parts with machined surfaces such as crankcase halves and valve covers. You will mar the surface and end up with leaks.

Make diagrams wherever similar-appearing parts are found. For instance, case cover screws are often not the same length. You may think you can remember where everything came from — but mistakes are costly. There is also the possibility you may be sidetracked and not return to work for days or even weeks — in which interval, carefully laid out parts may have been disturbed.

Tag all similar internal parts for location and mark all mating parts for position. Record number and thickness of any shims as they are removed. Small parts such as bolts can be identified by placing them in plastic sandwich bags. Seal and label the bags with masking tape.

Wiring should be tagged with masking tape and marked as each wire is removed. Again, don't rely on memory alone.

Disconnect battery ground cable before working near electrical connections and before disconnecting wires. Never run the engine with the battery disconnected; the alternator could be seriously damaged.

Protect finished surfaces from physical damage or corrosion. Keep gasoline and brake fluid off painted surfaces.

Frozen or very tight bolts and screws can often be loosened by soaking with penetrating oil, then sharply striking the bolt head a few times with a hammer and punch (or screwdriver for screws). Avoid heat unless absolutely necessary, since it may melt, warp, or remove the temper from many parts.

Avoid flames or sparks when working near a charging battery or flammable liquids such as brake fluid or gasoline.

No parts, except those assembled with a press fit, require unusual force during assembly. If a part is hard to remove or install, find out why before proceeding.

Cover all openings after removing components to keep dirt, small tools, parts, etc., from falling in.

When assembling 2 parts, start all fasteners, then tighten evenly.

Clutch plates, wiring connections, and brake shoes and drums should be kept clean and free of grease and oil.

When assembling parts, be sure all shims and washers are replaced exactly as they came out.

Whenever a rotating part butts against a stationary part, look for a shim or washer. Use new gaskets if there is any doubt about the condition of old ones. Generally you should apply gasket cement to one mating surface only so the parts may be easily disassembled in the future. A thin coat of oil on gaskets helps them seal effectively.

Heavy grease can be used to hold small parts in place if they tend to fall out during assembly. However, keep grease and oil away from electrical components or brake shoes and drums.

High spots may be sanded off a piston with sandpaper, but emery cloth and oil do a much more professional job.

Carburetors are best cleaned by disassembling them and soaking the parts in a commercial carburetor cleaner. Never soak gaskets and rubber parts in these cleaners. Never use wire to clean out jets and air passages; they are easily damaged. Use compressed air to blow out the carburetor only if float has been removed first.

A baby bottle makes a good measuring device for adding oil to forks and transmissions. Get one that is graduated in ounces and cubic centimeters.

Take your time and do the job right. Don't forget that a newly rebuilt motorcycle engine must be broken in the same as a new one. Keep engine rpm within the limits given in your owner's manual when you get back on the road.

SAFETY FIRST

Professional motorcycle mechanics can work for years and never sustain a serious injury. If you observe a few rules of common sense and safety, you can enjoy many safe hours servicing your own machine. You could hurt yourself or damage the bike if you ignore these rules.

1. Never use gasoline as a cleaning solvent.

2. Never smoke or use a torch in the vicinity of flammable liquids such as cleaning solvent in open containers.

3. Never smoke or use a torch in an area where batteries are being charged. Highly explosive hydrogen gas is formed during the charging process.

4. If welding or brazing is required on the machine, remove the fuel tank to a safe distance, at least 50 feet away. Welding on gas tanks requires special safety procedures and must be performed only by someone skilled in the process.

5. Use the proper sized wrenches to avoid damage to nuts and injury to yourself.

6. When loosening a tight or stuck nut, be guided by what would happen if the wrench should slip. Protect yourself accordingly.

7. Keep your work area clean and uncluttered.

8. Wear safety goggles during all operations involving drilling, grinding, or use of a cold chisel.

9. Never use worn tools.

10. Keep a fire extinguisher handy and be sure it is rated for gasoline and electrical fires.

PARTS REPLACEMENT

Honda makes frequent changes during a model year; some minor, some relatively major. When you order parts from the dealer or other parts distributor, always order by engine and chassis number. Write the numbers down and carry them in your wallet. Compare new parts to old before purchasing them. If they are not alike, have the parts person explain the difference to you.

TOOLS

Tool Kit

Most new models are equipped with fairly complete tool kits. The kit is located in a large compartment under the seat.

These tools are satisfactory for most small jobs and emergency roadside repairs. See **Figure 1**.

Shop Tools

For proper servicing, you will need an assortment of ordinary handtools. As a minimum, these include:

1. Metric combination wrenches	7. Phillips screwdrivers
2. Metric sockets	8. Slot (common) screwdrivers
3. Plastic mallet	9. Feeler gauges
4. Small hammer	10. Spark plug gauge
5. Snap ring pliers	11. Spark plug wrench
6. Pliers	12. Dial indicator

Special tools necessary are shown in the chapters covering the particular repair in which they are used.

Electrical system servicing requires a voltmeter, ohmmeter or other device for determining continuity, and a hydrometer for battery equipped machines.

Advanced tune-up and troubleshooting procedures require a few more tools.

1. *Timing gauge* (**Figure 2**). By screwing this instrument into the spark plug hole, piston position may be determined. The tool shown costs about 20 dollars, and is available from larger dealers and mail order houses. Cheaper ones,

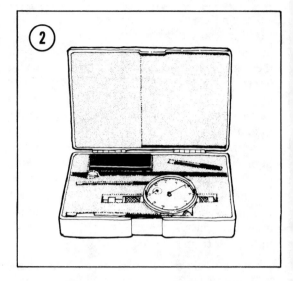

which utilize a vernier scale instead of a dial indicator, are also available. They are satisfactory, but are not quite so quick and easy to use.

2. *Hydrometer* (**Figure 3**). This instrument measures state of charge of the battery, and tells much about battery condition. Such an instrument is available at any auto parts store and through most larger mail order outlets. A satisfactory one costs less than 3 dollars.

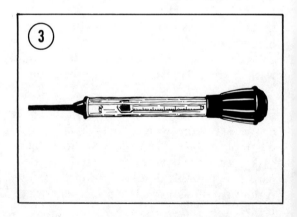

3. *Multimeter or VOM* (**Figure 4**). This instrument is invaluable for electrical system troubleshooting and service. A few of its functions may be duplicated by locally fabricated substitutes, but for the serious hobbyist, it is a must. Its uses are described in the applicable sections of this book. Prices start at around 10 dollars at electronics hobbyist stores and mail order outlets.

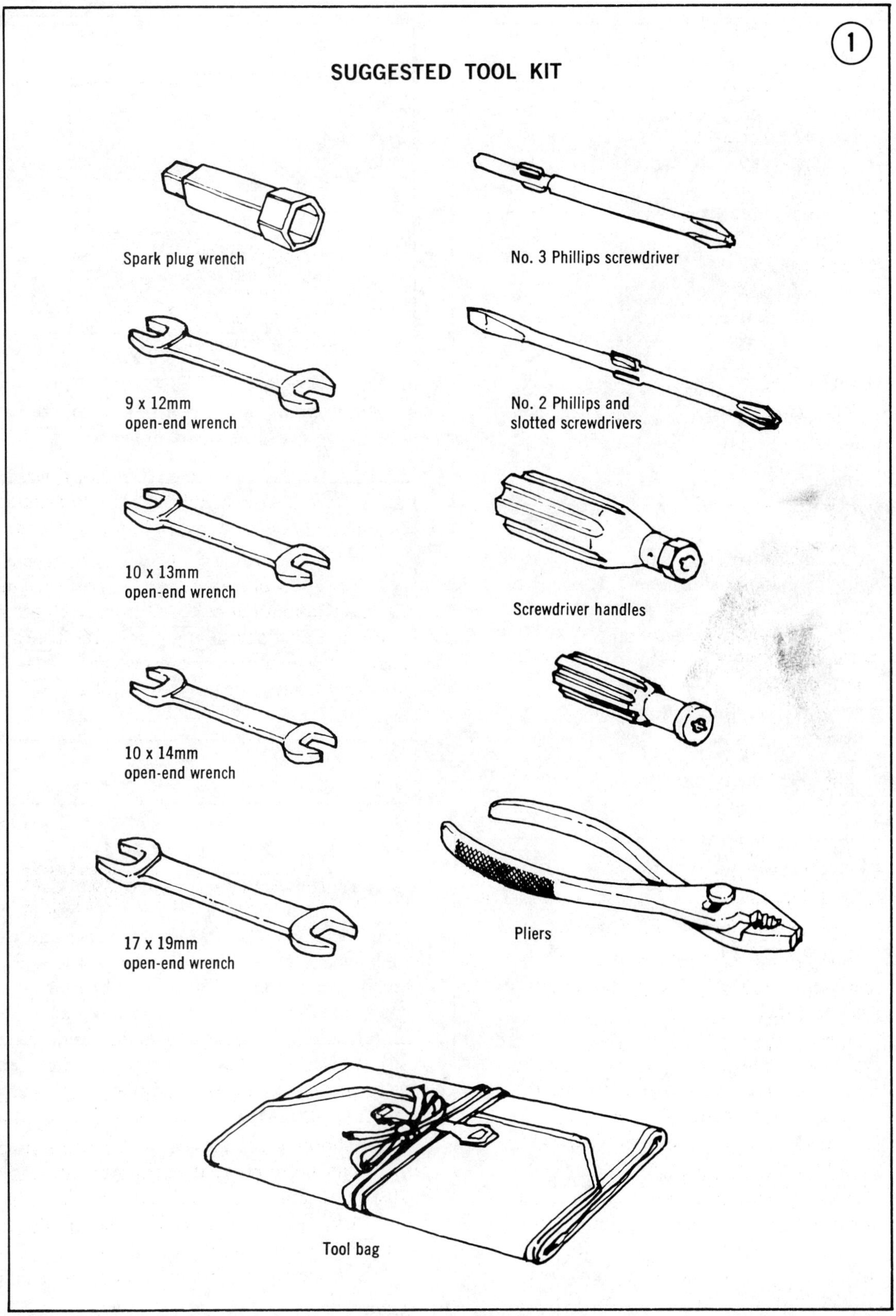

SUGGESTED TOOL KIT

Spark plug wrench

No. 3 Phillips screwdriver

9 x 12mm
open-end wrench

No. 2 Phillips and
slotted screwdrivers

10 x 13mm
open-end wrench

Screwdriver handles

10 x 14mm
open-end wrench

17 x 19mm
open-end wrench

Pliers

Tool bag

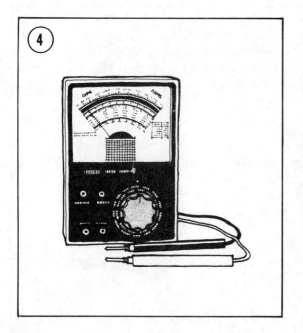

4. *Compression gauge* (**Figure 5**). An engine with low compression cannot be properly tuned and will not develop full power. A compression gauge measures engine compression. The one shown has a flexible stem, which enables it to reach cylinders where there is little clearance between the cylinder head and frame. Cheap ones start around 3 dollars, available at auto accessory stores or by mail order from large catalog order firms.

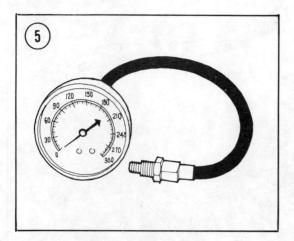

5. *Impact driver* (**Figure 6**). This tool makes removal of engine cover screws easy, and eliminates damaged screw slots. Good ones cost about 12 dollars at larger hardware stores.

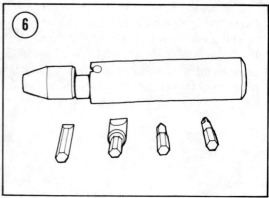

6. *Ignition gauge* (**Figure 7**). This tool measures point gap. It also has round wire gauges for measuring spark plug gap.

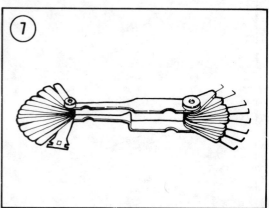

EXPENDABLE SUPPLIES

Certain expendable supplies are also required. These include grease, oil, gasket cement, wiping rags, cleaning solvent, and distilled water. Ask your dealer for the special locking compounds, silicone lubricants, and commerical chain lube products which make motorcycle maintenance simpler and easier. Solvent is available at most service stations and distilled water for the battery is available at most supermarkets.

SERIAL NUMBERS

You must know the model serial number for the sake of registration and when ordering special parts. These identification numbers are located in the same general area on all Honda models.

The engine number is on the crankcase between the front motor mount and frame.

The frame number is stamped on the steering head down-tube on the right-hand side. This same number is repeated on the central frame tube under the seat near the battery.

These numbers can be permanently recorded by placing a sheet of paper over the imprinted area and rubbing with the side of a pencil. Some motor vehicle registration offices will accept such evidence in lieu of inspecting the bike in person.

1

Table 1   GENERAL SPECIFICATIONS

	CB350	CB400
Dimensions		
Overall length	81.1 in. (2,060mm)	80.3 in. (2,040mm)
Overall width	30.1 in. (780mm)	27.8 in. (705mm)
Overall height	42.9 in. (1,090mm)	40.9 in. (1,040mm)
Wheelbase	53.3 in. (1,355mm)	53.3 in. (1,355mm)
Seat height	30.7 in. (780mm)	31.1 in. (790mm)
Foot peg height	11.8 in. (300mm)	13.0 in. (330mm)
Ground clearance	6.1 in. (155mm)	5.9 in. (150mm)
Dry weight	373 lb. (170 kg)	375 lb. (171 kg)
Engine		
Type	Air-cooled, 4-stroke, OHC engine	Air-cooled, 4-stroke, OHC engine
Cylinders	4-cylinders in-line	4-cylinders in-line
Bore and stroke	1.850 $\times$ 1.969 in. (47.0 $\times$ 50.0mm)	2.008 $\times$ 1.969 in. (51.0 $\times$ 50.0mm)
Displacement	21.1 cu. in. (347cc)	24.9 cu. in. (408cc)
Drive Train		
Clutch	Wet, multi-plate type	Wet, multi-plate type
Transmission	5-speed, constant mesh	6-speed, constant mesh
Gearshift pattern	Left foot return type	Left foot return type
Electrical		
Ignition	Battery and ignition coil	Battery and ignition coil
Starting system	Starting motor and kickstarter	Starting motor and kickstarter

	CB500	CB550
Dimensions		
Overall length	83.0 in. (2,105mm)	83.5 in. (2,120mm)
Overall width	32.5 in. (825mm)	32.5 in. (825mm)
Overall height	44.0 in. (1,117mm)	43.9 in. (1,115mm)
Wheelbase	55.5 in. (1,410mm)	55.3 in. (1,405mm)
Seat height	31.7 in. (805mm)	31.7 in. (805mm)
Foot peg height	12.4 in. (315mm)	12.4 in. (315mm)
Ground clearance	6.5 in. (165mm)	6.5 in. (165mm)
Dry weight	403.5 lb. (183 kg)	423.0 lb. (192 kg)
Engine		
Type	Air-cooled, 4-stroke, OHC engine	Air-cooled, 4-stroke, OHC engine
Cylinders	4-cylinders in-line	4-cylinders in-line
Bore and stroke	2.205 $\times$ 1.992 in. (56.0 $\times$ 50.6mm)	2.303 $\times$ 1.992 in. (58.5 $\times$ 50.6mm)
Displacement	30.38 cu. in. (498cc)	33.19 cu. in. (544cc)
Drive Train		
Clutch	Wet, multi-plate type	Wet, multi-plate type
Transmission	5-speed, constant mesh	5-speed, constant mesh
Gearshift pattern	Left foot return type	Left foot return type
Electrical		
Ignition	Battery and ignition coil	Battery and ignition coil
Starting system	Starting motor and kickstarter	Starting motor and kickstarter

CHAPTER TWO

PERIODIC MAINTENANCE
AND TUNE-UP

Regular maintenance is the best guarantee of a trouble-free motorcycle. An afternoon spent now, cleaning and adjusting your bike, can forestall costly mechanical problems in the future and unexpected breakdowns on the road.

This chapter explains all preventive maintenance, including engine tune-up, required for the Honda fours. Any owner with average mechanical ability can perform the procedures.

TOOLS

You will need the basic tools suggested in Chapter One. In addition, equipment required for a complete tune-up includes a static timing light, a strobe light, dwell tachometer, carburetor float gauge, sets of flat and round feeler gauges calibrated in millimeters, and a vacuum gauge set to balance the carburetors.

The only expensive item is the vacuum gauge set — about $30-75 — but a less expensive alternative is discussed in the fuel system chapter.

DAILY CHECKS

Before starting the engine for the first time each day, check the following.

Tire Pressures

1. For normal solo riding, inflate the front tire to 26 psi. Inflate the rear tire to 28 psi.

2. For normal double riding (with passenger), inflate the front tire to 26 psi and the rear tire to 32 psi.

3. For sustained high-speed riding, increase the tire pressures to 2 psi over normal.

4. Remove any embedded stones from the tires. Check each tire for bad cracks or cuts, and replace the tire if you find any (for the replacement procedures see Chapter Eight).

Front Brake Operation

1. Unscrew the top from the brake fluid reservoir on the handlebar and check the fluid level. If the reservoir is less than ½ full, add enough fluid to bring the level up to the line on the inside of the reservoir. Use brake fluid clearly marked DOT 3 or J-1703.

2. Pull the front brake lever. Check that it does not feel spongy and that the lever does not have too much travel.

3. With the gearbox in neutral and the front brake on, try to move the motorcycle back and forth, to check that the caliper pads are clamping the disc.

4. If the brake is spongy, or there is too much lever travel, bleed the brake hydraulic system (see *Front Brake System Bleeding* procedure, Chapter Eight). If caliper pads do not clamp the disc, see Chapter Eight.

Rear Brake Operation

1. Check the position of the rear brake pedal at rest. The top of the pedal should be slightly below the top of the front footpeg.

2. Hold a ruler vertical alongside the pedal, and push the pedal down by hand. The pedal should move ¾-1¼ in. (20-30mm). See **Figure 1**. The brake cam lever should then form an angle of 80-90° with the brake rod (**Figure 2**).

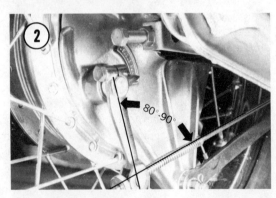

3. If brake pedal travel exceeds 1½ in. (40mm), adjust the linkage (see *Rear Brake Linkage Adjustment* procedure in this chapter).

4. If the angle between the brake cam lever and the brake rod exceeds 100° when the brake is applied, check the lining for wear (see Chapter Nine).

Lights and Horn

Check the following, with the engine running.
1. Pull the front brake lever and check that the brake light comes on.

2. Push the rear brake pedal, and check that the brake light comes on soon after depressing the pedal.

3. Turn the headlight switch to the ON position. Check to see that headlight and taillight are on.

4. Move the dimmer switch up and down between the high and low positions, and check to see that both headlight elements are working.

5. Push the turn signal switch to the left and right positions and check that all 4 turn signal lights are working.

6. Push the horn button and note that the horn blows loudly.

Clutch Operation

1. With the engine oil warm and the transmission in neutral, pull the clutch lever all the way to the handlebar and check to see that you can shift up into 2nd gear without a jolt or a clunking sound.

2. When you shift into 1st gear to ride away, check that you can let the ball end of the lever move at least ½ in. (12mm) from the handlebar before the clutch begins to engage. As you continue to let out the clutch, check that the clutch is fully engaged at least ½ in. (12mm) before the ball end of the lever reaches the end of its travel.

3. At rest, the clutch lever should have 1/16-1/8 in. (2-4mm) of slack.

4. If the clutch does not perform correctly, adjust the linkage (see *Clutch Linkage Adjustment* procedure in this chapter).

WEEKLY CHECKS

Front Brake Pad Wear

1. Have an assistant apply the front brake.

2. Shine a light between the caliper and the disc and inspect the brake pads (**Figure 3**).

3. If either pad has worn enough so that its red line is touching the disc, replace both pads as a set (**Figure 4**). See Chapter Eight.

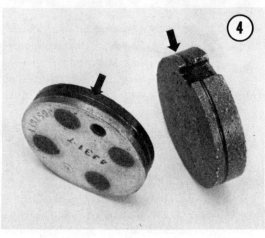

Wheel Spoke Tension

1. Tap each spoke with a wrench. The higher the pitch of sound it makes, the tighter the spoke. The lower the sound frequency, the looser the spoke. A "ping" is good; a "klunk" indicates a loose spoke.

2. If one or more spokes are loose, tighten them (see the *Spoke Tension and Wheel Balance* procedure in this chapter).

Tire Wear

1. With a depth gauge or a machinist's scale, measure the depth of the tread on each tire (**Figure 6**).

2. Replace the front tire when its tread is less than 0.04 in. (1.0mm) deep. Replace the rear tire when its tread is less than 0.08 in. (2.0mm) deep.

Battery Fluid Level

1. Lift the seat.

2. Check the electrolyte level in the battery (**Figure 5**).

3. If the electrolyte level is below the bottom line in any of the 6 cells, raise the seat and add enough distilled water to raise the level above the bottom line (but not above the top line) on the battery case. Do not use tap water.

PREVENTIVE MAINTENANCE SCHEDULE

Table 1 summarizes required preventive maintenance. Perform each item at the interval

specified. In addition, the following parts should be carefully inspected after 24 months.

   a. Front brake hydraulic hose
   b. Brake cable
   c. Front brake light switch
   d. Brake master cylinder and primary and secondary caps
   e. Disc brake caliper piston seal
   f. Carburetor rubber dust caps
   g. Fuel lines

CHASSIS CHECKS AND ADJUSTMENT

Steering Play Check

To be checked every 3,000 miles (5,000 km).
1. Prop up the motorcycle so that the front tire clears the ground.
2. Center the front wheel. Push lightly against the left handlebar grip to start the wheel turning to the right, then let go. The wheel should continue turning under its own momentum until the forks hit their stop.
3. Center the wheel, and push lightly against the right handlebar grip.
4. If, with a light push in either direction, the front wheel will turn all the way to the stop, the steering adjustment is not too tight.
5. Center the front wheel and kneel in front of it. Grasp the bottoms of the 2 front fork slider legs. Try to push them toward the engine. If no play is felt, the steering adjustment is not too loose.
6. If the steering adjustment is not correct, re-

adjust it (see the *Steering Play Adjustment* procedure below).

Steering Play Adjustment

1. Loosen the big steering stem cap nut on top of the top triple clamp.
2. Loosen the steering stem clamp bolt at the rear of the top triple clamp.
3. Loosen the 2 fork tube clamp bolts on the bottom triple clamp (**Figure 7**).

4. Fit a pin type wrench to the notched steering stem collar between the top triple clamp and the steering head (**Figure 8**).
5. Turn the collar clockwise to tighten the steering, or counterclockwise to loosen it.
6. Tighten the steering stem clamp bolt at the rear of the top triple clamp.
7. Torque the steering stem clamp bolt at the rear of the top triple clamp to 12-13 ft.-lb. (1.6-1.8 mkg). Check that the 2 fork tube clamp bolts on the top triple clamp are torqued to 12-13 ft.-lb.(1. 6-1.8 mkg).

Table 1   LUBRICATION AND PREVENTIVE MAINTENANCE

Every 1,000 miles (1,500 km)	Service spark plugs Lubricate and adjust final drive chain Lubricate control linkage
Every 2,000 miles (3,000 km)	Change engine oil
Every 3,000 miles (5,000 km)	Service contact breaker points and lubricate cam Adjust ignition timing Adjust valve tappet clearances Adjust cam chain Adjust clutch Service battery Clean fuel valve filter Check fuel tank and fuel lines Service air cleaner Adjust carburetors Check throttle valve operation Check handlebar holder Check front fork top plate Check front fork bottom case Grease and inspect swing arm Check swing arm Check rear shock absorber mounting bolts Check front and rear wheel spokes Check front and rear wheel rims and hubs Check front brake caliper and pad linings Check front brake fluid level (replace at 6,000 mile intervals) Check and adjust brake rear pedal Check rear brake stopper arm Check and lubricate rear brake cam Check frame Check steering play Check exhaust system Check side stand Check lights and switches Check horn Check speedometer and tachometer
Every 4,000 miles (6,000 km)	Change oil filter element
Every 6,000 miles (10,000 km)	Check final drive and driven sprockets Check front and rear wheels and axles Check and lubricate front and rear wheel bearings Check rear brake shoe linings Check front brake line Change front fork oil Check and grease steering head bearings Check steering handle lock Lubricate throttle cables Check ignition primary and secondary cables
Every 12,000 miles (20,000 km)	Compression test Clean oil screen filter

8. Hit each side of the bottom triple clamp from the top and bottom with a rubber mallet to reposition it on fork tubes and relieve strain.

9. Torque the 2 fork tube clamp bolts on the bottom triple clamp to 39-43 ft.-lb. (5.4-5.9 mkg).

10. Recheck the steering play per the steering play checking procedures listed earlier in this chapter.

Spoke Tension and Rim Truing

1. Prop motorcycle so wheel clears the ground.
2. For checking the rear wheel, remove the rear chain from the rear sprocket (for procedures, see Chapter Nine).
3. Position a dial gauge so that it bears against the side of the rim (**Figure 9**). Turn the wheel slowly, and write down the highest and lowest readings. Subtract the lowest from the highest reading to get the axial (side wobble) runout of the rim.

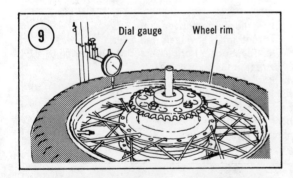

Dial gauge   Wheel rim

4. Position the dial gauge so that it bears against the inner face of the rim near the edge.

Turn the wheel slowly, and write down the highest and lowest readings. Subtract the lowest from the highest readings to get the radial (up-and-down wobble) runout of the rim.

5. A new wheel has an axial runout of less than 0.04 in. (1.0mm), and a radial runout of less than 0.04 in. (1.0mm).

6. If you measure more than 0.12 in. (3.0mm) of axial runout, or more than 0.08 in. (2.0mm) of radial runout, remove the axle from the wheel and check it for runout (for procedure, see Chapters Eight and Nine).

7. If axial runout is within tolerance, adjust spoke tension.

8. If you cannot true the rim with a reasonable amount of spoke tuning as follows, the rim is bent and must be replaced with a new one.

9. Mark the tire with a piece of chalk at the point where runout is greatest.

10. Note whether the reading at the point of greatest runout is a high number or a low number on the dial gauge. If the number is high, the rim is warped toward the side of the wheel being checked with the dial gauge. If low, it is warped toward the far side.

11. Loosen the 2 nearest spokes (½ turn each) on each side of the chalk mark that are laced to the side of the hub toward which the rim is warped.

12. Tighten the 2 nearest spokes (½ turn each) on each side of the chalk mark that are laced to the other side of the hub.

13. Check the axial runout again. Continue loosening or tightening those same spokes in the same sequence until the axial runout lies within the acceptable limits.

14. Tap each spoke in the wheel with a wrench, and listen to the sound, to check that you have not tightened or loosened any spoke too much. If considerable tightening of any spoke was required, you may need to remove the tire and grind off the protruding end of the spoke to prevent it from puncturing the tube.

15. If radial runout exceeds the limit, mark the tire with a piece of chalk at the point where runout is greatest.

16. Note whether the reading at the point of

greatest runout is a high number or a low number on the dial gauge. If the number is high, the rim is stretched away from the hub at that point. If the number is low, the rim is pulled toward the hub at that point.

17. If the number was high, tighten the 2 nearest spokes on each side of the chalk mark ½ turn each. Make another chalk mark on the opposite end of the tire, and loosen the 2 nearest spokes on each side of the new chalk mark ½ turn each.

18. If the dial gauge reading at the point of greatest runout was a low number, loosen the 4 spokes nearest the chalk mark, and tighten the 4 spokes at the opposite end of the wheel.

19. Check radial runout again. Continue loosening or tightening those same spokes in the same sequence until the runout lies within 0.040 in. (2.0mm). The same cautions apply as for correcting axial runout.

Wheel Balance

1. Spin the wheel. When it stops, mark the lowest part of the tire with a piece of chalk. Repeat the process 4 or 5 times. If the wheel stops in the same place (or nearly the same place) each time, it will need balancing.

2. If the wheel, after being spun, always comes to a stop in the same position (as indicated by a chalk mark on the lowest part of the tire), hang a 10 gram balance weight near the rim on the spoke at the opposite end of the wheel.

3. Spin the wheel and notice where it stops. If the 10 gram weight was not heavy enough to overcome the imbalance, try a 20 gram weight, and then a 30 gram weight.

4. After you have overcome the imbalance, spin the wheel again. Put a double chalk mark on the lowest part of the tire. Spin the wheel 6 more times. If the wheel comes to a stop several times in roughly the same position, hang a 10 gram weight on the spoke opposite that point on the wheel.

5. When the wheel is balanced and will stop at random, tap the weights down on the spoke nipple.

Tightness of Nuts and Bolts

To be checked every 3,000 miles (5,000 km), as follows.

1. Check for looseness of the following:
   a. Engine mount bolts
   b. Handlebar clamp bolts
   c. Top triple clamp bolts
   d. Bottom triple clamp bolts
   e. Front axle clamp nuts
   f. Shock absorber mounting nuts
   g. Swing arm pivot nut
   h. Rear brake backing plate torque link
   i. Rear axle nut

2. Check the engine cover screws for tightness.

3. Check the remaining nuts and bolts on the motorcycle for tightness. For torque figures, refer to specifications in the Appendix.

Rear Brake Linkage Adjustment

1. When it is at rest, the top of the brake pedal should be positioned about 1/16 in. (1.6mm) lower than the bottom of the right front footpeg. If it is not, loosen the locknut on the brake pedal stop bolt (**Figure 10**).

2. To lower the pedal, back out the stop bolt. To raise the pedal, screw in the stop bolt.

3. When the pedal is positioned correctly while at rest, tighten the stop bolt locknut.

4. Push down the rear brake pedal by hand. The brake cam lever and the brake rod should form an angle of 80-90°. If the angle they form is 100° or larger, remove the rear wheel (see Chapter Nine) and inspect the brake components for wear. If they are not worn past the acceptable limits, reassemble and install the wheel.

5. Scribe a line across the faces of the brake camshaft and the brake cam lever.

6. Disconnect the brake rod from the brake cam lever. Remove the mounting bolt from the lever.

7. Pull the brake cam lever off the camshaft splines, rotate the lever one tooth counterclockwise, and install it on the brake camshaft.

8. Attach the brake rod to the brake cam lever. Tighten the nut on the brake rod until the brake pedal has ¾-1¼ in. of travel when pushed down lightly by hand.

9. Check to see that the brake cam lever and the brake rod now form an angle of 80-90° when the brake is applied by hand.

10. Prop the motorcycle so the rear wheel clears the ground. Spin the wheel and check that the brake shoes are not binding against the drum, causing the wheel to make a hissing sound and to stop spinning too quickly. If the brake shoes are dragging, back off the brake rod nut a turn or so, and check to see if that solves the problem. If not, disassemble the brake and check the components.

OIL AND FILTER

Changing Frequency

Change the oil every 2,000 miles (3,000 km) or 2 months, whichever comes first. The time interval is as important as elapsed mileage. Acids formed by gasoline vapor blown by the piston rings will contaminate the oil even if the cycle is not run for several weeks.

If your motorcycle is run under dusty conditions the oil will get dirty faster. Accordingly, change the oil more often.

Quality and Viscosity

Use only a detergent oil with an API rating of SD (designated MS in the past) or better. These quality ratings are stamped on the top of the can. Try to use same brand of oil when topping up.

CAUTION
Never use oil additives in a Honda engine. The clutch is lubricated by the same oil used in the crankcase. The "honey" type of additives, e.g., STP, Stud., etc., will cause the clutch to slip.

Table 2 lists recommended oil viscosities for various ambient temperatures.

Table 2   RECOMMENDED OIL

Outside Temperature	Oil*
Above 59°F (15°C)	SAE 30, 30W or 20W-50
32°F to 59°F (0° to 15°C)	SAE 20 or 20W, SE
Below 32°F (0°C)	SAE 10W
*Must be rated SD or SE	

Draining Oil

1. Warm up the engine. Warm oil drains faster than cold and carries more accumulated impurities with it.

2. Place a catch pan of at least one gallon capacity under the crankcase and remove the filler cap.

3. Remove the drain plug with a 17mm socket. Location of the CB500/550 plug is shown in **Figure 11**, and the CB350/400 is shown in **Figure 12**. Allow the dirty oil to drain for about 10 minutes.

4. Crank the engine several times with the kickstarter to force out oil trapped in the inner recesses.

CAUTION
Do not permit the engine to start; keep the ignition off.

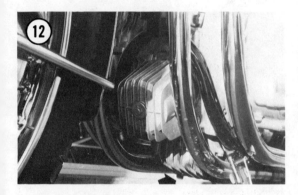

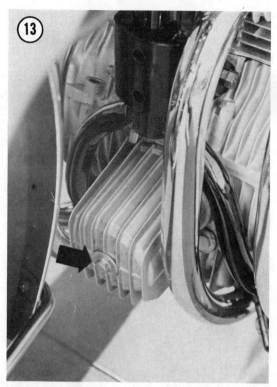

2

Changing Oil Filter

Replace the oil filter element every other oil change.

1. Remove the center bolt from the housing (**Figure 13**) and pull the assembly from the engine. Watch out for oil that will drip from the filter.

2. Throw away the dirty filter element and inspect the O-ring seal for damage. Clean the dirty oil and sludge from the inside of the housing with solvent and wipe or blow dry.

3. Install new filter element and new O-ring if required.

4. Install the assembly on the engine. Torque center bolt to 19-24 ft.-lb. (2.7-3.3 mkg).

Filling With Oil

1. Install the crankcase drain plug with its gasket. Be careful not to overtighten or it will be difficult to remove the next time. Torque to 25-29 ft.-lb. (3.5-4.0 mkg).

2. Fill the crankcase with the recommended oil (Table 2). The CB500 and CB550 hold 3.2 quarts (3 liters). The CB350 and CB400 hold 3.7 quarts (3.5 liters). Check the level with the dipstick.

3. Run the engine at 1,000-1,500 rpm for 2 minutes, then check for oil seepage around the drain plug and filter housing. Check the oil level and top up if necessary.

PERIODIC LUBRICATION

These procedures apply after the initial break-in period. For a lubrication schedule to use during the break-in period, see a dealer. Table 1 summarizes required lubrication.

Rear Chain

To be done every 1,000 miles (1,500 km) as follows:

1. Check that the rear chain is lightly oiled.

2. With the motorcycle on its centerstand, oil as much of the bottom chain run as you can reach with SAE 30 motor oil in a long-spout oil can or commercial chain lube. Concentrate on getting the oil down between the side plates of the chain links.

Control Linkage

To be done every 1,000 miles (1,500 km) or after washing the motorcycle, as follows:

Use a long-spout oil can to lubricate the points shown in **Figures 14 and 15**. Use SAE 30 motor oil.

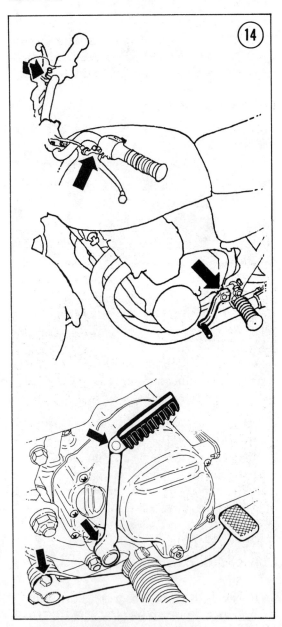

1. Remove the 2 screws that mount the breaker point cover. Remove the cover and its gasket.

2. Rub a small amount of high-temperature grease into the felt that bears against the breaker point cam. If you use too much grease, the cam will sling it into the points, fouling them.

3. Install gasket and cover.

Swing Arm

To be done every 3,000 miles (5,000 km) as follows:

1. Use a gun to force grease into the fitting on the swing arm, until the grease runs out both ends (fittings can be installed by a dealer if your model is not already so equipped).

2. Clean off excess grease.

Contact Breaker Points

To be done every 3,000 miles (5,000 km) or when the points are inspected, whichever comes first, as follows:

3. If grease will not run out of the ends of the swing arm, unscrew the grease fitting from the swing arm. Clean it, and make certain that the ball check valve is free. Reinstall fitting.

4. Apply the grease gun again. If grease does not run out both ends of the swing arm, remove the swing arm (see procedure in Chapter Ten—*Rear Suspension*). Clean out the old grease, install the swing arm, and lubricate it.

Fronk Fork Oil

To be checked every 6,000 miles (10,000 km) as follows:

1. Prop up the motorcycle so that the front tire just clears the ground.

2. Loosen a fork tube clamp bolt on one side of the top triple clamp (**Figure 16**).

3. Unscrew the fork tube plug (top fork bolt) from the fork tube on the side of triple clamp. If the oil is dirty, change it.

4. Remove the bottom fork plug, and drain oil into a pan.

5. Check that the top edge of the fork tube is flush with the top edge of the top triple clamp.

6. Torque the clamp bolt to 12-13 ft.-lb. (1.6-1.8 mkg).

7. Even though it was not loosened, check to see that the third clamp bolt in the top triple clamp is torqued to 12-13 ft.-lb. (1.6-1.8 mkg).

8. Even though they were not loosened, check to see that the 2 clamp bolts in the bottom triple clamp are torqued to 39-43 ft.-lb. (5.4-5.9 mkg).

9. Tighten the bottom fork plug.

10. For CB350 models, fill each fork leg with 125cc (4.2 oz.) of ATF (automatic transmission fluid); for CB400/500/550 models, fill each fork leg with 160cc (5.4 oz.) of SAE 10W-30 oil.

Clutch Cable Lubrication

To be done every 3,000 miles (5,000 km) as follows:

1. At the clutch lever mount, loosen the locknut and cable adjuster (**Figure 17**) to provide slack in the cable.

2. If there is enough slack in the cable, pull the cable housing (outer cable) free of the lever, and lift the inner cable out. Bend the inner cable around to match the slot in the lever, and pull the cable and its fitting out of the lever.

3. If there is not enough slack in the cable, loosen the locknut on the clutch adjusting screw.

This will provide enough slack in the clutch cable so that it can be freed from the handlebar lever.

4. At the top of the clutch cable, examine the exposed portion of the inner cable. If it is clean, hold the cable vertical and spray it with Dri-Slide or one of the thin spray-on chain lubricants. Hold the spray can close to the inner cable, near the top ferrule of the cable housing, so that the lubricant will run down between the inner cable and its housing. Spray the cable until it is lubricated along its entire length.

5. If the exposed portion of the inner cable is dirty, or the cable feels gritty while moving it up and down in its housing, spray it instead with a lubricant/solvent, such as LPS-25 or WD-40.

6. Attach the cable to the clutch lever, and then fit it to the lever mount. To adjust the clutch adjusting screw and/or the cable linkage, refer to the *Clutch, Adjustment* procedures in this chapter.

Front Brake Fluid Change

To be done every 6,000 miles (10,000 km), or whenever the fluid becomes dirty or watery.

1. Pull the rubber cap off the bleeder valve located on the brake caliper which clamps the disc.

2. Attach one end of a piece of clear plastic tubing to the nipple at the end of the bleeder valve. Stick the other end of the tubing into an empty can.

3. Unscrew the bleeder valve body enough to open the valve fully.

4. Squeeze and release the front brake lever until all of the fluid has been drained out of the reservoir, the line, and the caliper.

5. Screw in the bleeder valve body to close the valve. Pour out the used fluid and stick the bottom end of the tubing back into the can.

6. Unscrew the cap from the handlebar fluid reservoir. Fill the reservoir with fresh fluid.

7. Use only a disc brake fluid which is clearly marked DOT 3; the correct functioning of the brake depends upon it. Continue using the same brand each time the fluid is changed; do not mix brands. Use fluid only from a recently opened can.

8. Open the bleeder valve. Squeeze the brake lever and keep pressure on it. Close the valve, and quickly release the lever. Continue this operation until brake fluid starts coming out of the bleeder valve. See **Figure 18**. Add fluid as necessary to prevent reservoir from running dry.

9. Bleed air from the system. See the *Bleeding Front Brake System* procedure, Chapter Eight.

Throttle Cable

To be done every 6,000 miles (10,000 km), or when the cables begin to bind, as follows:

1. Loosen the nuts (at the carburetor pulley) and remove the 2 throttle cables from the pulley.

2. Remove the screws (at the handlebars) that assemble the twist grip housing. Remove the top half of the housing.

3. Remove the throttle cables from the twist grip, noting which cable goes where.

4. Examine the exposed parts of the inner cables. Pull each inner cable up and down in its

housing to determine by feel whether it is clean or gritty.

5. If the cables are clean, hold the top part of one cable vertical and spray it with Dri-Slide or one of the thin spray-on chain lubricants.

6. Hold the spray can close to the inner cable, near the top ferrule of the cable housing, so that the lubricant will run down between the inner cable and its housing. Spray the cable until the lubricant runs out of the bottom of the cable housing. Lubricate other cable in the same way.

7. If the cables are dirty, spray them instead with a lubricant/solvent, such as LPS-25 or WD-40. Continue spraying the upper portion of the inner cable until the lubricant, running out the bottom of the cable housing, is clean.

8. Lubricate the twist grip assembly with grease.

9. Reassemble throttle linkage in reverse order of disassembly. Refer to *Throttle Linkage* adjustment procedures, Chapter Six.

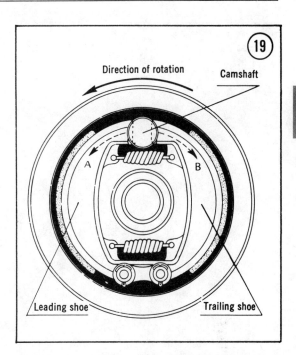

Rear Brake Cam

To be done every 12,000 miles (20,000 km), or whenever the rear wheel is removed.

1. Remove the rear wheel (for procedures, refer to Chapter Nine).

2. Take out the brake backing plate.

3. Wipe away the old grease, being careful not to get any of it on the brake shoes.

4. Sparingly apply high-temperature grease to the camming surfaces of the camshaft, the camshaft, the camshaft groove, the brake shoe pivots, and the ends of the springs (**Figure 19**). Do not get any grease on the brake shoes.

5. Reassemble the rear wheel and install it.

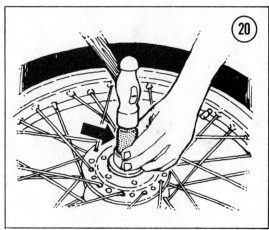

Wheel Bearings

Lubricate the front and rear wheel bearings every 12,000 miles (20,000 km) as follows:

1. Remove the wheels from the motorcycle and remove the bearings (**Figures 20 and 21**). For front and rear wheel removal and disassembly procedures, see Chapters Eight and Nine.

2. Clean the old grease out of the hub.

3. Wash each wheel bearing in kerosene and dry it, taking care not to spin it in the process.

4. Oil each bearing, and spin it by hand. See **Figure 22**. If it will not spin smoothly, is noisy, or has rough spots, replace it with a new one.

5. Pack the bearings with good quality bearing grease.

6. Grease the front hub speedometer gearbox.

7. Reassemble and install the wheel.

Steering Stem Bearing

To be done every 6,000 miles (10,000 km) as follows:

1. Remove the steering stem (**Figure 23**). Procedures are given in Chapter Ten.

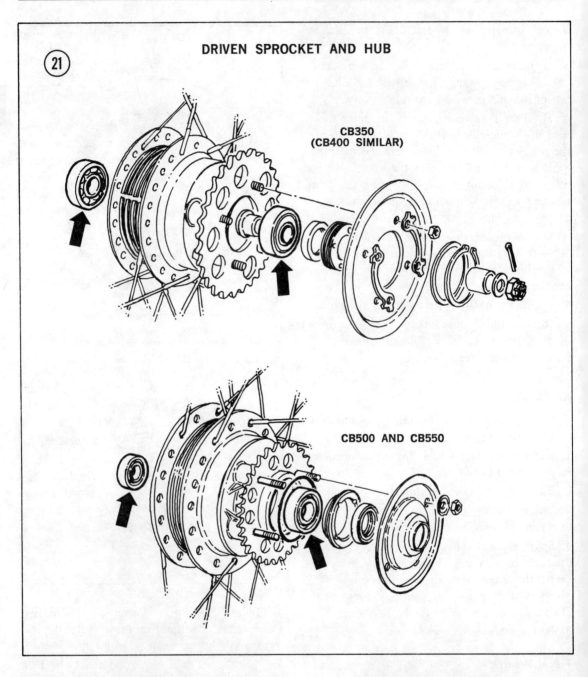

(21) **DRIVEN SPROCKET AND HUB**

**CB350
(CB400 SIMILAR)**

CB500 AND CB550

2. Clean the upper race, the lower race, and the balls of each bearing in a suitable solvent.

3. Inspect the balls and races of each bearing for wear or damage. If any component shows wear or damage, replace the entire bearing with new parts.

4. Coat all 4 races with grease, and position the balls on their races.

5. Install the steering stem.

ENGINE TUNE-UP

A complete tune-up should be performed every 3,000 miles (5,000 km) under normal conditions. More frequent tune-ups may be required if the bike is used for frequent stop-and-go driving.

Because different systems in an engine interact, the procedures should be performed in the following order:

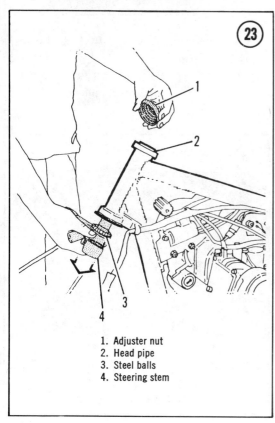

1. Adjuster nut
2. Head pipe
3. Steel balls
4. Steering stem

a. Check compression

b. Tighten cylinder head bolts

c. Adjust valve clearance

d. Work on ignition system and adjust

e. Adjust carburetor (if needed); see Chapter Six

COMPRESSION TEST

A compression tester measures pressure buildup in each cylinder. The results, when properly interpreted, can indicate general cylinder and valve condition.

This is one of the simplest, yet one of the most significant tests to determine engine condition. It should be performed every 12,000 miles (20,000 km) or prior to each tune-up.

The battery should be fully charged so that cranking rpm will exceed 250 rpm. To perform a compression check, proceed as follows:

1. Run the engine until normal operating temperature is reached; then, shut it off.

2. Pull the choke and throttle in their wide-open positions.

3. Remove all spark plugs.

4. Connect compression tester to one cylinder, following manufacturer's instructions.

5. Use a remote starter switch or have an assistant crank the engine until the reading on the compression tester stabilizes. This is usually about 8 revolutions.

6. Remove the tester and record the reading. Release air from tester.

7. Repeat above steps for each cylinder.

If compression reading does not differ between cylinders by more than 10 psi, the rings and valves are in good condition.

If a low reading (10% or more) is obtained on one cylinder, it indicates valve or ring trouble. To determine which, pour about a teaspoon of engine oil through the spark plug hole onto the top of the piston. Turn the engine over once to clear some of the excess oil, then take another compression test and record the reading. If the compression returns to normal, the valves are good but the rings are defective on that cylinder.

If compression does not increase, the valves require servicing. A valve could be hanging open but not be burned.

Low compression in 2 adjacent cylinders may indicate that the head gasket has blown between the cylinders and that gases are leaking from one cylinder to the other. Torque-tighten cylinder head bolts and take another set of readings. If the condition persists, replace head gasket.

VALVE ADJUSTMENT

Incorrect valve clearance between tappets and valve stems hampers performance and may damage the valves if the condition is prolonged. To forestall premature wear and a costly regrind, adjust clearances regularly.

Adjust the valves with the engine cold.

1. Turn the fuel valve off and disconnect both fuel lines. Raise seat and remove fuel tank. See Chapter Six.

2. Remove the breaker point cover.

3. Remove the 8 caps that cover the tappet access holes (arrows, **Figure 24**). There are 4 holes in back and 4 in front.

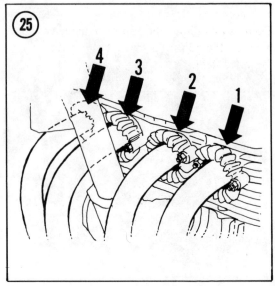

The cylinders are numbered 1 through 4 starting from the rider's left (**Figure 25**). Exhaust valves are at the front of the engine and intake valves at the back.

4. Slowly rotate the crankshaft clockwise with the kickstart pedal until the "T 1-4" mark, seen through the peephole in the breaker baseplate, is even with the outer index mark shown in **Figure 26**.

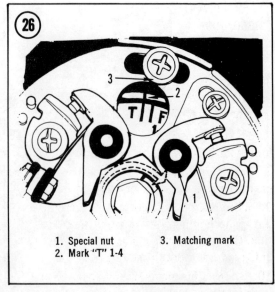

1. Special nut   3. Matching mark
2. Mark "T" 1-4

5. At this point, either No. 1 or No. 4 cylinder will be at the top dead center (TDC) of its compression stroke. Find out which one it is by feeling the rocker arms of both cylinders through the adjustment holes. The cylinder at TDC will have both its rocker arms loose, signifying that both intake and exhaust valves are closed.

6. Check the valve clearances as shown in **Figure 27** by sliding the appropriate feeler gauge between the adjusting screw tip and the top of the valve stem.

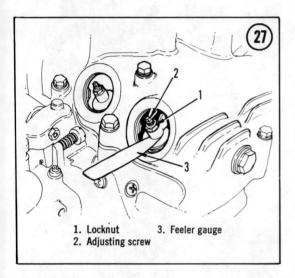

1. Locknut   3. Feeler gauge
2. Adjusting screw

The feeler blade should slide through with a slight amount of drag.

The standard clearances are:

CB350/400
    Intake (rear)   0.002 in. (0.05mm)
    Exhaust (front)   0.002 in. (0.05mm)

CB500/550
    Intake (rear)   0.002 in. (0.05mm)
    Exhaust (front)   0.003 in. (0.08mm)

7. To adjust, refer to Figure 27 again and loosen the locknut on the tappet adjusting screw.

8. Turn the adjusting screw clockwise to reduce clearance and counterclockwise to increase it.

9. When clearance is correct, tighten the locknut while holding the adjusting screw in position. Check clearance again to make sure tightening did not upset the setting.

10. These adjustments should be performed for both intake and exhaust valves of the cylinder that is at TDC.

11. Rotate the crankshaft 360° until the "T 1-4" mark once again is lined up with the index mark.

12. The other cylinder, either No. 1 or No. 4, is now at TDC. Check and adjust if necessary according to Steps 6 through 10.

13. Set up the valves for No. 2 and No. 3 cylinders by rotating the crankshaft until the "T 2-3" mark on the timing ring is aligned with the index line (**Figure 28**).

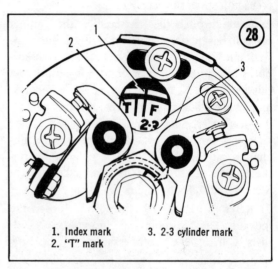

1. Index mark   3. 2-3 cylinder mark
2. "T" mark

14. Determine which cylinder is at TDC and then check and adjust the clearances.

15. Rotate the crankshaft another 360° until the "T 2-3" mark once again is lined up properly and adjust the valves for the final cylinder.

16. Replace the tappet hole caps with their gaskets. Do not overtighten. Torque to between 7.2-10 ft.-lb. (1-1.4 mkg). If you continue to have a tapping noise after carefully adjusting the rockers, it could be a bad rocker cover or excessive rocker end play. If this is the case, refer to Chapter Four for repair.

> NOTE: *If the cam chain tensioner is to be adjusted (next procedure), do not replace the caps for No. 1 cylinder or the breaker point cover.*

CAM CHAIN

The spring steel cam chain tensioner is faced with a layer of Teflon cemented to a base of heat resistant rubber which is vulcanized to the metal. The tensioner bears against the chain to absorb the shocks while the chain guide damps vibration.

A loose cam chain is noisy and can change valve timing. The tension is easy to set.

Adjustment

1. Using the kickstarter to rotate the camshaft, set the No. 1 cylinder to the top dead center of its compression stroke. Refer to Step 5 of the valve adjustment procedure.

2. Look through the peephole in the contact breaker baseplate. Continue to rotate the camshaft until the spring peg on the advancer assembly is just to the right of the timing mark. At this point the No. 1 cylinder is 15° after TDC and chain slack is at the rear of the engine, duplicating running condition.

A shortcut used by many professional mechanics on the CB350/400 is to actually run the engine at 2,500-3,000 rpm and perform Steps 3 and 4, following.

3. Refer to **Figures 29 and 30** and loosen the locknut. The tensioner bolt automatically adjusts itself to the correct pressure.

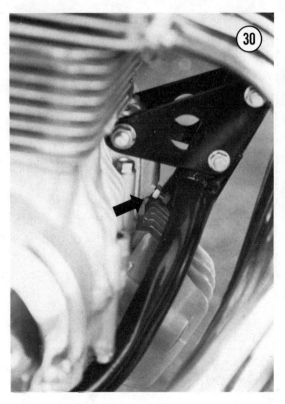

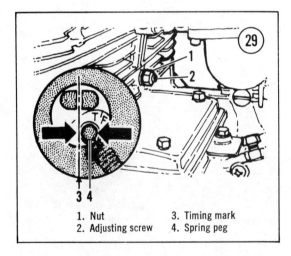

1. Nut	3. Timing mark
2. Adjusting screw	4. Spring peg

4. Tighten the locknut. Install the tappet hole caps and the breaker point cover.

SPARK PLUGS

Spark plugs are available in various heat ranges, hotter or colder than the plugs originally installed at the factory.

Select plugs of a heat range designed for the loads and temperature conditions under which the bike will run. Use of incorrect heat ranges can cause seized pistons, scored cylinder walls, or damaged piston crowns.

In general, use a lower numbered plug for low speeds, low loads, and low temperatures. Use a higher numbered plug for high speeds, high engine loads, and high temperatures.

> NOTE: *Use the highest numbered plug that will not foul.*

In areas where seasonal temperature variations are great, the factory recommends a "2-plug system"—a high numbered plug for hard summer riding and a lower numbered plug for slower winter operation.

The reach (length) of a plug is also important. A longer than normal plug could interfere with the valves and pistons causing permanent and severe damage. Refer to **Figures 31 and 32**.

The standard heat range spark plugs are:

	Bosch	NGK	ND	Champion
CB350/400	X290 T-17	NGK D8ESL	X24ES	A8Y-MC
CB500/550	X270 T-17	NGK D7ES	X22ES	A7Y-MC

Testing Plugs

A quick and simple test can be made to determine if the plug is correct for your type of

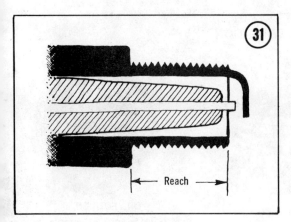

Reach

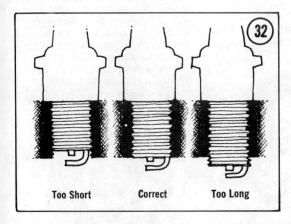

| Too Short | Correct | Too Long |

Removal/Installation

Remove and clean the spark plugs at least once every 1,000 miles (1,500 km) of riding. Electrode gap should be measured with a round feeler gauge and set at 0.024-0.028 in. (6-7mm) as shown in **Figure 34**.

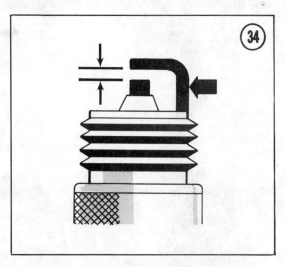

riding. Accelerate hard through the gears and maintain 7,000-8,000 rpm in 3rd gear. Shut the throttle off, and kill the engine at the same time, allowing the bike to slow, out of gear. Do not allow the engine to slow the bike. Remove the plug and check the condition of the electrode area. A spark plug of the correct heat range, with the engine in a proper state of tune, will appear light tan. See **Figure 33**. Always use a stock, used plug for testing. A new plug will not give an accurate reading.

If the insulator is white or burned, the plug is too hot and should be replaced with a colder one. Also check the setting of the carburetor for it may be too lean.

A too-cold plug will have sooty deposits ranging in color from dark brown to black. Replace with a hotter plug and check for too-rich carburetion or evidence of oil blow-by at the piston rings.

If any one plug is found unsatisfactory, discard the set.

Often heat and corrosion can cause the plug to bind in the head making removal difficult. Do not use force; the head is easily damaged.

Here is the proper way to replace a plug:

1. Blow out any debris which has collected in the spark plug wells. It could fall into the hole.
2. Gently remove the spark plug leads by pulling up and out. Do not jerk the wires or pull on the wire itself.
3. Apply penetrating oil to the base of the plug and allow it to work into the threads.
4. Back out the plugs with a socket that has a rubber insert designed to grip the insulator. Be careful not to drop the plugs into the cooling fins where they could become lodged.
5. Clean the seating area after removal and apply graphite to the thread to simplify future removal.
6. Clean the tips of the plugs with a sandblasting machine (some gas stations have them) or with a wire brush and solvent. This will work only one time. It is always better to replace plugs with new ones for best performance.
7. Always use a new gasket if old plugs are to be reused after cleaning.

SPARK PLUG CONDITION

NORMAL
- Identified by light tan or gray deposits on the firing tip.
- Can be cleaned.

CARBON FOULED
- Identified by black, dry fluffy carbon deposits on insulator tips, exposed shell surfaces and electrodes.
- Caused by too cold a plug, weak ignition, dirty air cleaner, too rich a fuel mixture, or excessive idling. Can be cleaned.

FUSED SPOT DEPOSIT
- Identified by melted or spotty deposits resembling bubbles or blisters.
- Caused by sudden acceleration. Can be cleaned.

GAP BRIDGED
- Identified by deposit buildup closing gap between electrodes.
- Caused by oil or carbon fouling. If deposits are not excessive, the plug can be cleaned.

LEAD FOULED
- Identified by dark gray, black, yellow, or tan deposits or a fused glazed coating on the insulator tip.
- Caused by highly leaded gasoline. Can be cleaned.

OVERHEATING
- Identified by a white or light gray insulator with small black or gray brown spots and with bluish-burnt appearance of electrodes.
- Caused by engine overheating, wrong type of fuel, loose spark plugs, too hot a plug, or incorrect ignition timing. Replace the plug.

OIL FOULED
- Identified by wet black deposits on the insulator shell bore electrodes.
- Caused by excessive oil entering combustion chamber through worn rings and pistons, excessive clearance between valve guides and stems, or worn or loose bearings. Can be cleaned. If engine is not repaired, use a hotter plug.

WORN
- Identified by severely eroded or worn electrodes.
- Caused by normal wear. Should be replaced.

PREIGNITION
- Identified by melted electrodes and possibly blistered insulator. Metallic deposits on insulator indicate engine damage.
- Caused by wrong type of fuel, incorrect ignition timing or advance, too hot a plug, burned valves, or engine overheating. Replace the plug.

8. Run the plug in finger-tight and tighten ¼ turn more with a wrench. Further tightening will only flatten the gasket and cause binding.

> NOTE: *A short piece of fuel line can be used to install the plug initially in areas where space is a problem.*

CONDENSER (CAPACITOR)

The condenser (capacitor) is a sealed unit and requires no maintenance. Be sure the connections are clean and tight.

The only proper test is to measure the resistance of the insulation with an ohmmeter. The value should be 5,000 ohms. A make-do test is to charge the capacitor by hooking the leads, or case and lead, to a 12V battery. After a few seconds, touch the leads together, or lead to case, and check for a spark, as shown in **Figure 35**. A damaged capacitor will not store electricity or spark.

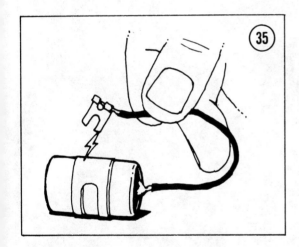

Most mechanics prefer to discard the condensers and replace them with new ones during engine tune-up.

BREAKER POINTS

Inspection

1. Remove the breaker point cover (the round plate on the side of the engine with "Honda" stamped on it) by removing the 2 Phillips head screws. If the cover does not come off easily, try tapping it loose with a rubber or rawhide mallet.

> CAUTION
> *Do not use a metal hammer.*

2. Pry open the points gently with a finger and check the 2 sets for alignment and wear. Replace the points if they are severely pitted or worn.

Cleaning

1. Gray discoloration of the contacts is normal. Dress the surfaces with a point file. Never use sandpaper or emery cloth for this purpose.

2. Blow away the residue and then clean the contacts with chemical point cleaner or a piece of unwaxed stiff paper such as a business card. Make certain the contacts are absolutely clean. Even fingerprint oil can affect performance.

3. If the same points are to be used, skip the next section on removal and replacement procedure. If new points will be installed, it is recommended that the 2 condensers also routinely be replaced. These parts usually are sold in sets.

Replacement

1. Disconnect the yellow and blue leads at the junction box located near the center of the frame. Refer to **Figure 36**, and remove the 6mm hex bolt and its washer. Then loosen the 3 breaker plate holding screws and lift out unit.

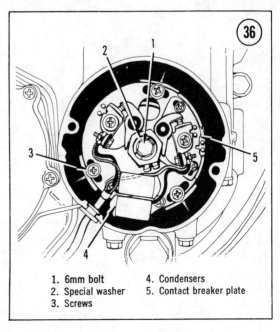

1. 6mm bolt	4. Condensers
2. Special washer	5. Contact breaker plate
3. Screws	

2. Remove the points and condensers (arrows, **Figure 37**). Install new parts. Make sure that the points arm spring and the coil/condenser wires are on the outside of the fiber washers away from a ground or base plate.

Adjusting Gap

There are 2 methods for measuring point gap; the static procedure using a feeler gauge and the dwell tachometer method. In either case, the points must be adjusted manually.

Static Gap Adjustment

1. Rotate the crankshaft (use a 23mm socket on the big retainer bolt in the center shaft) until points for No. 1 and No. 4 cylinders are fully open. See **Figure 38**.

2. The point gap should be 0.012-0.016 in. (0.04mm). Check with a wire feeler gauge.

3. To adjust, loosen the lockscrew (1) in

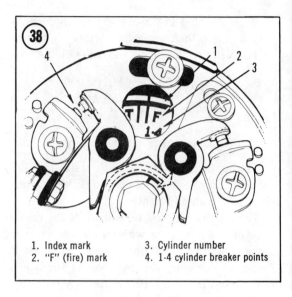

1. Index mark	3. Cylinder number
2. "F" (fire) mark	4. 1-4 cylinder breaker points

Figure 39. Set the tip of a screwdriver in the notch in the point arm and shift it by gently prying against the 2 leverage buttons set into the plate on which the points rest.

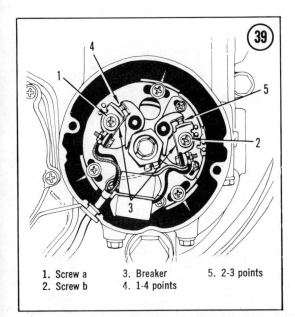

1. Screw a   3. Breaker   5. 2-3 points
2. Screw b   4. 1-4 points

4. When the gap is correct, tighten the lock-screw. Check the gap a final time with the gauge which should slip between the contact points with a slight amount of drag.

> NOTE: *Tightening the lockscrew may change the point gap. The points may have to be adjusted several times.*

5. To adjust the other set of points (for cylinders No. 2 and No. 3), rotate the crankshaft clockwise until points are fully open. Repeat Steps 3 and 4 this time loosening screw "b" (2), Figure 39.

6. Finally, lubricate the cam with a thin coating of special cam grease. Do not apply an excessive amount or it will contaminate the contact surfaces and lead to premature failure.

> NOTE: *Adjust ignition timing as described later.*

Dwell Procedure

Dwell is the number of degrees that the breaker point cam rotates while the points remain closed. The longer the dwell, the smaller the point gap. The shorter the dwell, the wider the gap.

The dwell should be between 92 and 98 degrees if the points are clean and correctly adjusted. A dwell meter is an extremely accurate tool for measuring point gap. Of course,

the points must still be adjusted statically if the distance is incorrect.

Figure 40 shows one type of dwell meter suitable for motorcycle engines. Make sure the meter is calibrated for small gasoline engines of 2 cylinders (one point set controls 2 cylinders). If read on a 4-cylinder scale, the correct dwell would be 46-49 degrees.

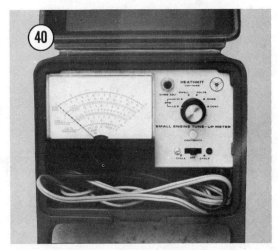

1. Hook up the meter according to its instructions—usually one lead attaches to the points and the other grounds to the engine.

2. Start the engine and read the dwell angle on the meter.

3. If the points require adjustment, refer to the static adjusting procedure.

IGNITION TIMING

There are 2 methods used to adjust ignition timing—the static procedure and the more precise method using a stroboscopic (strobe) light.

Static Method

The static method requires something that can signal when an electronic circuit is opened or closed. This can be a buzz box (ignition on), an ohmmeter (ignition off), or a continuity light (ignition on). This latter, often called a timing light, is the least expensive. It is available for under $2 at parts stores.

A homemade timing light consists of a 12-volt light bulb, a socket to hold it, and 2 wires attached to the socket with alligator clips at the ends of each wire.

1. As shown in **Figure 41**, the cylinders controlled by each set of points are stamped next to the breaker set on the base plate. Start the timing procedure with the set for No. 1 and No. 4 cylinders.

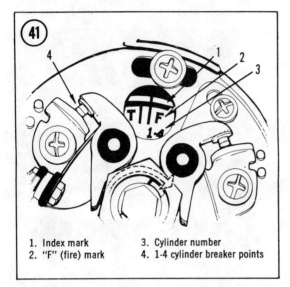

1. Index mark
2. "F" (fire) mark
3. Cylinder number
4. 1-4 cylinder breaker points

2. Hook up the timing light at the blue wire. Ground the other lead as shown in **Figure 42**.

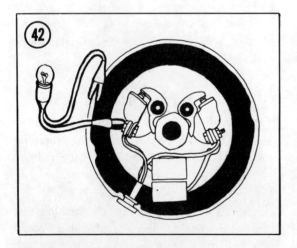

3. **Figure 43** is a view through the peephole in the base plate with the timing marks visible. Rotate crankshaft with a wrench on the 23mm retaining bolt of center shaft until the "1-4 F" mark is even with the index, or matching, mark on the outer ring. At this instant the points

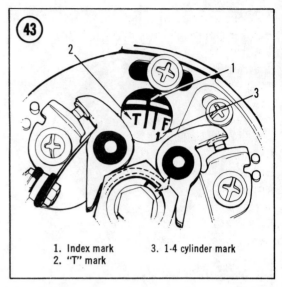

1. Index mark
2. "T" mark
3. 1-4 cylinder mark

should begin to open and the timing light should go on. If it does not, the timing is off.

4. To adjust, refer to **Figure 44** and loosen the 3 base plate locking screws (6, Figure 42). Rotate the plate to retard or advance the timing until the light flickers. Tighten the 3 screws, being careful not to change the adjustment. Check the point gap before proceeding to the next step to make sure it has not changed.

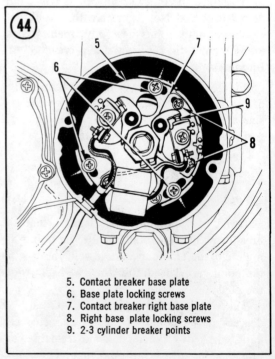

5. Contact breaker base plate
6. Base plate locking screws
7. Contact breaker right base plate
8. Right base plate locking screws
9. 2-3 cylinder breaker points

5. Connect the timing light to the other set of breaker points which control cylinders No. 2 and No. 3.

6. Rotate the crankshaft ½ revolution until the "2-3 F" mark is aligned with the index mark inscribed on the outer ring.

7. If the light does not flicker at this point, adjust by loosening the 2 right base plate locking screws (8, Figure 44). Note that these are different from the screws used to make the earlier adjustment.

8. Disconnect the timing light and turn off the ignition. Replace the point cover unless advance is to be checked (below).

Stroboscopic (Strobe Light) Timing Method

A strobe light enables the timing to be checked under actual running conditions. Such lights are commonly available, but beware of inexpensive ones because they usually are not durable or produce a weak light.

A homemade adapter will simplify this task and eliminate the risk of possible personal injury.

Obtain one foot (30.0 cm) of solid wire core spark plug wire, an old spark plug, and 3 terminal ends (one male and two female). Cut the wire in half and strip all 4 ends to expose ½ in. of bare conductor. To one piece, solder a male and female terminal to each end. See **Figure 45**.

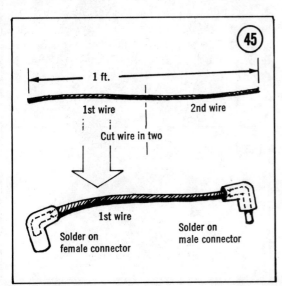

To the other wire piece, solder on the remaining female terminal. Solder the opposite end to the center electrode of the old spark plug. Wrap the entire electrode end of the old plug with solid copper wire and solder in place. See **Figure 46**. Connect the old spark plug to the female end of the first piece of wire and insert this between the spark plug and cap on the engine. You can now hook up the strobe light at the exposed point of the old plug. See **Figure 47**. If 2 of these adapters are made, you can switch back and forth between cylinders No. 3 and No. 4 while the engine is running to speed up the operation.

WARNING
Do not allow the exposed end of the old plug to get near the frame, exhaust headers, or other metal. Do not touch the exposed end with your bare fingers or you will receive a severe shock.

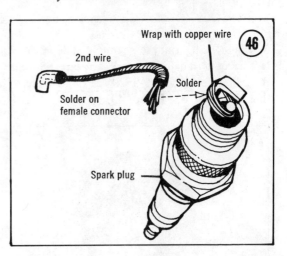

1. Connect the light according to its instructions. The light's spark plug lead should be connected to the plug either in cylinder No. 1 or No. 4.

2. Start the engine and set it at idling speed—between 1,000 and 1,200 rpm.

3. Aim the flashing light at the peephole in the breaker base plate. The "1-4 F" mark should appear to line up with the outer index mark when illuminated by the light.

4. If the marks do not line up, adjust the timing according to Step 5 under *Static Timing*.

5. Increase the engine speed to 2,500 rpm to check the timing advance mechanism.

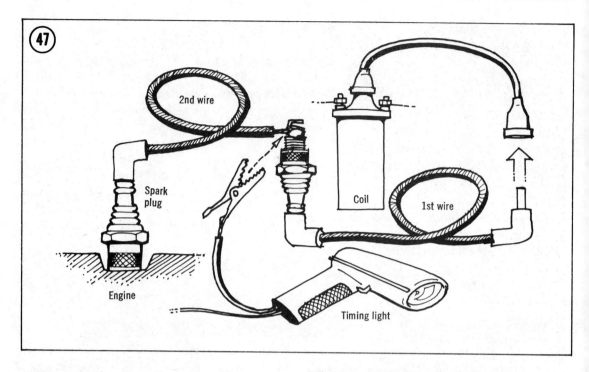

6. Point the light at the peephole. The advance is correct if the index mark appears between the 2 lines located 23.5-26.5°, or in advance, of the "F" mark. See **Figure 48**.

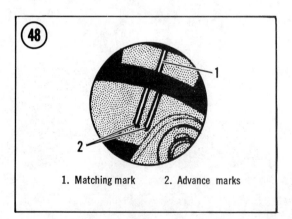

1. Matching mark   2. Advance marks

7. Shut off the engine and connect the plug lead to either the No. 2 or No. 3 cylinder spark plug.

8. Repeat the operations for checking the timing at idle and at 2,500 rpm and adjust if necessary.

AIR CLEANER SERVICE

A clogged air cleaner can decrease the efficiency and life of the engine. It should be checked at each oil change, or more often if the motorcycle is operated under dusty conditions.

1. Raise the seat and remove the tool kit and top air cleaner cover.

2. Lift up the spring retaining clip or loosen wing nuts and then remove the filter element (**Figure 49**).

3. Replace the element if it is clogged with dirt or caked with oil or if the bonding material is cracked.

4. Light dust can be shaken off the element by tapping it while using a soft brush on the outside. If compressed air is available, force it through the filter from the inside as shown in **Figure 50**.

5. Install the unit in reverse order.

CARBURETOR ADJUSTMENT

Unless the carburetors have been disassembled, they normally should not require adjustment. They should be worked on only as a last resort when all other possible causes of problems, such as rough idling or misfiring, have been checked out. See Chapter Six for maintenance and repair.

EMISSION CONTROL DEVICES

No regular maintenance is required other than cleaning, replacement of filter, or replacement of valve. It is recommended that a qualified shop make any repairs.

CLUTCH

If the clutch slips when it is engaged, or if the motorcycle creeps forward with the clutch disengaged, then free play is out of adjustment.

Adjustment

1. Measure free play at the tip of the lever, as shown in **Figure 51**. It should be between 0.4 in. and 0.8 in. (10mm and 20mm).

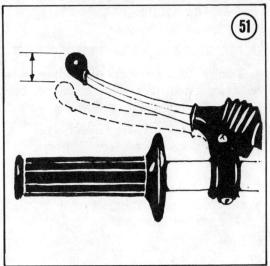

2. Major adjustment, if needed, should be made at the lower end of the clutch cable and fine adjustment at the grip end. See **Figure 52**.

> NOTE: *The following 2 steps apply to adjustment of lower end of clutch cable on CB350/400 models.*

3. Refer to **Figure 53** and loosen the lock bolts on the cable adjuster.

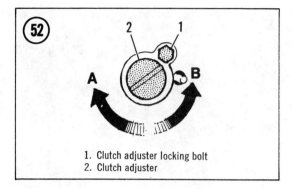

1. Clutch adjuster locking bolt
2. Clutch adjuster

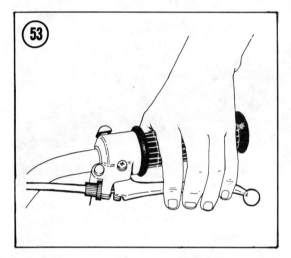

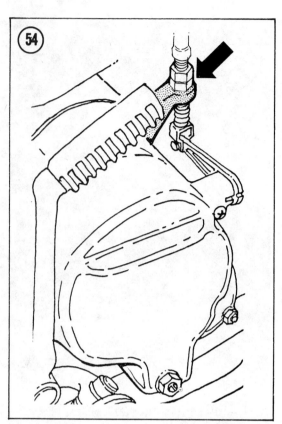

4. Turn the adjuster, **Figure 54**, until a slight resistance is felt, then turn the adjuster back about 0.12 in. (3mm) and retighten the lock bolt.

> NOTE: *The following 2 steps apply to adjustment of lower end of clutch cable on CB550/500.*

5. Refer to **Figure 55** and align the index mark on the clutch lever with the one on the right crankcase cover.

6. Loosen the locknut and turn the adjuster counterclockwise until it feels tight. Then back off about ¼ turn and tighten the locknut.

BATTERY CHECK

The battery is the heart of the electrical system. Its condition should be checked regularly.

Battery charging procedures are covered in the electrical system chapter.

1. Remove the right side cover by pulling it free of its rubber mounts.

2. Check the electrolyte level. **Figure 56** shows the maximum and minimum marks. If necessary, top up with distilled water only. Be careful not to overfill.

> **CAUTION**
> *Painted surfaces will be damaged if corrosive battery electrolyte is spilled on them. Flush away all spills with water, and neutralize with baking soda if necessary.*

3. Inspect the terminals for corrosion. Flush off any oxidation with a solution of baking soda and water. Coat the terminals lightly with Vaseline or a silicone grease to retard new corrosion.

DRIVE CHAIN SERVICE

Cleaning and Lubrication

Follow the recommended service intervals listed in this chapter. More frequent attention is required when the machine has been ridden over dusty or muddy terrain.

Failure to clean the chain regularly will result in faster chain wear.

1. Remove the chain and clean it with solvent and a stiff brush.

> **CAUTION**
> *Always check both sprockets every time the chain is removed. If any wear is visible on the teeth, replace the sprocket. Never install a new chain over worn sprockets or a worn chain over new sprockets.*

2. Rinse thoroughly in clean solvent and dry with a clean rag or compressed air.

3. Put the chain in a pail of melted grease and then hang it to drain excess lubricant. As an alternative, use one of the chain lubes sold by most motorcycle dealers.

Inspection

1. After cleaning the chain, examine it carefully for wear or damage. If any signs are visible, replace the chain.

2. Lay the chain alongside a ruler (**Figure 57**) and compress the links together. Then stretch them apart. If more than ¼ in. (0.6mm) of movement is possible, replace the chain; it is too worn to be used again.

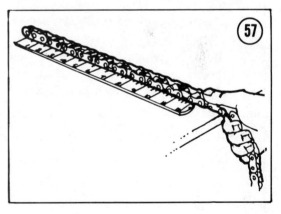

3. Check the inner faces of the inner plates. They should be lightly polished on both sides. If they show considerable wear on both sides, the sprockets are not aligned. Adjust alignment as described in the following section.

Adjustment

1. Loosen the rear axle nut 3 turns.

2. Turn the chain adjuster nuts equally until the

chain has ¾ in. (20mm) slack on the bottom run with the rider on the machine (**Figure 58**) and the chain at its tightest point. Rotate the chain to its loosest point. If more than an inch (25mm) of play is evident, replace the chain.

3. Make sure that the sprockets are aligned by sighting along the top run of the chain. A straight chain is readily visible from the rear sprocket.

4. Tighten the axle nut and recheck alignment and slack.

5. Tighten the brake anchor bolt.

WINTER STORAGE

Several months of inactivity can cause serious problems and a general deterioration of bike condition. This is especially important in areas of extreme cold weather. During the winter months it is advisable to specially prepare a bike for "hibernation."

Selecting a Storage Area

Most cyclists store their bikes in their home garage. Facilities suitable for long-term storage are readily available for rent or lease in most areas. In selecting a building, consider the following points:

1. The storage area must be dry, free from dampness and excessive humidity. Heating is not necessary but the building should be well insulated to minimize extreme temperature variations.

2. Buildings with large window areas should be avoided, or such windows should be masked (a good security measure) if direct sunlight can fall on the bike.

3. Buildings in industrial areas, where factories emit corrosive fumes, are not desirable, nor are facilities near bodies of salt water.

4. The area should be selected to minimize the possibility of loss by fire, theft, or vandalism. It is strongly recommended that the area be fully insured, perhaps with a package covering fire, theft, vandalism, weather, and liability. The advice of your insurance agent should be solicited on these matters. The building should be fireproof and items such as the security of doors and windows, alarm facilities, and proximity of police should be considered.

Preparing Bike for Storage

Careful pre-storage preparation will minimize deterioration and will ease restoring the bike to service in the spring. The following procedure is recommended:

1. Wash the bike completely, making certain to remove any accumulation of road salt that may have collected during the first weeks of winter. Wax all painted and polished surfaces.

2. Run the engine for 20-30 minutes to stabilize oil temperature. Drain oil regardless of mileage

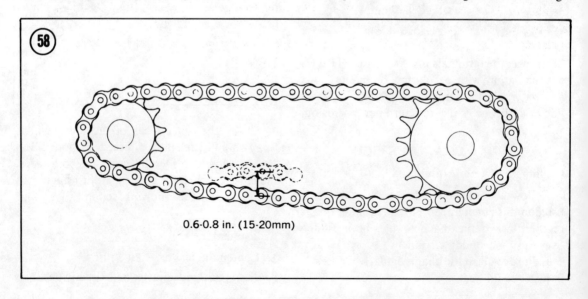

0.6-0.8 in. (15-20mm)

since oil change and replace with normal quantity of fresh oil.

3. Remove battery and coat cable terminals with petroleum jelly. If there is evidence of acid spillage in the battery box, neutralize with baking soda, wash clean, and repaint. Batteries should be kept in an area where they will not freeze, and where they can be recharged every 2 weeks. If the battery cannot be recharged regularly, drain out all electrolyte and store off the floor, preferably on a shelf.

4. Drain all gasoline from the fuel tank, settling bowl, and carburetor float bowls. Leave fuel cock on RESERVE position.

5. Remove spark plugs and add a small quantity of oil to each cylinder. Turn the engine a few revolutions by hand. Install spark plugs.

6. Insert a paper card, lightly saturated with silicone oil, between the points.

7. Check tire pressures. Move machine to storage area and store on centerstand with both wheels off the ground. If preparation is performed in an area remote from the storage facility, the bike should be trucked, not ridden, into storage.

Inspection During Storage

Try to inspect bike weekly while in storage. Any deterioration should be corrected as soon as possible. For example, if corrosion of bright metals parts is observed, cover them with a light film of grease or silicone spray after a thorough polishing.

Restoring Bike to Service

A bike that has been properly prepared, and stored in a suitable area, requires only light maintenance to restore it to service. It is advisable, however, to perform a spring tune-up.

1. Before removing the bike from the storage area, reinflate tires to the correct pressures. Air loss during storage may have nearly flattened the tires, and moving the bike can cause damage to tires, tubes, or rims.

2. When the bike is brought to the work area, immediately install the battery (fully charged) and fill the fuel tank. (The fuel cock should be on the RESERVE position; do not move yet.) If the battery was drained, it can be refilled by a dealer and recharged.

3. Check the fuel system for leaks. Remove carburetor float bowl or open the float bowl drain cock and allow several cups of fuel to pass through the system. Move the fuel cock slowly to the CLOSE position, remove the settling bowl and empty any accumulated water.

4. Perform normal tune-up, described earlier, adjust valve clearance, apply oil to camshaft, and, when checking spark plugs, add a few drops of oil to the cylinder. Be especially certain to degrease ignition points if an oily card was used to inhibit oxidation during storage; use a non-petroleum solvent such as tricholorethylene.

5. Check safety items, i.e., lights, horn, etc., as oxidation of switch contacts and/or sockets during storage may make one or more of these critical devices inoperative.

6. Test ride and clean the motorcycle.

CHAPTER THREE

TROUBLESHOOTING

Diagnosing mechanical problems is relatively simple if you use orderly procedures and keep a few basic principles in mind.

The troubleshooting procedures in this chapter analyze typical symptoms, and show logical methods of isolating causes. These are not the only methods. There may be several ways to solve a problem, but only a systematic, methodical approach can guarantee success.

Never assume anything. Don't overlook the obvious. If you are riding along and the bike suddenly quits, check the easiest, most accessible problem spots first. Is there gasoline in the tank? Is the gas petcock in the ON or RESERVE position? Has a spark plug wire fallen off? Check the ignition switch. Sometimes the weight of keys on a key ring may turn the ignition off suddenly.

If nothing obvious turns up in a cursory check, look a little further. Learning to recognize and describe symptoms will make repairs easier for you or a mechanic at the shop. Describe problems accurately and fully. Saying that, "it won't run," isn't the same as saying, "it quit on the highway at high speed and wouldn't start," or that, "it sat in my garage for 3 months and then wouldn't start."

Gather as many symptoms together as possible to aid in diagnosis. Note whether the engine lost power gradually or all at once, what color smoke (if any) came from the exhaust, and so on. Remember that the more complicated a machine is, the easier it is to troubleshoot because symptoms point to specific problems.

After the symptoms are defined, areas which could cause problems are tested and analyzed. Guessing at the cause of a problem may provide the solution, but it can easily lead to frustration, wasted time, and a series of expensive, unnecessary part replacements.

You don't need fancy equipment or complicated test gear to determine whether repairs can be attempted at home. A few simple checks could save a large repair bill and time lost while the bike sits in a dealer's service department. On the other hand, be realistic and don't attempt repairs beyond your abilities. Service departments tend to charge heavily for putting together a disassembled engine that may have been abused. Some won't even take on such a job—so use common sense, don't get in over your head.

OPERATING REQUIREMENTS

An engine needs 3 basics to run properly: correct gas/air mixture, compression, and a spark at the right time. If one or more are missing, the engine won't run. The electrical system is the weakest link of the three. More problems result from electrical breakdowns than from any other source. Keep that in mind before you begin tampering with carburetor adjustments and the like.

If a bike has been sitting for any length of time and refuses to start, check the battery for a charged condition first, and then check the gasoline delivery system. This includes the tank, fuel petcocks, lines, and the carburetors. Rust may have formed in the tank, obstructing fuel flow. Gasoline deposits may have gummed up carburetor jets and air passages. Gasoline tends to lose its potency after standing for long periods. Condensation may contaminate it with water. Drain old gas and try starting with a fresh tankful.

TROUBLESHOOTING INSTRUMENTS

Chapter One lists many of the instruments needed and detailed instructions on their use.

STARTING DIFFICULTIES

Check gas flow first. Remove the gas cap and look into the tank. If gas is present, pull off a fuel line at the carburetor and see if gas flows freely. If none comes out, the fuel tap may be shut off, blocked by rust or foreign matter, or the fuel line may be stopped up or kinked. If the carburetor is getting usable fuel, turn to the electrical system next.

Make sure the ignition switch is on and the fuse is good.

Check that the battery is charged by turning on the lights or by beeping the horn. Refer to your owner's manual for starting procedures with a dead battery. Have the battery recharged if necessary.

Pull off a spark plug cap, remove the spark plug, and reconnect the cap. Lay the plug against the cylinder head so its base makes a good connection, and turn the engine over with the kickstarter. A fat, blue spark should jump across the electrodes. If there is no spark, or only a weak one, there is electrical system trouble. Check for a defective plug by replacing it with a known good one. Don't assume a plug is good just because it's new.

Once the plug has been cleared of guilt, but there's still no spark, start backtracking through the system. If the contact at the end of the spark plug wire can be exposed, it can be held about ⅛ inch from the head while the engine is turned over to check for a spark. Remember to hold the wire only by its insulation to avoid a nasty shock. If the plug wires are dirty, greasy, or wet, wrap a rag around them so you don't get shocked. If you do feel a shock or see sparks along the wire, clean or replace the wire and/or its connections.

If there's no spark at the plug wire, look for loose connections at the coil and battery. If all seems in order there, check next for oily or dirty contact points. Clean points with electrical contact cleaner, or a strip of paper. On battery ignition models, with the ignition switch turned on, open and close the points manually with a screwdriver.

No spark at the points with this test indicates a failure in the ignition system. Refer to Chapter Seven for checkout procedures for the entire system and individual components. Refer to Chapter Two for checking and setting ignition timing.

Note that spark plugs of the incorrect heat range (too cold) may cause hard starting. Set gaps to specifications. If you have just ridden through a puddle or washed the bike and it won't start, dry off plugs and plug wires. Water may have entered the carburetor and fouled the fuel under these conditions, but wet plugs and wires are the more likely problem.

If a healthy spark occurs at the right time, and there is adequate gas flow to the carburetor, check the carburetor itself at this time. Make sure all jets and air passages are clean, check float level, and adjust if necessary. Shake the float to check for gasoline inside it, and replace or repair as indicated. Check that the carburetors are mounted snugly, and no air is leaking past the manifold. Check for a clogged air filter. Compression, or the lack of it, usually enters the picture only in the case of older engines. Worn or broken pistons, rings, and cylinder bores could prevent starting. Generally, a gradual power loss and harder starting will be readily apparent in this case.

Compression may be checked in the field by

turning the kickstarter by hand and noting that adequate resistance is felt.

An accurate compression check gives a good idea of the condition of the basic working parts of the engine. To perform this test, you need a compression gauge. The motor should be warm.

1. Remove the plug on the cylinder to be tested and clean out any dirt or grease

2. Insert the tip of the gauge into the hole, making sure it is seated correctly.

3. Open the throttle all the way and make sure the chokes on the carburetors are open.

4. Crank the engine several times and record the highest pressure reading on the gauge. Run the test on each of the cylinders.

5. The normal compression for all models is 155-170 psi. If the readings are significantly lower than 155 psi as a group, or if they vary more than 10 psi between any 2 cylinders, proceed to the next step.

6. Pour a tablespoon of motor oil into the suspect cylinder and record the compression.

If oil raises the compression significantly—10 psi in an old engine—the rings are worn and should be replaced. No, or low compression could be indicative of a holed piston, broken rings, or a bent valve.

Valve adjustments should be checked next. Sticking, burned, or broken valves may hamper starting. As a last resort, check valve timing.

STARTER

Starter system troubles are relatively easy to isolate. The following are common symptoms and causes.

1. *Engine cranks very slowly or not at all.* On older models, turn on the headlight. If the light is very dim, the battery or connecting wires are probably at fault. Check the battery. Check the wiring for breaks, shorts, or dirty connections.

If the battery or connecting wires are not at fault, turn the headlight on and try to crank the engine. If the light dims drastically, the starter is probably shorted to ground. Remove it and test as described.

If the light remains bright, or dims only slightly when trying to start the engine, the trouble may be in the starter, relay, or wiring. Perform the following steps to isolate the cause.

WARNING
Disconnect the coil wire to prevent accidental starting. Keep away from moving parts when working near the engine.

a. If the starter doesn't respond at all, connect a 12-volt test lamp between the starter terminal and ground. Turn the ignition key to START. If the lamp lights, the starter is probably at fault. Remove it and test the unit. If the lamp doesn't light, the problem is somewhere in the starting circuit. Perform the next steps.

b. Connect a jumper wire between the battery and starter terminals on the starter relay. If the starter doesn't respond at all, the relay is probably defective. If the starter cranks normally, perform the next step.

c. Connect a test lamp between the starter terminal on the starter relay and ground. Turn the ignition key to START. If the lamp doesn't light, check the ignition switch and associated wiring. Turn the key to START and work it around in the switch. If the lamp lights erratically, the ignition switch is probably defective.

d. If the problem still has not been isolated, check all wiring in the starting circuit with an ohmmeter or other continuity tester. See the wiring diagrams in Chapter Seven.

2. *Starter turns, but does not engage.* This problem may be caused by a defective starter drive mechanism, or broken gear teeth. Remove and inspect the starter as described in Chapter Seven.

3. *Loud grinding noises when starter runs.* This may mean the teeth are not meshing properly, or it may mean the starter drive mechanism is damaged. In the first case, remove the starter and examine the gear teeth. In the latter case, remove the starter and replace the starter drive mechanism.

POOR IDLING

Poor idling may be caused by incorrect carburetor adjustment, incorrect timing, or ignition system defects. Check the gas cap vent for an obstruction.

MISFIRING

Misfiring can be caused by a weak spark or dirty plugs. Check for fuel contamination. Run the engine at night to check for spark leaks along the plug wires and under the spark plug cap.

WARNING
Do not run engine in dark garage to check for spark leaks. There is considerable danger of carbon monoxide poisoning.

If misfiring occurs only at certain throttle settings, refer to the fuel system chapter for the specific carburetor circuits involved. Misfiring under heavy load, as when climbing hills or accelerating, is usually caused by faulty spark plugs.

FLAT SPOTS

If the engine seems to die momentarily when the throttle is opened and then recovers, check for a dirty main jet in the carburetor, water in the fuel, or an excessively lean mixture.

POWER LOSS

Poor condition of rings, pistons, or cylinders will cause a lack of power and speed. Ignition timing should be checked.

OVERHEATING

If the engine seems to run too hot all the time, be sure you are not idling it for long periods. Air-cooled engines are not designed to operate at a standstill for any length of time. Heavy stop-and-go traffic is hard on a motorcycle engine. Spark plugs of the wrong heat range can burn pistons. An excessively lean gas mixture may cause overheating. Check ignition timing. Don't ride in too high a gear. Broken or worn rings may permit compression gases to leak past them, heating heads and cylinders excessively. Check oil level and use the proper grade lubricants. See Chapter Two.

ENGINE NOISES

Experience is needed to diagnose accurately in this area. A large screwdriver can be used like a stethoscope. Hold the handle to your ear and the blade against the cylinder or cases. Noises are hard to differentiate and harder yet to describe. Deep knocking noises usually mean main bearing failure. A slapping noise generally comes from loose pistons. A light knocking noise during acceleration may be a bad connecting rod bearing. Pinging should be corrected immediately or damage to pistons will result. Compression leaks at the head-cylinder joint will sound like a rapid on-and-off squeal.

PISTON SEIZURE

Piston seizure is caused by incorrect piston clearances when fitted, fitting rings with improper end gap, too thin an oil being used, incorrect spark plug heat range, or incorrect ignition timing. Overheating from any cause may result in seizure.

EXCESSIVE VIBRATION

Excessive vibration may be caused by loose motor mounts, worn engine or transmission bearings, loose wheels, worn swing arm bushings, a generally poor running engine, broken or cracked frame, or one that has been damaged in a collision. See also *Poor Handling* in this chapter.

CLUTCH SLIP OR DRAG

Clutch slip may be due to worn plates, improper adjustment, or glazed plates. A dragging clutch could result from damaged or bent plates, improper adjustment, or even clutch spring pressure.

All clutch problems, except adjustments or cable replacement, require removal to identify the cause and make repairs.

1. *Slippage*—This condition is most noticeable when accelerating in high gear at relatively low speed. To check slippage, drive at a steady speed in fourth or fifth gear. Without letting up the accelerator, push in the clutch long enough to let engine speed increase (1 or 2 seconds). Then let the clutch out rapidly. If the clutch is good, engine speed will drop quickly or the bike will jump forward. If the clutch is slipping, engine speed will drop slowly and the bike will not jump forward.

3

Slippage results from insufficient clutch lever free-play, worn friction plates or weak springs. Riding the clutch can cause the disc surfaces to become glazed, resulting in slippage.

2. *Drag or failure to release*—This trouble usually causes difficult shifting and gear clash especially when downshifting. The cause may be excessive clutch lever free-play, warped or bent plates, stretched clutch cable, or broken or loose disc linings.

3. *Chatter or grabbing*—Check for worn or misaligned steel plate and clutch friction plates.

TRANSMISSION

Transmission problems are usually indicated by one or more of the following symptoms:

   a. Difficulty shifting gears

   b. Gear clash when downshifting

   c. Slipping out of gear

   d. Excessive noise in neutral

   e. Excessive noise in gear

Transmission symptoms are sometimes hard to distinguish from clutch symptoms. Be sure the clutch is not causing the trouble before working on the transmission.

POOR HANDLING

Poor handling may be caused by improper tire pressures, a damaged frame or swing arm, worn shocks or front forks, weak fork springs, a bent or broken steering stem, misaligned wheels, loose or missing spokes, worn tires, bent handlebars, worn wheel bearings, dragging brakes, bent frame, or bad steering bearings and races.

BRAKE PROBLEMS

Sticking brakes may be caused by broken or weak return springs, improper cable or rod adjustment, or dry pivot and cam bushings. Grabbing brakes may be caused by greasy linings which must be replaced. Brake grab may also be due to out-of-round drums or linings which have broken loose from the brake shoes. Glazed linings or glazed brake pads will cause loss of stopping power.

ELECTRICAL PROBLEMS

Bulbs which continuously burn out may be caused by excessive vibration, loose connections that permit sudden current surges, poor battery connections, installation of the wrong type bulb or a faulty voltage regulator.

A dead battery or one which discharges quickly may be caused by a faulty alternator or rectifier. Check for loose or corroded terminals. Shorted battery cells or broken terminals will keep a battery from charging. Low water level will decrease a battery's capacity. A battery left uncharged after installation will sulphate, rendering it useless.

A majority of light and horn, or other electrical accessory problems, are caused by loose or corroded ground connections. Check those first, and then substitute known good units for easier troubleshooting.

TROUBLESHOOTING GUIDE

The following summarizes the troubleshooting process. Use it to outline possible problem areas, then refer to the specific chapter or section involved.

Loss of Power

1. *Poor compression*—Check for worn piston rings and cylinders, worn head gaskets, bent valves, and incorrect valve adjustment.

2. *Overheated engine*—Check lubricating oil supply; check for clogged cooling fins, incorrect ignition timing, a slipping clutch, carbon in the combustion chamber, and improper carburetor synchronization.

3. *Improper mixture*—Check for dirty air cleaner, restricted fuel flow, clogged gas cap vent hole, and improper carburetor synchronization.

4. *Miscellaneous*—Other causes could be dragging brakes, tight wheel bearings, a defective chain, or a clogged exhaust system.

Steering Problems

1. *Hard steering*—Incorrect tire pressures, incorrect steering damper adjustment, worn steering stem head and/or bearings.

2. *Pulls to one side*—Problem may be caused by unequal shock absorbers, incorrect drive chain adjustment, improper front/rear wheel alignment, unbalanced tires, a defective swing arm, or a defective steering head.

3. *Shimmy*—Can be caused by improper drive chain adjustment, loose or missing spokes, deformed wheel rims, worn wheel bearings, or incorrect wheel balance.

Gearshifting Difficulties

1. *Clutch*—Check for proper clutch adjustment, condition of clutch springs, friction plates, steel plates; also check oil quantity.

2. *Transmission*—Check oil level, oil grade; check return spring or pin, gear change lever or spring, drum position plate, change drum, and change forks.

Brake Troubles

1. *Poor brakes*—May be caused by worn lining, incorrect brake adjustment, oil or water on brake lining or pads, loose linkage or cables, or a hydraulic leak or low fluid.

2. *Noisy brakes*—May be caused by a worn or scratched lining, scratched brake drum, dirt in brakes, glazed drum or pads, or improper mounting.

3. *Unadjustable brakes*—Caused by worn lining or pads, worn drum or disc, worn brake cams, or drum and lining not true.

CHAPTER FOUR

ENGINE

The four-cylinder engines have a mystique of technological advancement and complexity about them which has scared many a home mechanic away from performing his own work. In most ways the small fours are simple in construction and easy to maintain. The trick is to think of each cylinder as if it were the only one or one of two. In other words, take each operation in turn.

Most operations will take longer than for a single or twin cylinder bike. Mechanics charge for their time rather than for the type of job. You'll save money by doing the work yourself and have the added satisfaction of knowing the work was done properly.

SERVICING ENGINE IN FRAME

The following parts can be serviced while the engine is mounted in the frame:

   a. Cylinder head
   b. Camshaft and chain tensioner
   c. Cylinders and pistons
   d. Electrical systems
   e. Oil pump and filter
   f. Gear shift mechanism
   g. Clutch
   h. Carburetors

EXHAUST SYSTEM (TYPICAL)

Muffler and Exhaust Pipe Removal/Installation

1. Loosen the bolts which hold the muffler(s) to the frame.

2. Loosen the 8 nuts holding the exhaust collars in place.

3. Remove the 4 exhaust pipe collars. See **Figure 1**.

4. Loosen the muffler band bolts and exhaust pipes on the 4-into-one system. See **Figure 2**. Standard models have 4 separate mufflers and pipes.

5. Remove the 2 separate exhaust pipes on a 4-into-one system.

6. Remove the mufflers and pipes.

7. Clean the pipes and reverse this procedure to reinstall or for replacement.

Cleaning

The exhaust system can be cleaned without removing the mufflers or tailpipes. Follow periodic intervals specified in Chapter Two or perform as the need arises. The average 4-stroke exhaust system requires infrequent cleaning because there is not the oil-fouling or carbon build-up associated with a 2-stroke engine.

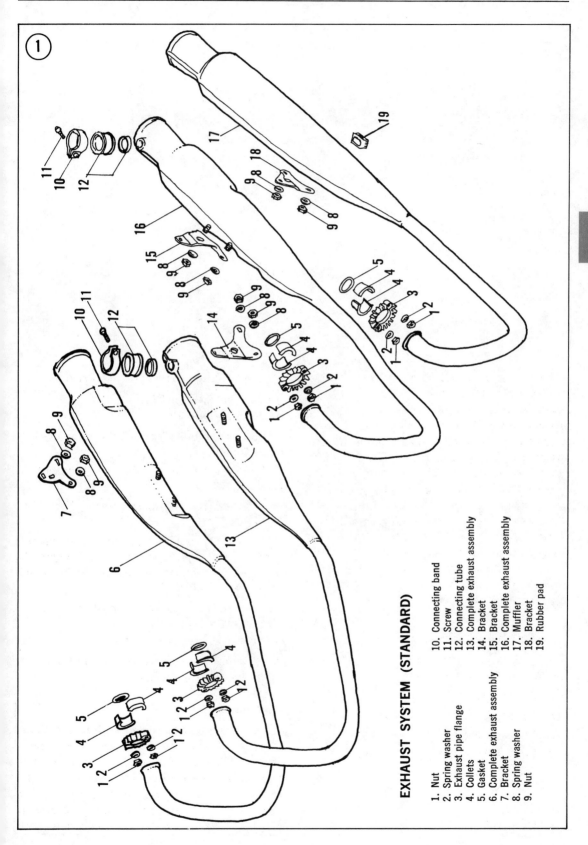

EXHAUST SYSTEM (STANDARD)

1. Nut
2. Spring washer
3. Exhaust pipe flange
4. Collets
5. Gasket
6. Complete exhaust assembly
7. Bracket
8. Spring washer
9. Nut
10. Connecting band
11. Screw
12. Connecting tube
13. Complete exhaust assembly
14. Bracket
15. Bracket
16. Complete exhaust assembly
17. Muffler
18. Bracket
19. Rubber pad

4

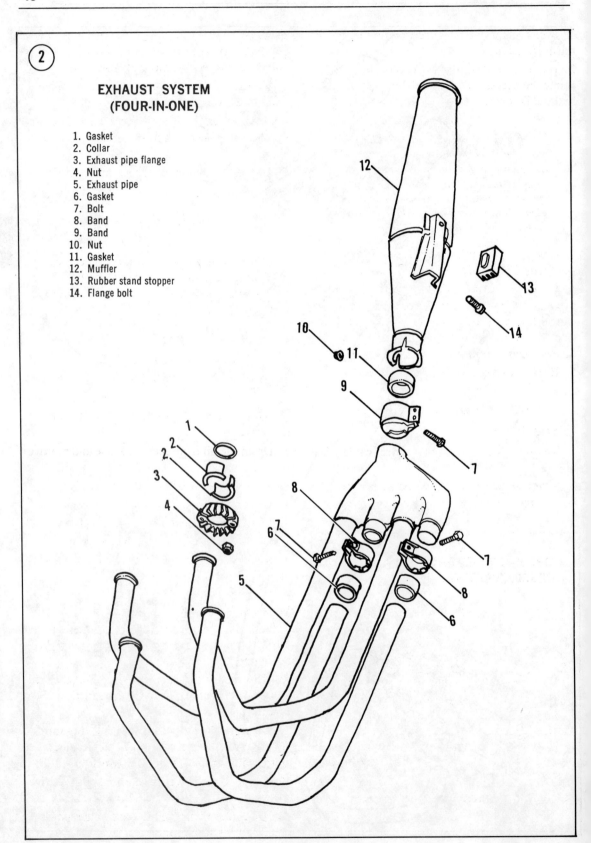

**EXHAUST SYSTEM
(FOUR-IN-ONE)**

1. Gasket
2. Collar
3. Exhaust pipe flange
4. Nut
5. Exhaust pipe
6. Gasket
7. Bolt
8. Band
9. Band
10. Nut
11. Gasket
12. Muffler
13. Rubber stand stopper
14. Flange bolt

1. Remove the baffle setscrews at the end of the muffler(s).

2. Pull the baffle out of the end of the muffler. It may be necessary to twist the baffle slightly if buildup is severe.

CAUTION
Do not run the engine with the baffles removed. The engine has been designed to run properly at one fuel setting which can be upset by any change in the exhaust or induction system. An unbaffled engine will run lean and hot causing premature failure.

3. Clean heavy buildup off the baffles with a wire brush. Soak in solvent if necessary.

4. Clean the inside of the muffler(s) with a piece of old control cable frayed at one end and chucked in a drill at the other. The flailing action will scrape away any carbon. Blow out any dust with compressed air.

5. Install baffle(s) and replace setscrew(s).

TACHOMETER DRIVE CABLE

Oil Seal Repair

1. Remove the tachometer drive cable. See **Figure 3**.

2. Screw a long, narrow wood screw into the hole alongside the tachometer drive shaft and

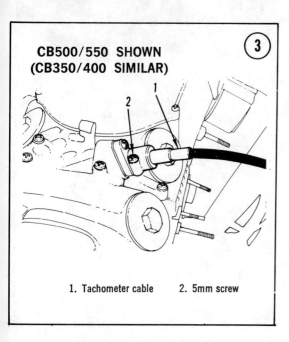

CB500/550 SHOWN
(CB350/400 SIMILAR)

③

1. Tachometer cable   2. 5mm screw

seal. As the screw is turned, the seal will slowly come out. If care is taken, the only thing which will get damaged is the already bad seal.

3. Coat a new seal with Armor All or silicone and place it on the tachometer drive shaft.

4. Seat the seal using a piece of tubing or a thin wall socket placed over the tachometer drive shaft.

5. Install the tachometer drive cable.

ENGINE REMOVAL
(CB350/400)

Figure 4 illustrates various operations to remove the engine. They should be performed in numerical order. These illustrations are self-explanatory.

ENGINE REMOVAL
(CB500/550)

1. Turn off the fuel valve and disconnect the lines to the fuel tank. Raise the seat and remove the tank.

2. Drain the oil from the crankcase and remove the filter.

3. Remove the mufflers and exhaust pipes.

4. Disconnect spark plug wires at plugs.

5. Disconnect the battery ground strap.

6. Disconnect tachometer cable. See Figure 3.

7. Remove the air cleaner element and then its case by loosening the 6mm bolts.

8. Disconnect the throttle cable at the carburetors. See **Figure 5**.

9. Remove the carburetors by loosening the screws at the insulator and air cleaner chamber. See **Figure 6**.

10. Disconnect the starter cable at the solenoid and the alternator wiring at the junction. See **Figure 7**.

11. Remove the gearshift pedal, starting motor cover, and left crankcase cover. Disconnect the clutch cable at the lifter. See **Figure 8**.

12. Remove the drive chain and the final drive sprocket.

13. Disconnect the yellow and blue contact breaker leads at the connector.

4

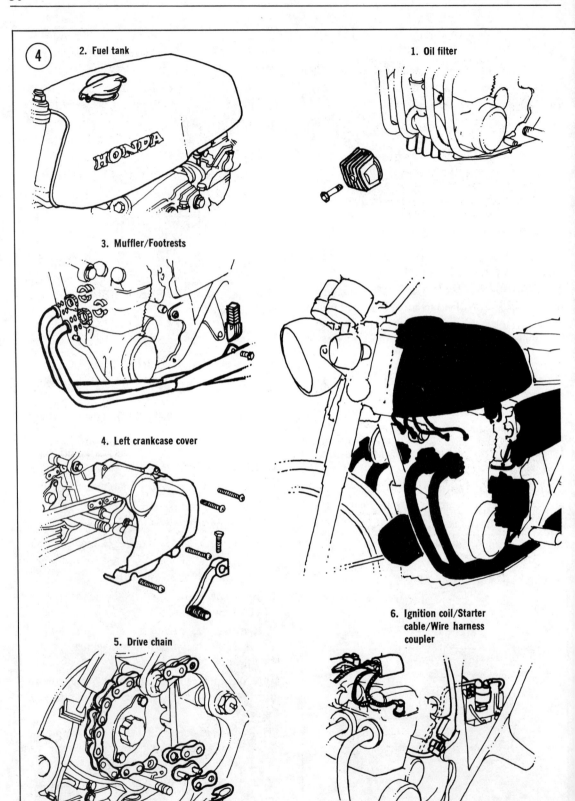

④

2. Fuel tank

1. Oil filter

3. Muffler/Footrests

4. Left crankcase cover

5. Drive chain

6. Ignition coil/Starter
cable/Wire harness
coupler

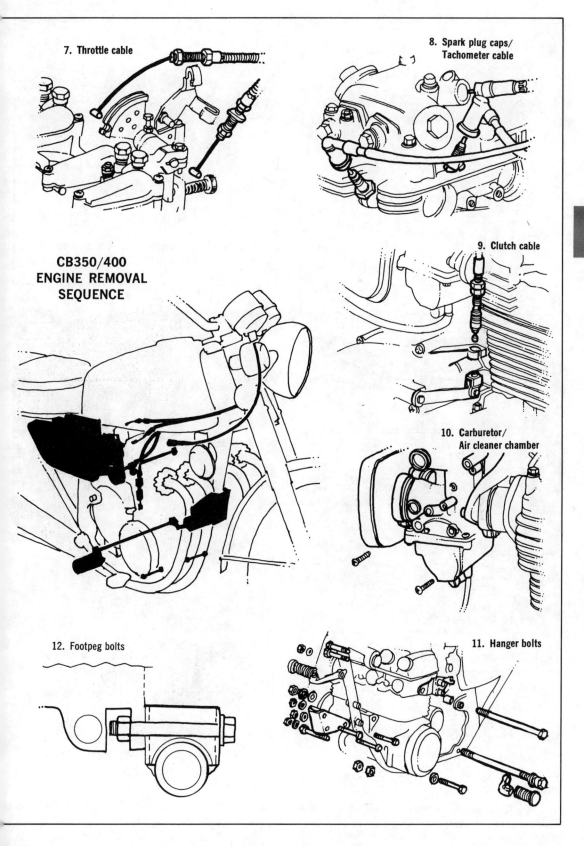

7. Throttle cable

8. Spark plug caps/ Tachometer cable

9. Clutch cable

CB350/400 ENGINE REMOVAL SEQUENCE

10. Carburetor/ Air cleaner chamber

12. Footpeg bolts

11. Hanger bolts

4

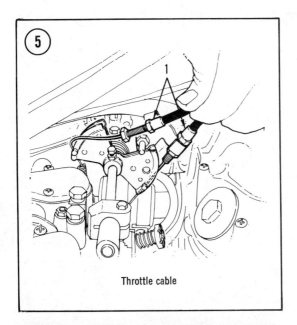

Throttle cable

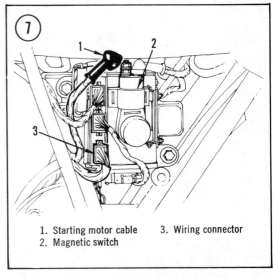

1. Starting motor cable   3. Wiring connector
2. Magnetic switch

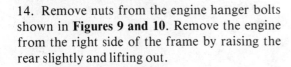

14. Remove nuts from the engine hanger bolts shown in **Figures 9 and 10**. Remove the engine from the right side of the frame by raising the rear slightly and lifting out.

Engine Installation (Typical)

Install the engine by reversing removal procedure. Pay particular attention to the following points.

1. Battery ground cable terminal is installed along with rear mounting bolt, **Figure 11**.

2. Do not pinch the alternator or starter wiring when left crankcase cover is reinstalled.

3. Connect each pair of mufflers with proper band, **Figure 12**.

4. Adjust the clutch, drive chain, and carburetors after the engine is installed.

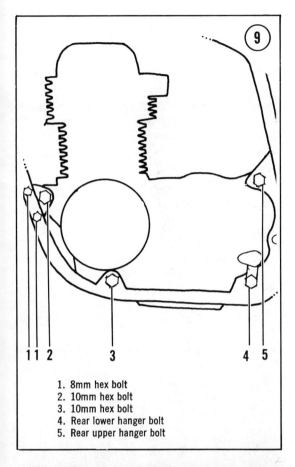

1. 8mm hex bolt
2. 10mm hex bolt
3. 10mm hex bolt
4. Rear lower hanger bolt
5. Rear upper hanger bolt

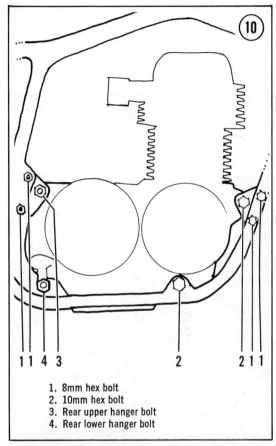

1. 8mm hex bolt
2. 10mm hex bolt
3. Rear upper hanger bolt
4. Rear lower hanger bolt

CYLINDER HEAD

Refer to **Figures 13 through 16** for the following procedures.

Removal

1. Remove fuel tank, mufflers, spark plugs, and breather cover (**Figure 17**). Disconnect tachometer cable.

2. Remove the caps from the 8 valve tappet access holes and loosen the rocker arm adjusting screws.

3. Remove the cylinder head cover, **Figure 18**. Take care to loosen the screws and bolts uniformly to relieve stress gradually.

4a. *CB500/550*. Relieve cam chain tension. See **Figure 19**. Loosen the locknut, turn the adjusting screw clockwise as far as it will go (about 90 degrees) and tighten locknut.

4b. *CB350/400*. Relieve cam chain tension (**Figure 20**). Remove the chain tensioner holder by unscrewing the bolts and then removing the tension "slipper."

5. Remove the point cover and rotate the crankshaft (use a 23mm socket on the special nut, **Figure 21**) until one of the cam sprocket mounting bolts comes into view. Remove the bolt. Then rotate the crankshaft a full turn and remove the other bolt.

6. Remove the cam sprocket from the camshaft, **Figure 22**, and remove the cam chain from the sprocket. Use wire to hold the cam chain so it does not slip into the crankcase. Remove the cam.

7. Remove the carburetors. See Chapter Six.

8. CB500/550 (**Figure 23**): Loosen the cam chain tensioner mounting bolt.

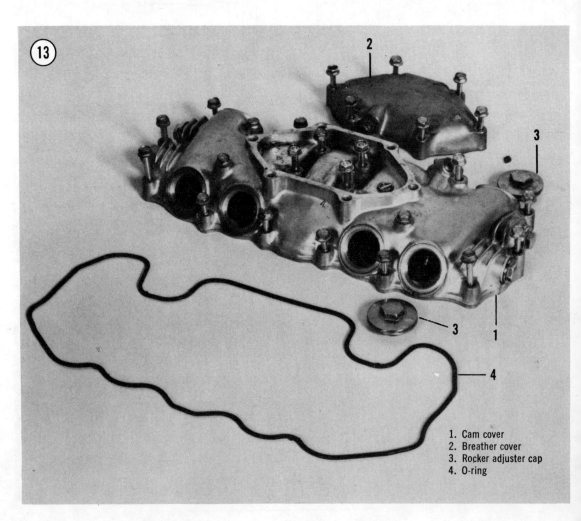

1. Cam cover
2. Breather cover
3. Rocker adjuster cap
4. O-ring

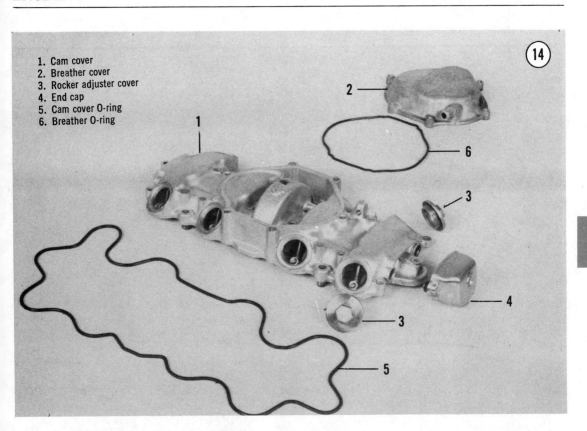

1. Cam cover
2. Breather cover
3. Rocker adjuster cover
4. End cap
5. Cam cover O-ring
6. Breather O-ring

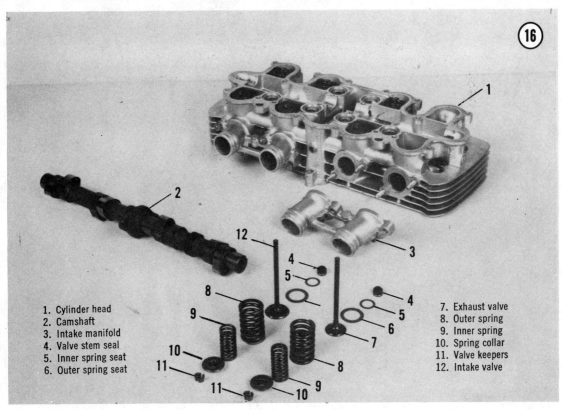

1. Cylinder head
2. Camshaft
3. Intake manifold
4. Valve stem seal
5. Inner spring seat
6. Outer spring seat

7. Exhaust valve
8. Outer spring
9. Inner spring
10. Spring collar
11. Valve keepers
12. Intake valve

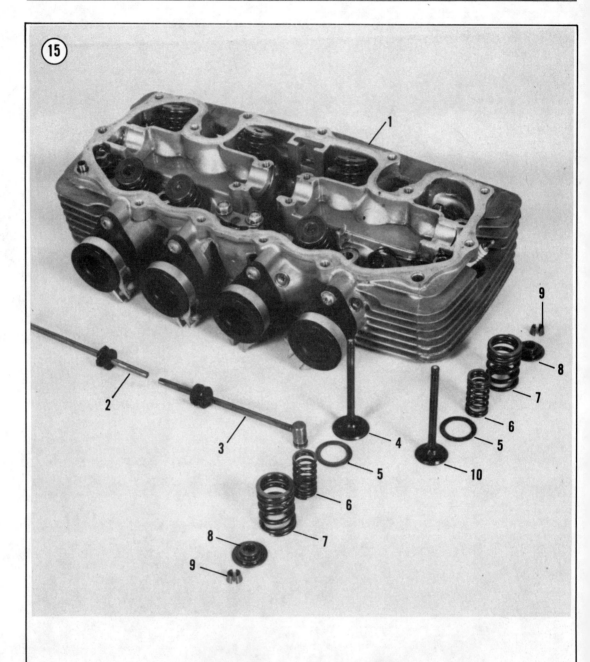

⑮

1. Cylinder head
2. Left oil manifold
3. Right oil manifold
4. Intake valve
5. Spring seat
6. Inner spring
7. Outer spring
8. Spring collar
9. Valve keepers
10. Exhaust valve

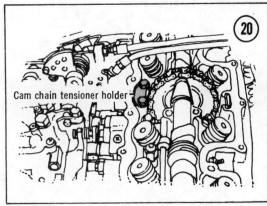

Cam chain tensioner holder

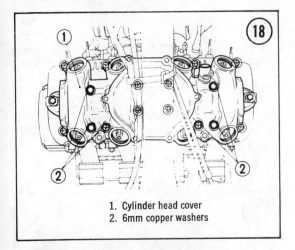

1. Cylinder head cover
2. 6mm copper washers

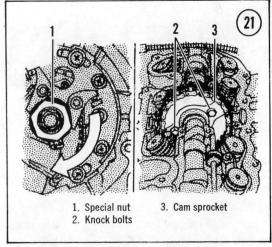

1. Special nut
2. Knock bolts
3. Cam sprocket

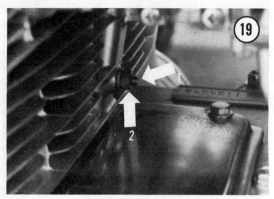

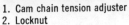

1. Cam chain tension adjuster
2. Locknut

9. Loosen the 12 cylinder head nuts in a crisscross pattern as shown in **Figure 24** to relieve the stresses equally.

10. Lift cylinder head off.

Installation

1. Place the cylinder head on the block, being careful not to drop the cam chain into the crankcase. Install all new seals, gaskets, and O-rings, even if old ones look good.

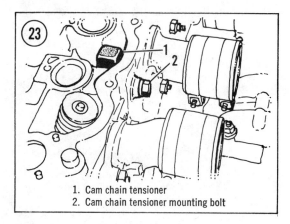

1. Cam chain tensioner
2. Cam chain tensioner mounting bolt

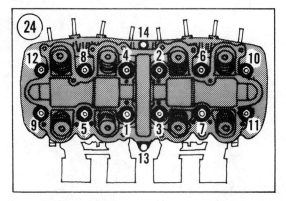

2. Tighten cylinder head nuts in the sequence shown in **Figure 25**, ultimately torquing them down to 14.5-16.6 ft.-lb. (2.0-2.2 mkg).

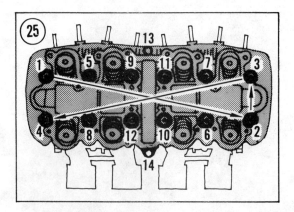

3. Slide the camshaft, together with the cam chain sprocket, into place from the right side and install the chain. Leave the sprocket free to turn on the shaft.

4. Remove the point cover and rotate the crankshaft until the "T 1-4" timing mark is

aligned with the index mark when viewed through the peephole in the base plate.

5a. *CB500/550* (**Figure 26**): Set the camshaft so that the center of the notch on the right end is lined up with the surface of the cylinder head. Secure the sprocket to the shaft with 2 bolts.

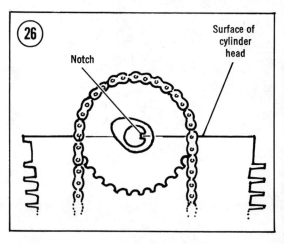

5b. *CB350/400* (**Figure 27**): Align the sprocket so that the 2 matching lines are even with the surface of the cylinder head. Secure the sprocket to the shaft with the 2 bolts.

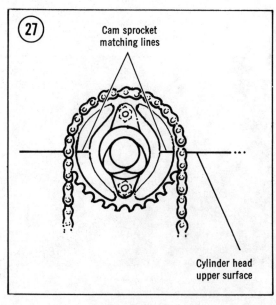

6. Install the cylinder head cover and torque it to 5.1-8.7 ft.-lb. (0.7-1.2 mkg) with the difference between each bolt no greater than 1.5 ft.-lb. (0.2 mkg).

CAUTION

*Reach through the opening and pull up on rocker arms so that tappet adjuster comes into contact with the valve end, or damage will result (**Figure 28**).*

7. Adjust cam chain tension (see Chapter Two). Adjust the valves.

CAUTION

Before starting the engine, rotate the crankshaft slowly by hand to check for binding and metal-to-metal contact. If contact or binding are felt or heard, stop turning the crankshaft. Recheck your work to find the cause.

VALVE TRAIN

Figures 29 and 30 show valve train.

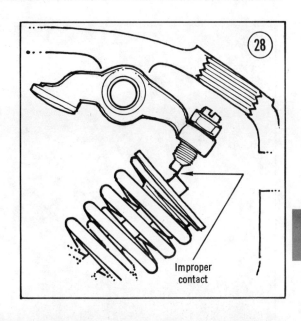

Improper contact

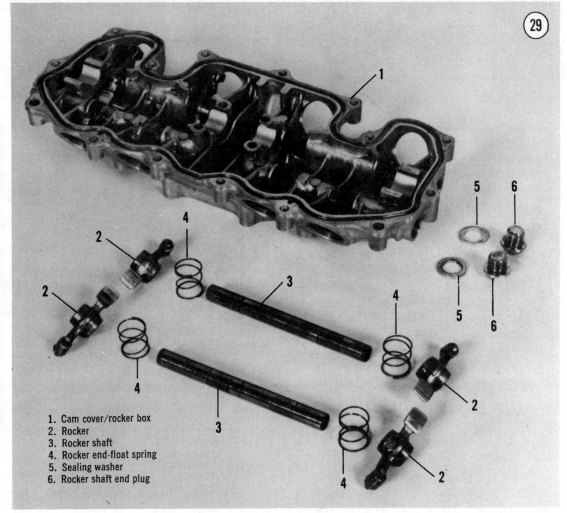

1. Cam cover/rocker box
2. Rocker
3. Rocker shaft
4. Rocker end-float spring
5. Sealing washer
6. Rocker shaft end plug

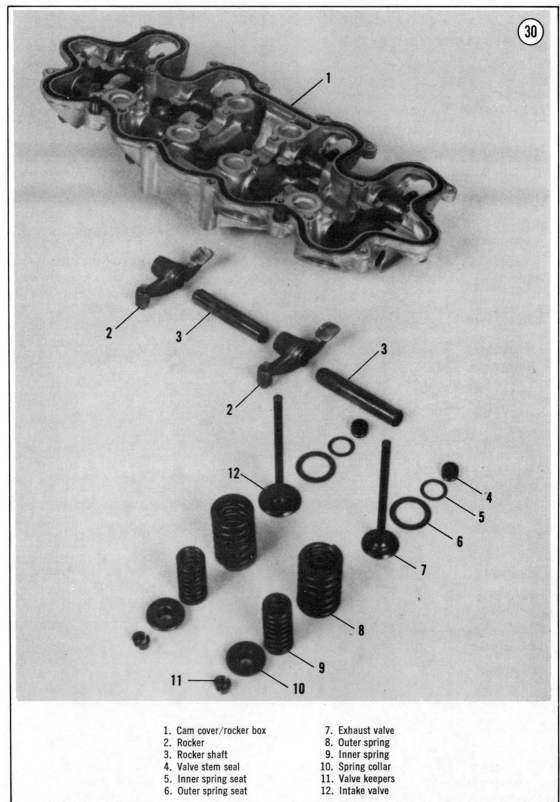

30

1. Cam cover/rocker box
2. Rocker
3. Rocker shaft
4. Valve stem seal
5. Inner spring seat
6. Outer spring seat
7. Exhaust valve
8. Outer spring
9. Inner spring
10. Spring collar
11. Valve keepers
12. Intake valve

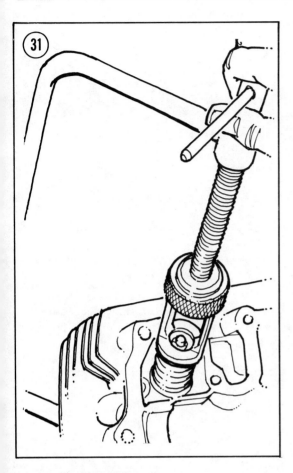

Valve Removal/Installation

1. Remove the valve keepers using a valve spring compressor as shown in **Figure 31**.

2. Remove the valves.

3. Remove the valve guides if necessary. Replace old valve guide oil seals. Do not reuse old ones.

Valve Lapping

Valve lapping is a simple operation which can restore the valve seal without costly machining if the amount of wear or distortion is not too great. The process is as follows:

1. Coat the valve seating area with a lapping compound such as carborundum or Clover Brand.

2. Insert the valve in its guide.

3. Grasp the valve using a valve lapping tool (an inexpensive item available at any automotive store) or an old piece of fuel line and rotate the valve back and forth.

4. Frequently check the mating surface to see if a uniform gray has been created on both surfaces. Stop as soon as this happens, to avoid removing too much material.

5. Thoroughly clean the valves and guides with solvent to remove all grinding compound. Any compound left on the valves or in the guides could wear out the valve stem and the guide or find its way into the cylinder and ruin the seal of the rings and bore.

Valve Inspection

1. Measure the clearance between the valve stem and its guide with a dial gauge as shown in **Figure 32**. Replace the valve and guide as a set if worn beyond 0.004 in. (0.10mm) for exhaust valves and 0.003 in. (0.08mm) for intake valves. Use a valve guide driver to insert the guide into the cylinder head. Then ream out the guide to the proper inside diameter. See **Table 1**. Be sure to maintain the correct valve stem-to-valve guide clearances (**Table 2**).

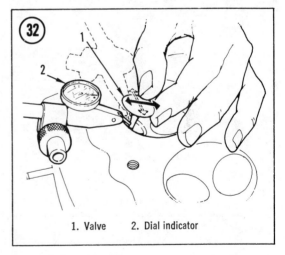

1. Valve   2. Dial indicator

Table 1   VALVE GUIDE DIAMETER

Model	Diameter
CB500	
Intake and exhaust	0.217-0.218 in. (5.513-5.538mm)
CB550	
Intake	0.215 in. (5.45mm)
Exhaust	0.214 in. (5.43mm)
CB350/400	
Intake and exhaust	0.218-0.219 in. (5.538-5.564mm)

Table 2   VALVE STEM-TO-GUIDE CLEARANCE

Model	Clearance
CB500/550, CB350/400	
Intake	0.0004-0.0018 in. (0.008-0.045mm)
Exhaust	0.001-0.002 in. (0.030-0.050mm)

2. Measure contact of the valve with its seat. Coat the valve face with a thin application of bluing, red lead, or similar preparation. Press the valve against its seat and rotate it one turn only. The coating should show a band of uniform width around the seat and the valve.

Measure the band with a caliper as shown in **Figure 33**. The valve seat width should be as given in **Table 3**.

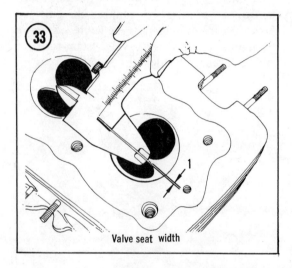

Valve seat width

Table 3   VALVE SEAT WIDTH

Model	Width
CB500/550	0.039-0.059 in. (1.0-1.5mm)
CB350/400	0.028-0.059 in. (0.7-1.5mm)

If the band is irregular, lap the valve with suitable compound and take the measurement a second time. If results still are not satisfactory the head must be replaced.

3. Measure the runout of the valve with a dial indicator as shown in **Figure 34**, with the valve wedged in a V-block. If runout is greater than 0.002 in. (0.05mm) the valve must be replaced.

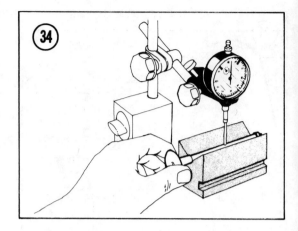

4. Inspect the edge of the valve for burned spots and replace if necessary.

5. Measure the free length of the valve spring with a vernier caliper as shown in **Figure 35**. Replace the springs if the free length is less than the limits given in **Table 4**.

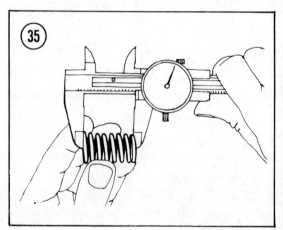

6. Check the flatness of the cylinder head by placing a straightedge across the surface, as in **Figure 36**, and checking the clearance with a feeler blade. If clearance is greater than 0.012 in. (0.3mm) the head should either be machined or replaced.

Rocker Arm Shaft Removal/Installation

Remove the rocker arm shaft from the cylinder head cover, **Figure 37**, by screwing the appropriate size bolt into the end of the shaft. CB500/550 takes a 6mm bolt. CB350/400 takes a 10mm bolt.

Installation is the reverse of this procedure.

Table 4   VALVE SPRING LENGTH

Model	Spring Length
CB550	
Inner	1.40 in. (35.7mm)
Outer	1.59 in. (40.4mm)
CB500	
Inner	1.36 in. (34.5mm)
Outer	1.54 in. (39.0mm)
CB400	
Inner	1.14 in. (29.0mm)
Outer	1.36 in. (34.5mm)
CB350	
Inner	1.06 in. (27.0mm)
Outer	1.28 in. (32.5mm)

On the CB500/550, check that rockers do not have more than 0.004-0.008 in. (0.01-0.02mm) of end play and that the rocker shafts are tight in the cover. If the rocker shafts have up and down play, replace the cover with a 1977 model.

CYLINDER BARRELS

Refer to **Figures 38 through 41** for the following procedures.

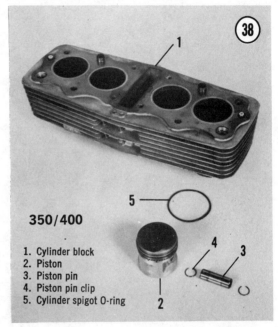

350/400

1. Cylinder block
2. Piston
3. Piston pin
4. Piston pin clip
5. Cylinder spigot O-ring

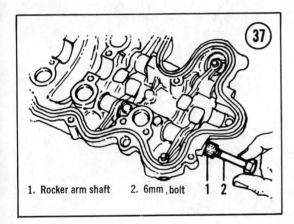

1. Rocker arm shaft   2. 6mm bolt

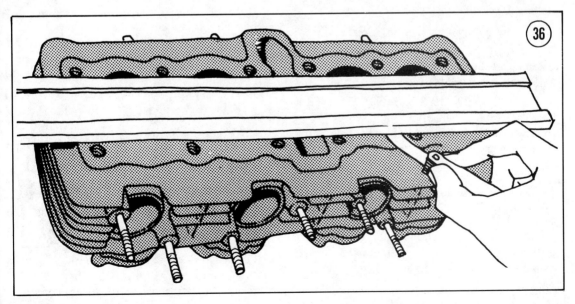

500/550

1. Cylinder block
2. Piston
3. Piston pin
4. Piston pin clip
5. Cylinder spigot O-ring
6. Cylinder base gasket
7. Oil gallery O-ring

Removal/Installation

1. Remove cylinder head as described earlier.

2. Remove the cam chain guide. On the CB500/550 (**Figure 42**), raise the guide slightly and rotate it 90° while lifting it up and out.

3. On the CB500/550 (**Figure 43**), remove the locknut from the cam chain tensioner adjuster, referring back to Figure 16, and then remove the tensioner itself from the head.

4. Remove the cylinder barrels. If stuck to the block, tap with a soft mallet. See Figure 44.

5. Install a new cylinder gasket. See Figure 38.

6. Use clothes hanger wire bent in a "U" shape to hold the pistons as shown in **Figure 45**. Use a piston ring compressor tool, **Figure 45**, to insert all 4 pistons into the cylinder bores at the same time.

NOTE: *A hose clamp can be used in place of a ring compressor.*

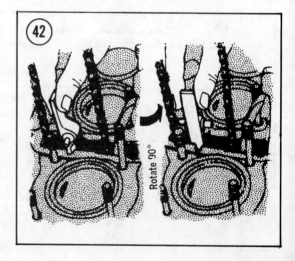

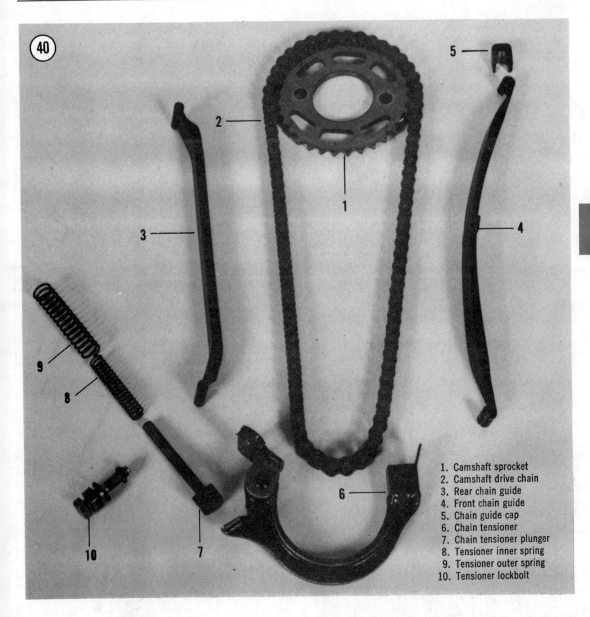

40

1. Camshaft sprocket
2. Camshaft drive chain
3. Rear chain guide
4. Front chain guide
5. Chain guide cap
6. Chain tensioner
7. Chain tensioner plunger
8. Tensioner inner spring
9. Tensioner outer spring
10. Tensioner lockbolt

4

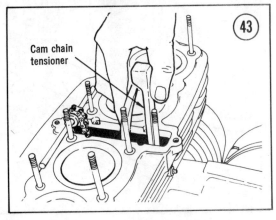

Cam chain tensioner

43

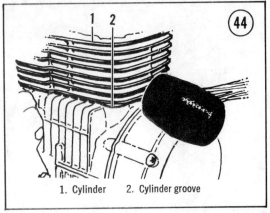

44

1. Cylinder   2. Cylinder groove

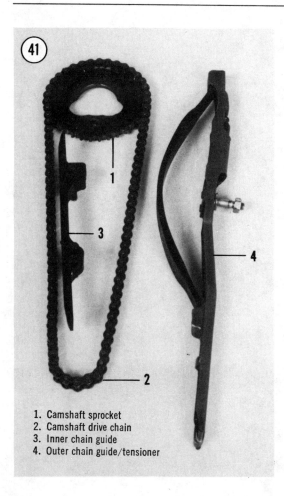

1. Camshaft sprocket
2. Camshaft drive chain
3. Inner chain guide
4. Outer chain guide/tensioner

7. Install the cam chain tensioner in the cylinder (**Figure 46**). Hold it down by hand, install the O-ring and washer, and tighten the locknut.

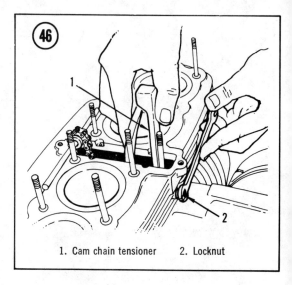

1. Cam chain tensioner   2. Locknut

NOTE: *Steps 8 and 9 apply to the CB500/550 only.*

8. Install the cam chain guide as shown in **Figure 47**.

9. Install cylinder head as described earlier.

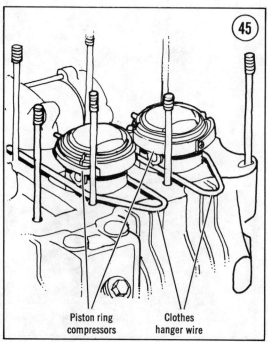

Piston ring compressors   Clothes hanger wire

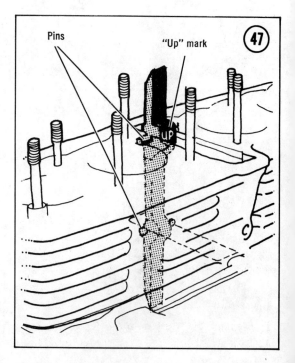

Pins   "Up" mark

Inspection

Measure the inside diameter of each cylinder along both the (x) and (y) axes (**Figure 48**) with a cylinder gauge at the top, center, and bottom.

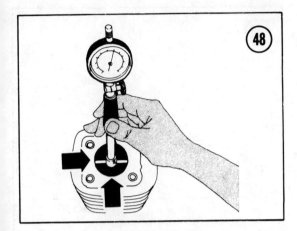

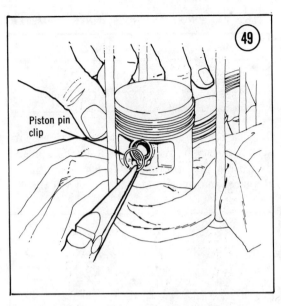

A rebore will be necessary if the cylinders are worn beyond the dimensions in **Table 5**.

Four standard oversized pistons are available: 0.010 in. (0.25mm), 0.020 in. (0.50mm), 0.030 in. (0.75mm), and 0.040 in. (1.0mm).

in **Figure 50**. Replace if worn beyond limits given in **Table 6**.

2. Measure the inside diameter of the wrist pin hole. Replace if worn beyond the limits given in **Table 7**.

Table 5   CYLINDER WEAR LIMITS

Model	Wear Limit
CB550	2.307 in. (58.6mm)
CB500	2.207 in. (56.1mm)
CB400	2.012 in. (51.1mm)
CB350	1.854 in. (47.1mm)

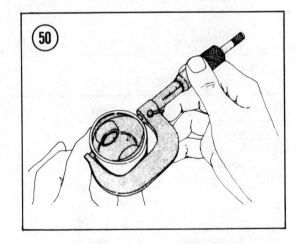

PISTONS AND RINGS

Refer to Figures 38 through 39 for the following procedures.

Piston Removal

Refer to **Figure 49** and remove the wrist pin clip, the pin itself, and then the piston. Drape a rag under the piston so the clips do not fall into the crankcase.

Inspection

1. Measure the outside diameter of the piston at its skirt, 90 degrees to the wrist pin, as shown

Table 6   PISTON DIAMETER

Model	Wear Limit
CB550	2.300 in. (58.35mm)
CB500	2.199 in. (55.85mm)
CB400	2.002 in. (50.75mm)
CB350	1.844 in. (46.85mm)

Table 7   WRIST PIN HOLE INNER DIAMETER

Model	Wear Limit
CB500/550	0.594 in. (15.08mm)
CB350/400	0.514 in. (13.05mm)

3. Measure the end gap of the piston ring by inserting it into the cylinder as shown in **Figure 51** and using the appropriate feeler gauge blade. Replace if worn beyond limits given in **Table 8**.

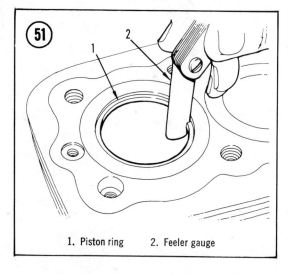

1. Piston ring   2. Feeler gauge

Table 8   PISTON RING END GAP

Model	Wear Limit
CB550	
Top ring	0.028 in. (0.7mm)
Second ring	0.028 in. (0.7mm)
Oil ring	0.043 in. (1.1mm)
CB500	
Top ring	0.030 in. (0.8mm)
Second ring	0.020 in. (0.5mm)
Oil ring	0.020 in. (0.5mm)
CB400	
Top ring	0.006 in. (0.15mm)
Second ring	0.006 in. (0.15mm)
Oil ring	0.008 in. (0.2mm)
CB350	
Top ring	0.028 in. (0.7mm)
Second ring	0.028 in. (0.7mm)
Oil ring	0.028 in. (0.7mm)

4. Measure the side clearance of the piston ring (while installed on the piston) as shown in **Figure 52**. Replace if worn beyond limits given (**Table 9**).

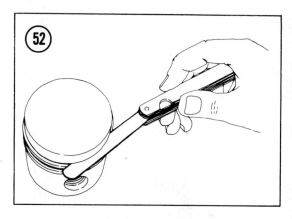

Table 9   PISTON RING SIDE CLEARANCE

Model	Wear Limit
CB500/550	
Top ring	0.007 in. (0.18mm)
Second ring	0.006 in. (0.15mm)
Oil ring	0.006 in. (0.15mm)
CB350/400	
Top ring	0.006 in. (0.15mm)
Second ring	0.006 in. (0.15mm)
Oil ring	0.006 in. (0.15mm)

5. Check the piston for damage. If the ring grooves are worn the pistons should be replaced. Scrape the carbon from the piston crowns.

Piston Ring Installation

Piston rings should be installed as a set with manufacturer's mark facing the top, **Figure 53A**. Roll the rings in the grooves beforehand to ensure that clearance is correct. Some models have a 3-piece oil scraper ring as shown in **Figure 53B**.

The gaps in the rings (**Figure 54**) should be staggered 120 degrees with none being either exactly in line or 90 degrees opposed from the wrist pin.

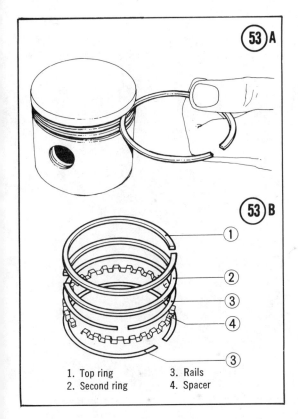

1. Top ring   3. Rails
2. Second ring   4. Spacer

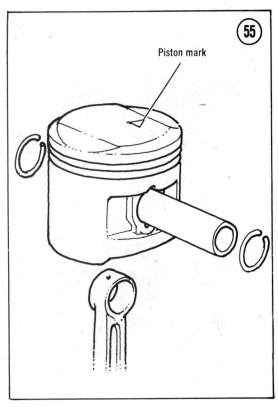

Piston mark

4

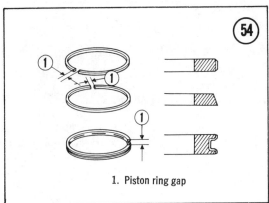

1. Piston ring gap

Piston Installation

Install the pistons so that the triangular arrow mark is pointed toward the front, or exhaust side, of the engine as shown in **Figure 55**. Use new wrist pin clips.

CAMSHAFT

Removal/Installation

Perform Steps 1-6 of *Cylinder Head, Removal/Installation*.

Inspection

1. The surfaces of the camshaft bearings should be smooth and shiny. See **Figure 56**. If the surfaces are scratched or worn, the head must be replaced.

2. Measure the height of each cam lobe with a micrometer as shown in **Figure 57**. Replace shaft if worn beyond the serviceable limit (measurements less than those given in **Table 10**).

3. Refer to **Figure 58** for the setup to measure runout of the camshaft. Support the shaft between 2 blocks and measure the bend at the center journal with a dial gauge. Replace the shaft if runout is greater than 0.004 in. (0.1mm).

4. Inspect the camshaft for cracks and replace if necessary.

OIL PUMP AND FILTER

Oil Pump Removal

Refer to **Figures 59, 60, and 61** for the following procedures.

1. Drain the engine oil. See Chapter Two.

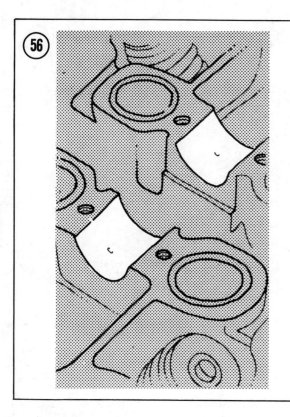

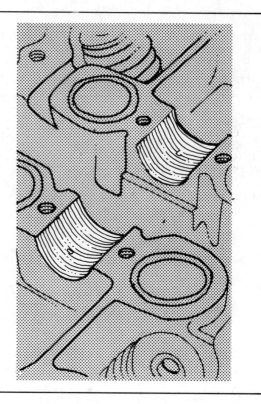

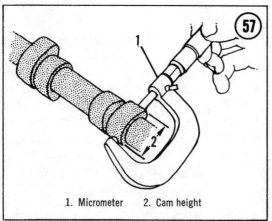

1. Micrometer   2. Cam height

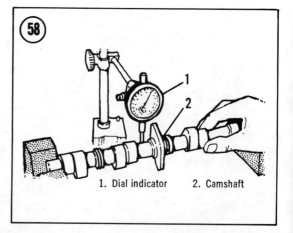

1. Dial indicator   2. Camshaft

Table 10   CAM LOBE HEIGHT

Model	Wear Limit
CB500/550	
Intake cam	1.411 in. (35.85mm)
Exhaust cam	1.3569 in. (34.45mm)
CB350/400	
Intake cam	1.1029 in. (28.00mm)
Exhaust cam	1.1029 in. (28.00mm)

2a. *CB500/550*. Remove the starter motor cover.

2b. *CB350/400*. Remove the gearshift pedal and the left footrest.

3. Remove the left crankcase cover.

4. Disconnect the oil pressure switch lead.

5a. *CB500/550*. Remove the oil pump by removing bolts and screws shown in **Figure 62**.

5b. *CB350/400*. Remove oil pump by removing mounting bolts and screws. See **Figure 63**.

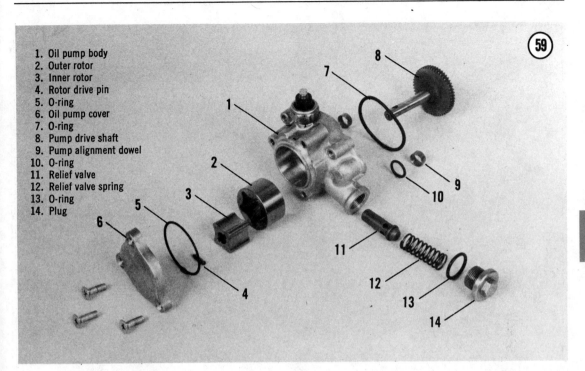

1. Oil pump body
2. Outer rotor
3. Inner rotor
4. Rotor drive pin
5. O-ring
6. Oil pump cover
7. O-ring
8. Pump drive shaft
9. Pump alignment dowel
10. O-ring
11. Relief valve
12. Relief valve spring
13. O-ring
14. Plug

4

59

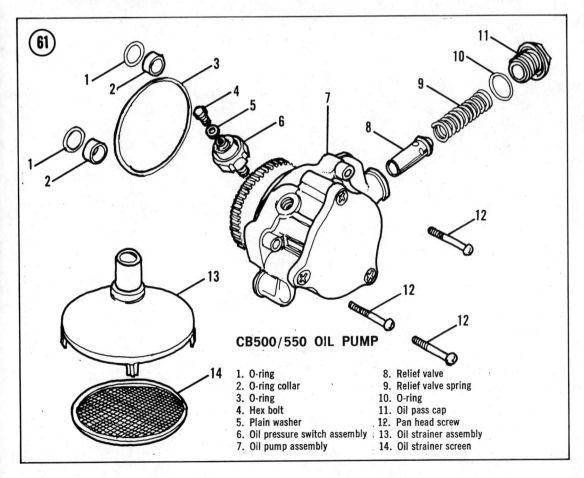

CB500/550 OIL PUMP

1. O-ring
2. O-ring collar
3. O-ring
4. Hex bolt
5. Plain washer
6. Oil pressure switch assembly
7. Oil pump assembly
8. Relief valve
9. Relief valve spring
10. O-ring
11. Oil pass cap
12. Pan head screw
13. Oil strainer assembly
14. Oil strainer screen

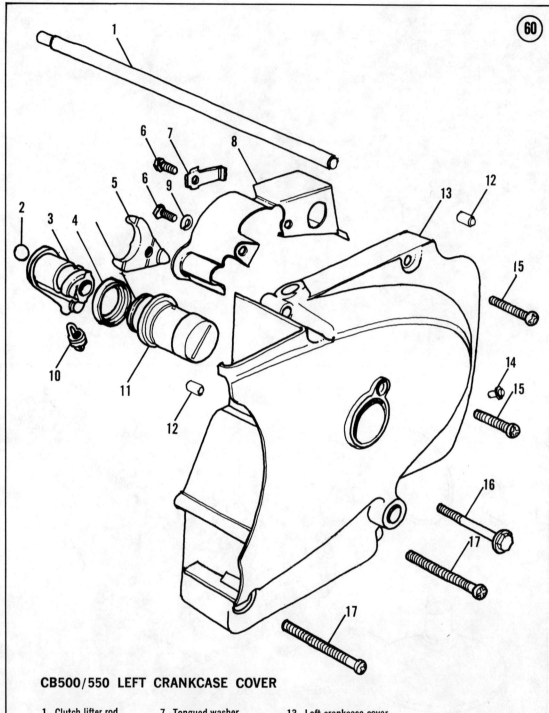

CB500/550 LEFT CRANKCASE COVER

1. Clutch lifter rod
2. Steel ball
3. Clutch actuator
4. Oil seal
5. Adjuster bracket
6. Hex bolt
7. Tongued washer
8. Case protector
9. Lockwasher
10. Clutch lever spring
11. Clutch adjustor
12. Dowel pin
13. Left crankcase cover
14. Grease nipple
15. Pan head screw
16. Flange bolt
17. Pan head screw

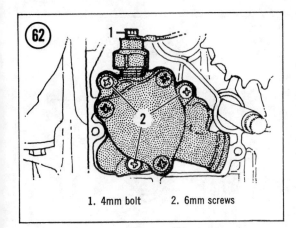

1. 4mm bolt   2. 6mm screws

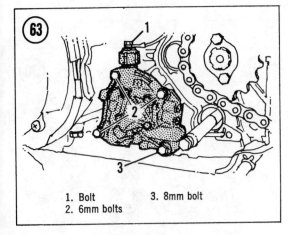

1. Bolt   3. 8mm bolt
2. 6mm bolts

Oil Pump Inspection

1. Measure the clearance between the inner and outer rotors with a feeler gauge blade as shown in **Figure 64**. Replace if worn beyond 0.013 in. (0.35mm) for CB500/550 and 0.012 in. (0.30mm) for CB350/400.

2. Measure clearance between outer rotor and pump body as shown in **Figure 65**. Replace pump if worn beyond 0.014 in. (0.35mm).

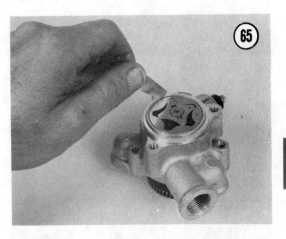

3. Check the operation of the relief valve (**Figure 66**, CB500/550), which should move freely, and examine the seat for foreign objects.

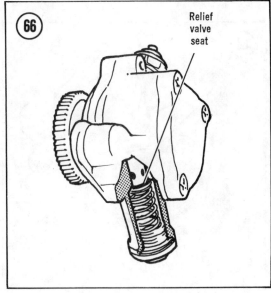

Relief valve seat

4. Clean and inspect the screen filter and replace if damaged.

Installation

Installation is the reverse of removal. Observe the following when installing.

1. CB500/550 (**Figure 67**): Align the punch marks on the inner and outer rotors.

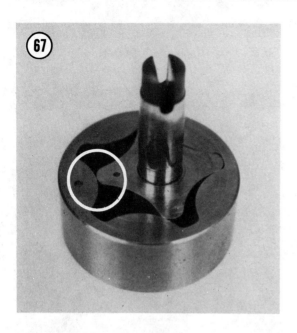

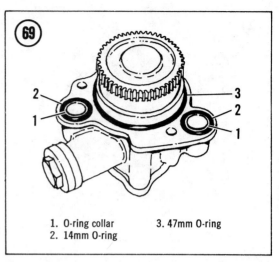

1. O-ring collar   3. 47mm O-ring
2. 14mm O-ring

2. Install the O-rings in the proper locations. See **Figures 68 and 69** for CB500/550 and **Figure 70** for CB350/400.

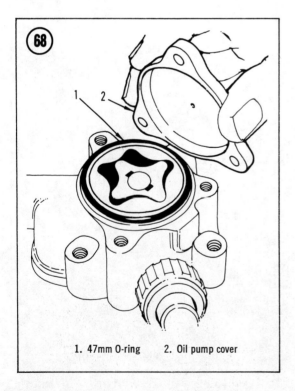

1. 47mm O-ring   2. Oil pump cover

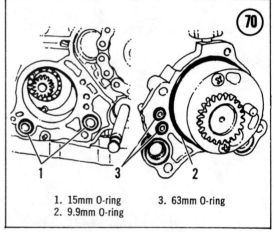

1. 15mm O-ring   3. 63mm O-ring
2. 9.9mm O-ring

Oil Screen Filter

Remove the oil pan to expose the screen filter (**Figure 72**).

CRANKCASE

Disassembly (CB350/400)

Refer to **Figure 73** for these steps.

1. Remove the engine from the frame. Drain oil from crankcase. Remove cylinder head, cylinders, and pistons.

2. Remove the alternator rotor with a puller.

3. In order, remove the right footrest, kickstarter pedal, gearshift pedal, right crankcase cover, and gearshift spindle. See **Figure 74**.

Oil Filter

Refer to **Figure 71** and unscrew the center bolt to remove.

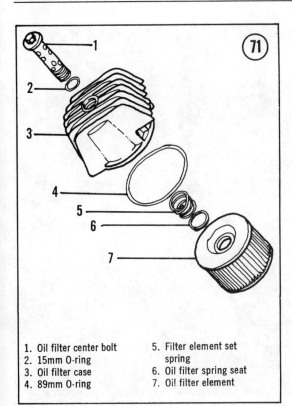

1. Oil filter center bolt
2. 15mm O-ring
3. Oil filter case
4. 89mm O-ring
5. Filter element set spring
6. Oil filter spring seat
7. Oil filter element

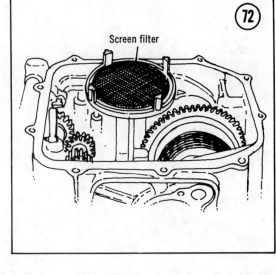

4. Refer to **Figure 75** and disassemble the positive stopper, gearshift drum stopper, and neutral stopper arm.

5. Remove the contact breaker and spark advancer. See **Figure 76**.

6. Remove the oil pump.

350/400

1. Footrest
2. Kickstarter
3. Crankcase cover

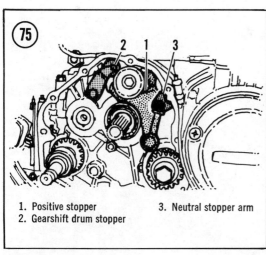

1. Positive stopper   3. Neutral stopper arm
2. Gearshift drum stopper

7. Refer to **Figure 77**. Remove the 12mm bolt (1) and slide secondary drive gear off the primary shaft.

8. Pull out the primary shaft to the right side.

9. Refer to **Figure 78** and remove the internal circlip, the ball bearing, and the 25mm collar.

10. Loosen the bolts from the lower crankcase in a crisscross pattern from the inside outward to relieve stresses equally.

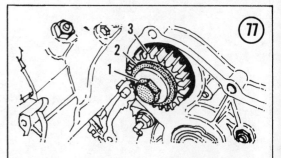

1. Bolt   3. Secondary drive gear
2. Primary shaft lockwasher

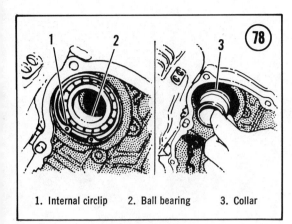

1. Internal circlip   2. Ball bearing   3. Collar

Disassembly (CB500/550)

Refer to **Figure 79** for this procedure.

1. Remove the engine. Drain the oil. Remove cylinder head, cylinders, and pistons.

2. Remove the alternator rotor with a puller as shown in **Figure 80**.

3. Refer to **Figure 81** and remove the 6mm bolt and the 5mm screws. Remove the breaker assembly and spark advancer.

4. Remove the clutch and gearshift arm according to the instructions in Chapter Five. Remove right crankcase cover. See **Figure 82**.

4

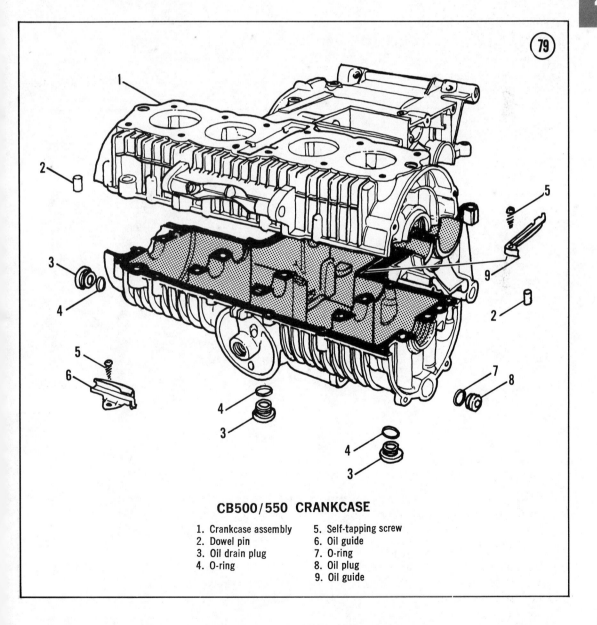

CB500/550 CRANKCASE

1. Crankcase assembly
2. Dowel pin
3. Oil drain plug
4. O-ring
5. Self-tapping screw
6. Oil guide
7. O-ring
8. Oil plug
9. Oil guide

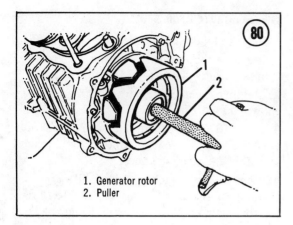

1. Generator rotor
2. Puller

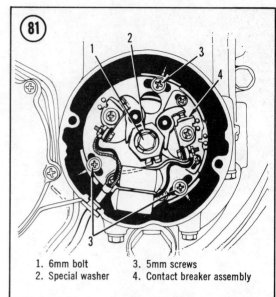

1. 6mm bolt   3. 5mm screws
2. Special washer   4. Contact breaker assembly

5. Remove starter (**Figure 83**).

6. Remove the oil pan. See **Figures 84 and 85**.

7. Remove the lower crankcase by unscrewing the ten 8mm bolts and the twelve 6mm bolts.

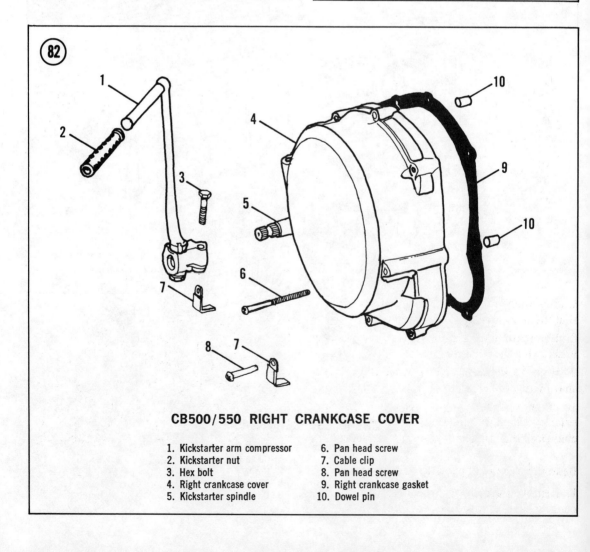

CB500/550 RIGHT CRANKCASE COVER

1. Kickstarter arm compressor   6. Pan head screw
2. Kickstarter nut   7. Cable clip
3. Hex bolt   8. Pan head screw
4. Right crankcase cover   9. Right crankcase gasket
5. Kickstarter spindle   10. Dowel pin

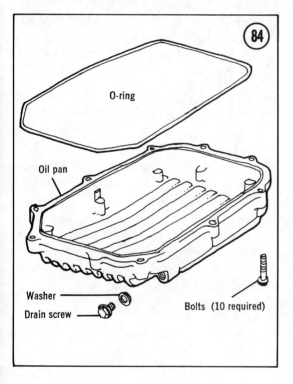

O-ring

Oil pan

Washer

Drain screw

Bolts (10 required)

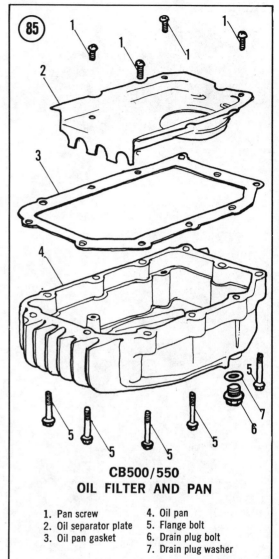

**CB500/550
OIL FILTER AND PAN**

1. Pan screw
2. Oil separator plate
3. Oil pan gasket
4. Oil pan
5. Flange bolt
6. Drain plug bolt
7. Drain plug washer

Loosen the 8mm bolts in a crisscross pattern so that the stresses are relieved equally.

8. Refer to **Figure 86** and remove the plate by unscrewing the two 6mm bolts.

9. Refer to **Figure 87** and remove the primary shaft with a puller.

10. Remove the starting clutch from the primary chain (**Figure 88**). Then remove the chain and the cam chain from the crankshaft.

Bearing Selection (Typical)

1. Remove the bearings, then assemble the upper and lower crankcases.

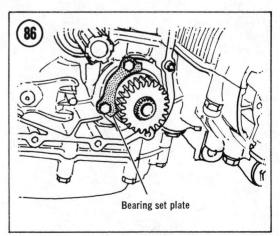

Bearing set plate

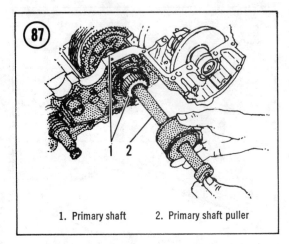

1. Primary shaft   2. Primary shaft puller

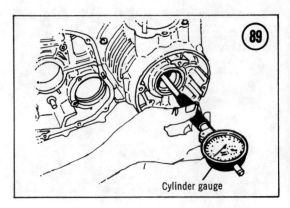

Cylinder gauge

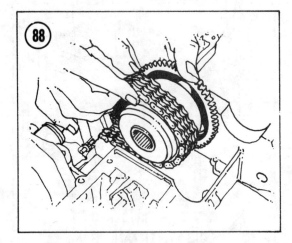

2. Measure the inside diameter of the bearing seats with a cylinder gauge, shown in **Figure 89**.

3. Measure the diameter of the crankshaft journals with a micrometer (**Figure 90**).

4. New bearings are sized according to either a letter or color code. Determine the correct replacement bearing by referring to **Table 11** for CB350/400 bearings or **Table 12** for CB500/550 bearings.

The letter and figure codes stamped on the lower crankcase and crankshaft (**Figure 91**) are factory production references and should not be confused with the bearing codes.

5. **Figure 92** shows the weight codes for connecting rods. When replacing rods, make sure the new one is the same weight code as the old.

6. Select connecting rod bearings by measuring the outside diameter of the crankshaft pin (**Figure 93**) and noting the code number on the big end of the rod. Select the proper bearing from **Table 13**.

Crankcase Assembly

Refer to Figures 74 and 80. Assemble the crankcase in reverse order of disassembly, noting the following.

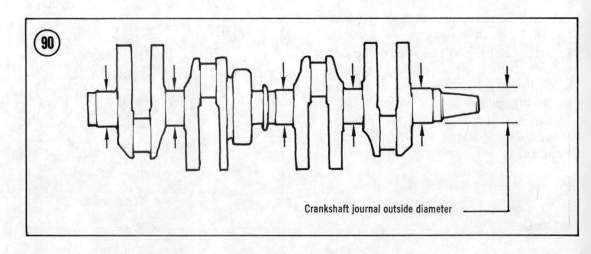

Crankshaft journal outside diameter

Table 11 CRANKSHAFT JOURNAL DIAMETER (CB350/400)

Crankcase Bearing Inside Diameter	Crankshaft Journal Outside Diameter		
	1.2594 in.-1.2598 in. (31.99mm-32.00mm)	1.2590 in.-1.2594 in. (31.98mm-31.99mm)	1.2586 in.-1.2590 in. (31.97mm-31.98mm)
1.3780 in.-1.3783 in. (35.000mm-35.008mm)	E (Red)	D (Yellow)	C (Green)
1.3783 in.-1.3786 in. (35.008mm-35.016mm)	D (Yellow)	C (Green)	B (Brown)
1.3786 in.-1.3789 in. (35.016mm-35.024mm)	C (Green)	B (Brown)	A (Black)

Table 12   CRANKSHAFT JOURNAL DIAMETER (CB500/550)

Crankcase Bearing Diameter	1.2987 in. - 1.2992 in. (32.99mm - 33.00mm)	1.2983 in. - 1.2987 in. (32.98mm - 32.99mm)
1.4179 in. - 1.4182 in. (36.016mm - 36.024mm)	B (Brown)	A (Black)
1.4176 in. - 1.4179 in. (36.008mm - 36.016mm)	C (Green)	B (Brown)
1.4173 in. - 1.4176 in. (36.000mm - 36.008mm)	D (Yellow)	C (Green)

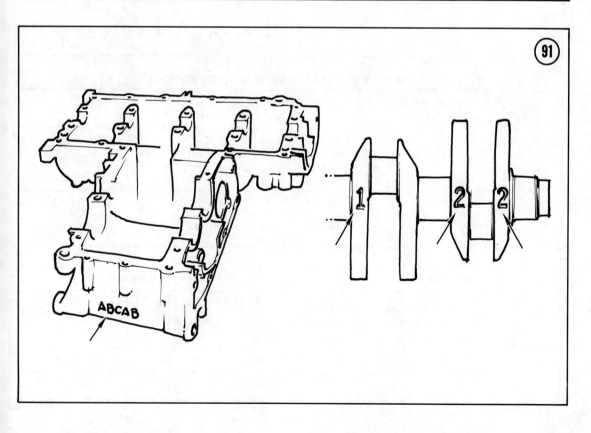

91

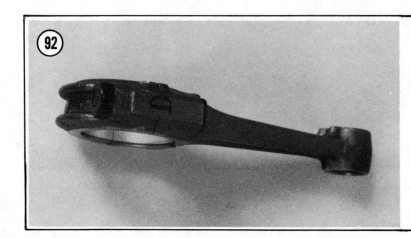

Code	Weight (gr.)
A	281—285
B	286—290
C	291—295
D	296—300
E	301—305
F	306—310
G	311—315

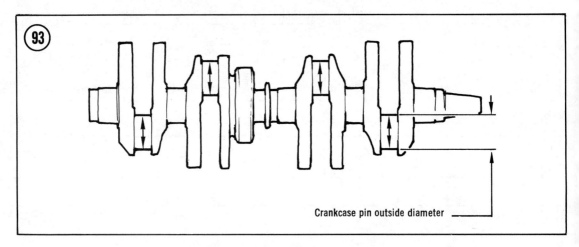

Crankcase pin outside diameter

Table 13   CONNECTING ROD SPECIFICATIONS

Model	Connecting Rod Code Number	Crankshaft Pin O.D.		
		1.2594 in.-1.2598 in. (31.99mm-32.00mm)	1.2590 in.-1.2594 in. (31.98mm-31.99mm)	1.2587 in.-1.2590 in. (31.97mm-31.98mm)
CB350/ CB400	1	E (Red)	D (Yellow)	C (Green)
	2	D (Yellow)	C (Green)	B (Brown)
	3	C (Green)	B (Brown)	A (Black)

	Connecting Rod Code Number	Crankshaft Pin Diameter	
		1.3776 in.-1.3780 in. (34.99mm-35.00mm)	1.3772 in.-1.3776 in. (34.98mm-34.99mm)
CB500/ CB550	1	B (Brown)	A (Black)
	2	C (Green)	B (Brown)
	3	D (Yellow)	C (Green)

1. Apply a thin coat of gasket paste to the mating surface of the lower crankcase and a coat of engine oil on bearing surfaces.

2. Torque the mounting bolts in the sequence shown in **Figure 94** to 16.63-18.08 ft.-lb. (2.3-2.5 mkg).

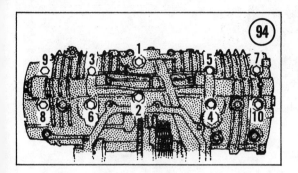

CRANKSHAFT AND CONNECTING RODS

Removal/Installation

The crankshaft is removed during crankcase disassembly. Refer to *Crankcase* section in this chapter.

Figures 95 and 96 show details of the crankshaft and connecting rods.

Inspection (Typical)

1. Measure the crankshaft runout at the center journal with a dial gauge as shown in **Figure 97**. Support the crank on V-blocks and then rotate it against the guage to read the amount of bend. Replace the crankshaft if the runout is greater than 0.002 in. (0.05mm).

2. Measure the crankshaft journal wear with "Plastigage" or the equivalent. Place a piece of Plastigage on the bearing as shown in **Figure 98** and install the crankshaft. Then assemble the upper and lower crankcase and torque the bolts to the regular 16.6-18.1 ft.-lb. (2.3-2.5 mkg). Disassemble the crankcase and measure the Plastigage.

If the clearance is greater than 0.003 in. (0.08mm) the bearing should be replaced. The procedure for selecting bearings is covered below.

4

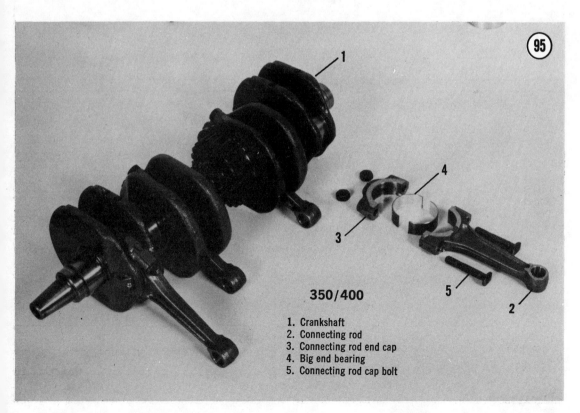

350/400

1. Crankshaft
2. Connecting rod
3. Connecting rod end cap
4. Big end bearing
5. Connecting rod cap bolt

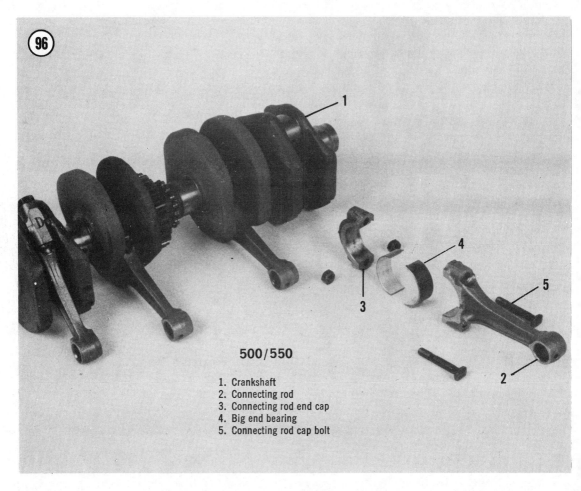

500/550

1. Crankshaft
2. Connecting rod
3. Connecting rod end cap
4. Big end bearing
5. Connecting rod cap bolt

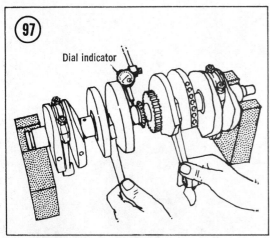

Dial indicator

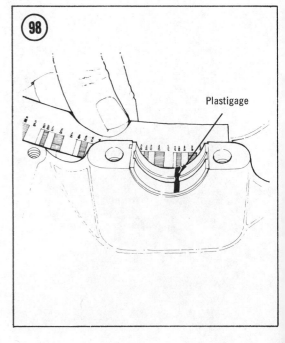

Plastigage

3. Inspect the crankshaft journals for any scratches or uneven wear. If any journal is worn out-of-round, or if the end taper exceeds 0.0002 in. (0.005mm), the crank should be replaced.

4. Measure the inside diameter of the small ends of the connecting rods with an inside dial gauge as shown in **Figure 99**. Replace if worn beyond 0.593 in. (15.08mm) for CB500/550 and 0.516 in. (13.10mm) for CB350/400.

5. Measure the side clearances of the connecting rods with a feeler gauge. The rods should be mounted on the crankshaft as in **Figure 100**.

Replace the rods if they are worn beyond 0.014 in. (0.35mm) for CB500/550 and 0.006 in. (0.15mm) for CB350/400.

6. Measure the wear of the large ends of the connecting rods as follows:

a. Remove the bearing cap (**Figure 101**) and place a piece of Plastigage on the surface of the bearing.

b. Install the cap and torque to 14.5-15.9 ft.-lb. (2.0-2.2 mkg).

c. Disassemble and measure the clearance on the gauge. Replace the bearing if it is worn beyond 0.003 in. (0.08mm). Bearing selection is covered earlier in this chapter.

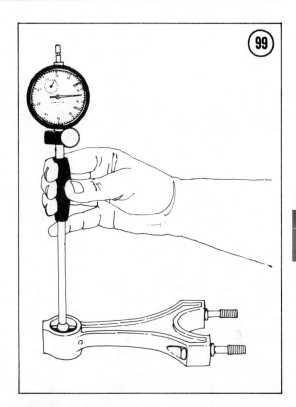

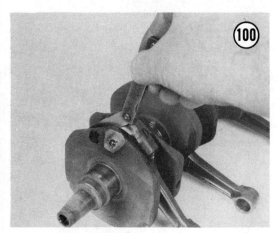

CHAPTER FIVE

CLUTCH AND TRANSMISSION

CLUTCH

The clutch is a wet multi-plate type which operates immersed in engine oil. Refer to **Figures 1, 2, and 3** for the following service procedures.

CAUTION
Oil additives of the "honey" type (STP, Stud, etc.) are too slippery and can cause near instantaneous clutch slipping and failure. Further, the additives are penetrative and cannot be removed from the discs. The only solution is to remove the clutch, flush the crankcase with kerosene, and replace the discs with new ones.

Disassembly

1. Drain oil from the crankcase.

2. Remove the right footrest, kickstarter pedal, and clutch cover.

3. Refer to **Figure 4** and remove the clutch pressure plate and clutch springs.

4. Remove the 25mm snap ring (**Figure 5**) and shims (if any). Then pull the clutch assembly from the shaft.

5a. *CB350/400* (**Figure 6**): Remove the circlip from the clutch center. Disassemble clutch plate B (see exploded view), the disc spring, and the disc spring seat.

5b. *CB500/550*: Disassemble the disc, plate, and center from the outer clutch.

6. Remove the clutch lever and adjuster lever from the crankcase cover.

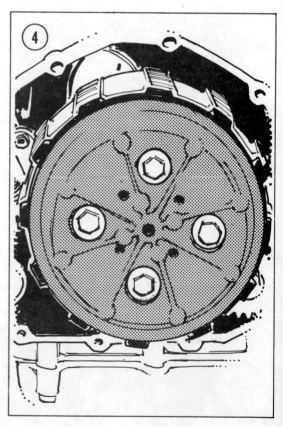

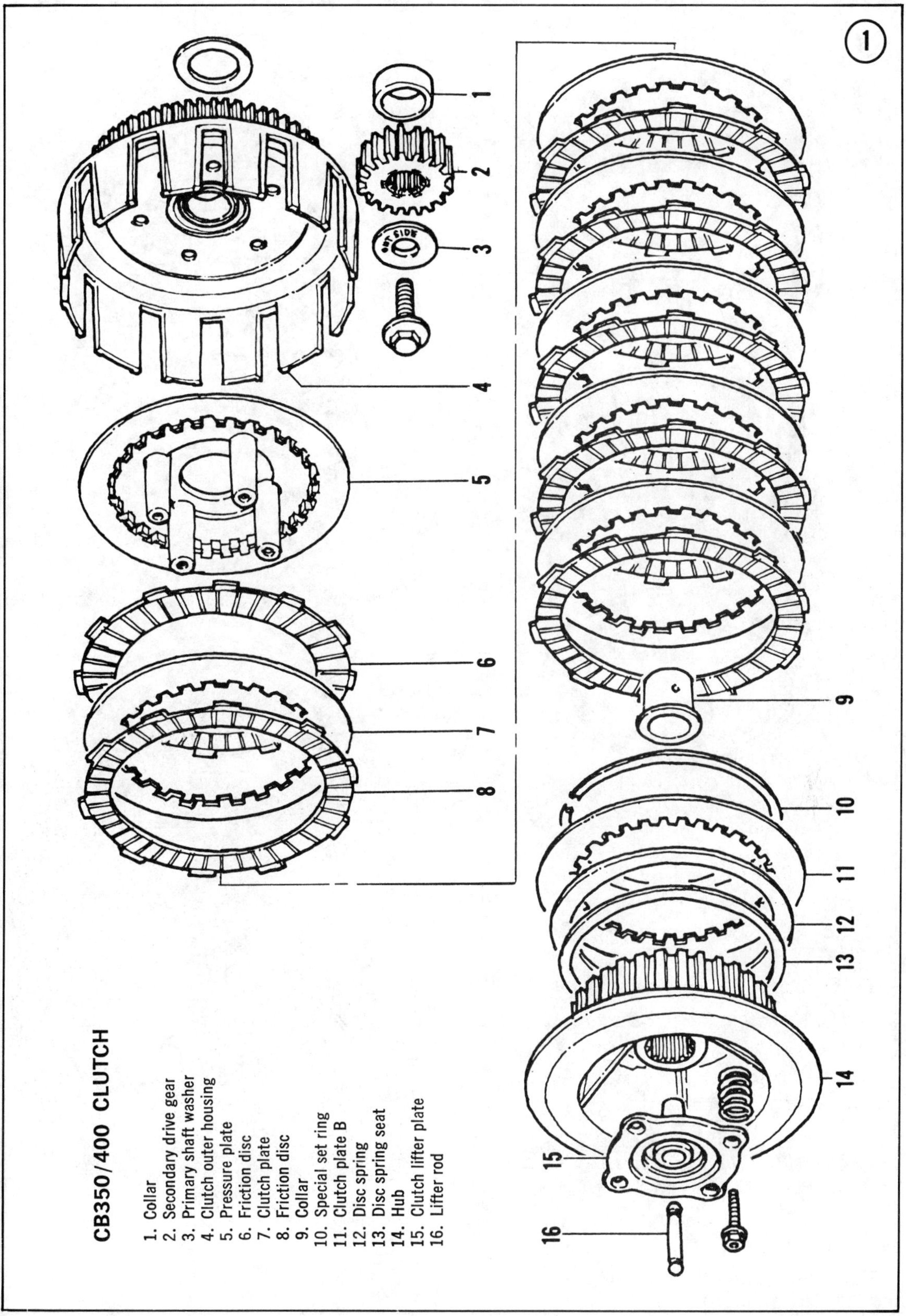
1
CB350/400 CLUTCH
1. Collar
2. Secondary drive gear
3. Primary shaft washer
4. Clutch outer housing
5. Pressure plate
6. Friction disc
7. Clutch plate
8. Friction disc
9. Collar
10. Special set ring
11. Clutch plate B
12. Disc spring
13. Disc spring seat
14. Hub
15. Clutch lifter plate
16. Lifter rod
OUT SIDE

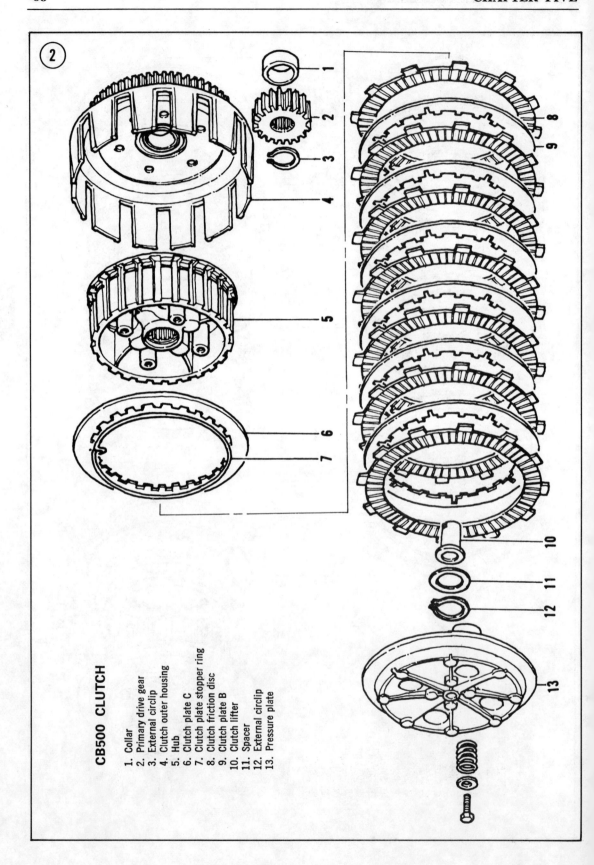

CB500 CLUTCH

1. Collar
2. Primary drive gear
3. External circlip
4. Clutch outer housing
5. Hub
6. Clutch plate C
7. Clutch plate stopper ring
8. Clutch friction disc
9. Clutch plate B
10. Clutch lifter
11. Spacer
12. External circlip
13. Pressure plate

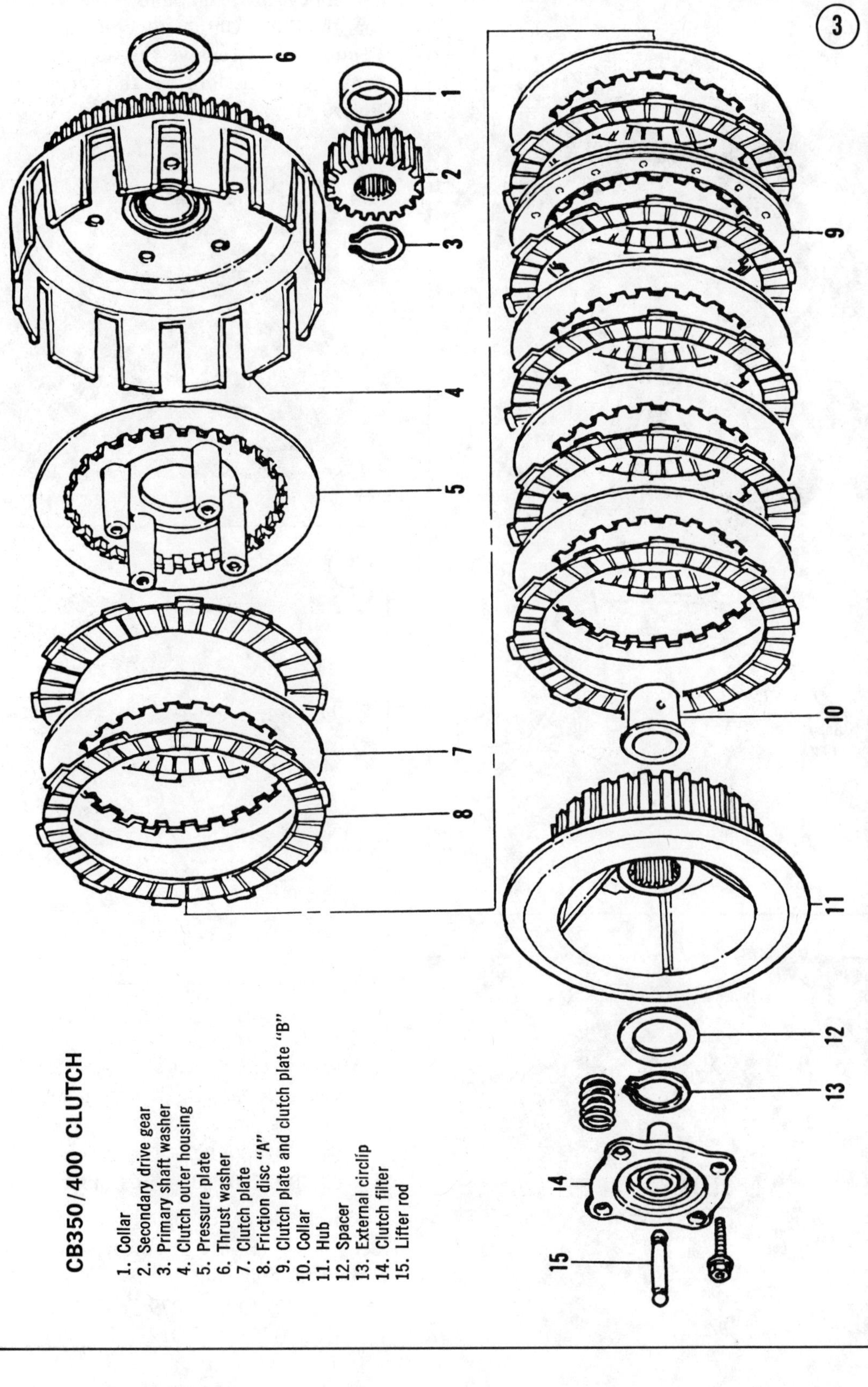

CB350/400 CLUTCH

1. Collar
2. Secondary drive gear
3. Primary shaft washer
4. Clutch outer housing
5. Pressure plate
6. Thrust washer
7. Clutch plate
8. Friction disc "A"
9. Clutch plate and clutch plate "B"
10. Collar
11. Hub
12. Spacer
13. External circlip
14. Clutch filter
15. Lifter rod

7. *CB500/550*: Disconnect the clutch cable from the lifter. Unscrew the adjuster lock bolt (**Figure 7**) and remove the adjuster from the crankcase cover. Pull out the clutch lifter rod (**Figure 8**).

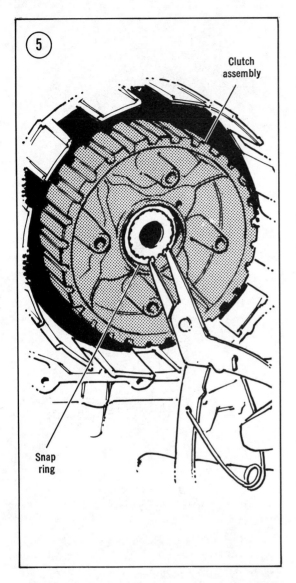

Clutch assembly

Snap ring

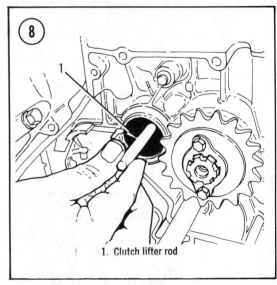

1. Clutch lifter rod

Inspection

1. Measure the thickness of the friction disc with a vernier caliper. Replace if worn beyond the following limits:

    CB350/400: 0.091 in. (2.3mm)
    CB500/550: 0.11 in. (3.0mm)

2. Check the clutch plate for warping with a feeler gauge (**Figure 9**) and replace if distorted beyond the following limits:

    CB350/400: 0.0079 in. (0.2mm)
    CB500/550: 0.012 in. (0.3mm)

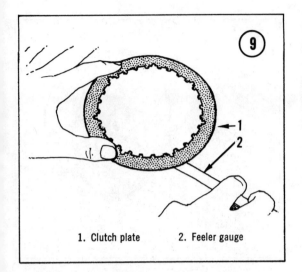

1. Clutch plate   2. Feeler gauge

1. Refer to **Figure 12** for the proper direction in which to install the disc spring seat and clutch disc spring.

3. Measure the uncompressed length of the clutch spring with a vernier caliper and replace if less than the following limits:

CB350/400: 1.339 in. (34.0mm)
CB500/550: 1.20 in. (30.5mm)

4a. *CB350/400*: Refer to **Figure 10** and measure the clearance between the center and clutch plate B. If it is not between 0.004-0.02 in. (0.1-0.5mm), replace clutch plate.

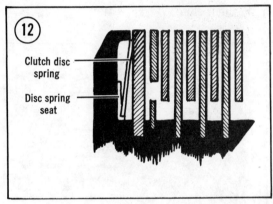

Clutch disc spring

Disc spring seat

2. Do not forget to install the 25mm thrust washer.

3. Alternate the friction discs and the clutch plates when placing them in the outer clutch with the 8mm friction disc going on last.

Assembly (CB500/550)

Assemble the clutch in the reverse order of disassembly, referring to the exploded drawing and noting the following.

1. Refer to **Figure 13** and insert the lifter rod into the main shaft with the spherical end toward the right side.

2. Grease the clutch lifter and, together with the adjuster, mount on the left crankcase cover. Tighten the lock bolt and reconnect the clutch cable to the lifter.

3. Place the steel ball in the lifter and mount the left crankcase cover with the 4 screws.

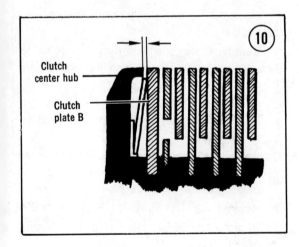

Clutch center hub

Clutch plate B

4b. *CB500/550* (**Figure 11**): Replace the outer clutch if any of the mounting rivets are loose.

Assembly (350/400)

Assemble in reverse order of disassembly, referring to the exploded drawing and noting the following steps.

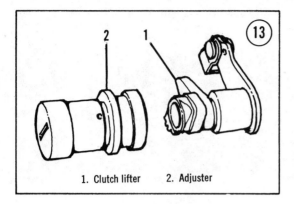

1. Clutch lifter   2. Adjuster

4. Lubricate the friction discs with motor oil and place them in the clutch center, alternating with the clutch plates. Then place the assembly in the outer clutch (**Figure 14**).

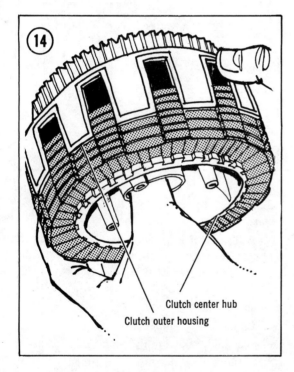

Clutch center hub
Clutch outer housing

5. Mount the clutch on the main shaft and install the snap ring.

6. Mount a dial gauge so that it bears against the end of the clutch assembly and measure for looseness along the shaft. If the assembly can move back and forth more than 0.004 in. (0.1mm), install a shim between the snap ring and the clutch assembly (**Figure 15**). Shims are made in 0.1mm, 0.3mm, and 0.5mm thicknesses.

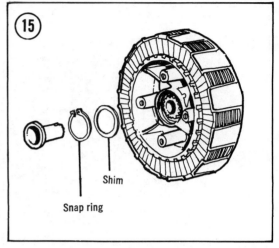

Shim

Snap ring

7. Refer to Figure 15 and insert the joint into the main shaft. Mount the clutch plate with the 4 springs, washers, and bolts.

8. Install the clutch cover.

TRANSMISSION

This section covers servicing of the transmission, kickstarter, and primary shaft.

Disassembly

Refer to **Figures 16 through 20** for this procedure.

1. Remove the engine from the frame (Chapter Four). Remove the clutch and disassemble the lower crankcase (Chapter Four).

2. Remove the transmission countershaft and main shaft from the upper crankcase and remove the gears.

3. Refer to **Figures 21, 22, and 23** for details of the kickstarter. Remove the 2 springs and remove the assembly from the lower crankcase.

4. Remove the primary shaft (Figure 19 or 20).

5. Remove the 20mm snap ring and primary drive gear (**Figure 24**).

6. Remove the side collar and the ball bearing.

7. Remove the 30mm snap ring, the primary driven sprocket, starting clutch, and rubber shock dampers.

8. Refer to **Figure 25** and remove the outer starting clutch by unscrewing the flathead screws.

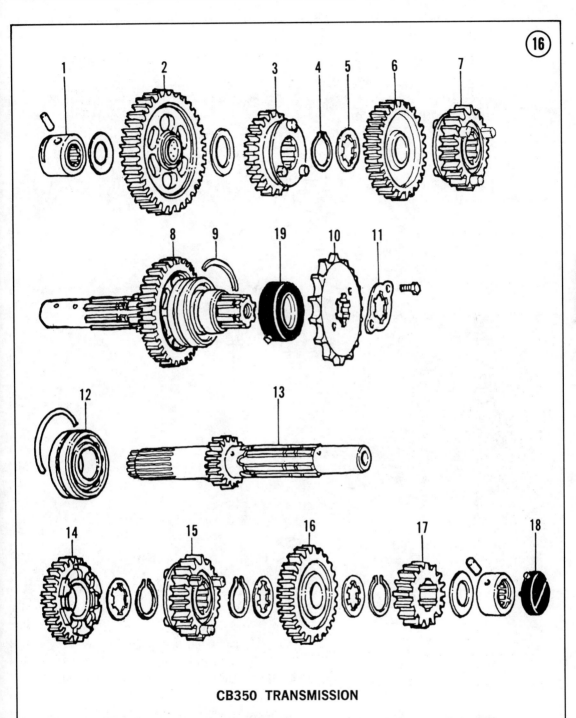

⑯

5

CB350 TRANSMISSION

1. Needle bearing
2. Countershaft 1st gear
3. Countershaft 4th gear
4. Circlip
5. Thrust washer
6. Countershaft 3rd gear
7. Countershaft 5th gear
8. Countershaft
9. Bearing set ring
10. Drive sprocket
11. Drive sprocket fixing plate
12. Ball bearing
13. Transmission mainshaft
14. Mainshaft 4th gear
15. Mainshaft 3rd gear
16. Mainshaft 5th gear
17. Mainshaft 2nd gear
18. Oil seal
19. Oil seal

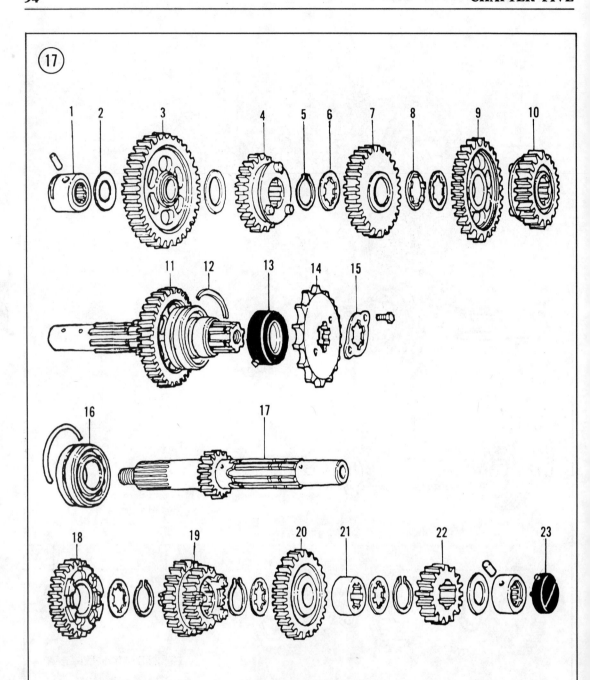

CB400 TRANSMISSION

1. Needle bearing
2. Thrust washer
3. Countershaft gear
4. Countershaft 5th gear
5. Circlip
6. Thrust washer
7. Countershaft 4th gear
8. Lockwasher
9. Countershaft 3rd gear
10. Countershaft top gear
11. Countershaft
12. Bearing set ring
13. Oil seal
14. Drive sprocket
15. Sprocket plate
16. Ball bearing
17. Main shaft
18. Main shaft 5th gear
19. Main shaft 3rd and 4th gear
20. Main shaft top gear
21. Bushing
22. Main shaft 2nd gear
23. Oil seal

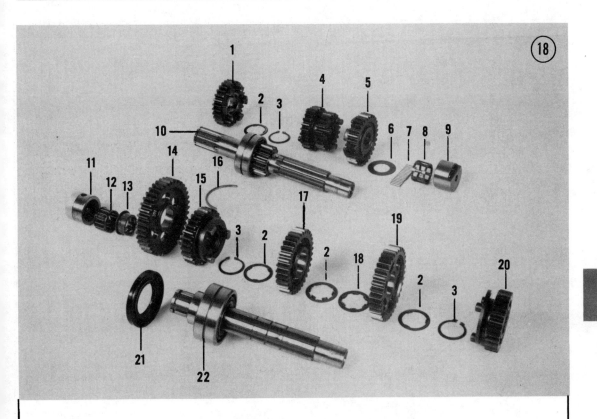

1. Mainshaft 4th gear
2. Spacer
3. Snap ring
4. Mainshaft 2nd and 3rd gear
5. Mainshaft top gear
6. Spacer
7. Bearing rollers
8. Bearing cage
9. Bearing race
10. Mainshaft (with bearing)
11. Bearing race
12. Roller bearing assembly
13. Bushing
14. Countershaft 1st gear
15. Countershaft 4th gear
16. Bearing set ring
17. Countershaft 3rd gear
18. Lock ring
19. Countershaft 2nd gear
20. Countershaft top gear
21. Countershaft end seal
22. Countershaft (with bearing)

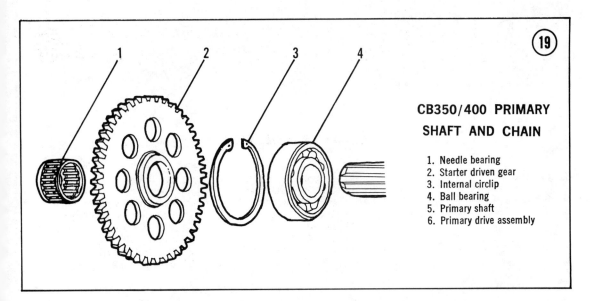

CB350/400 PRIMARY
SHAFT AND CHAIN

1. Needle bearing
2. Starter driven gear
3. Internal circlip
4. Ball bearing
5. Primary shaft
6. Primary drive assembly

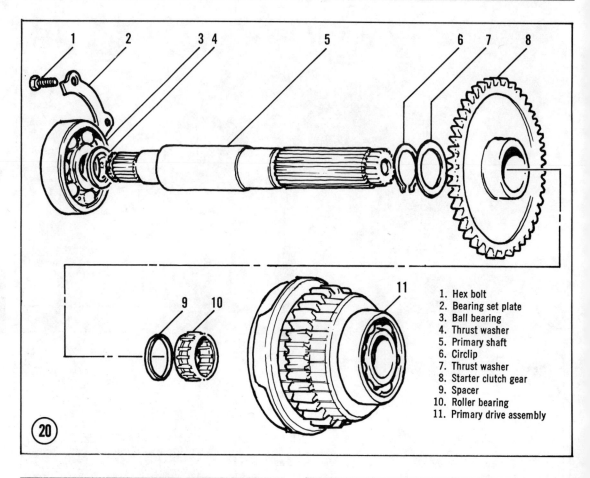

1. Hex bolt
2. Bearing set plate
3. Ball bearing
4. Thrust washer
5. Primary shaft
6. Circlip
7. Thrust washer
8. Starter clutch gear
9. Spacer
10. Roller bearing
11. Primary drive assembly

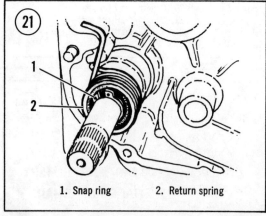

1. Snap ring   2. Return spring

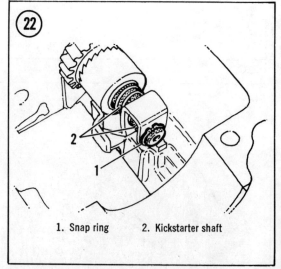

1. Snap ring   2. Kickstarter shaft

Inspection

1. Measure backlash of the transmission gears by setting the pointer of a dial indicator against the gear tooth as shown in **Figure 26**. Replace if backlash exceeds 0.008 in. (0.2mm).

2. Replace gears that are obviously worn or whose lugs are damaged.

3. Ensure that the gears slide smoothly along the splines.

4. Check the kickstarter ratchet for smooth functioning.

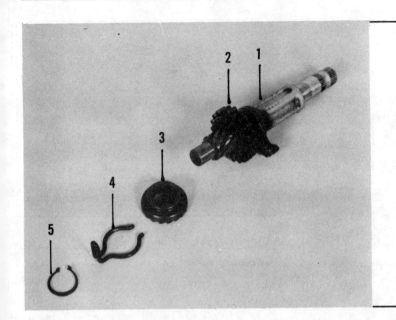

1. Kickstarter shaft
2. Kickstarter drive gear
3. Ratchet
4. Stop clip
5. Snap ring

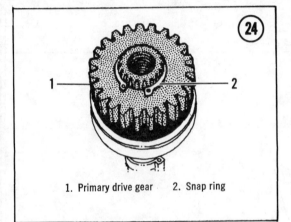

1. Primary drive gear   2. Snap ring

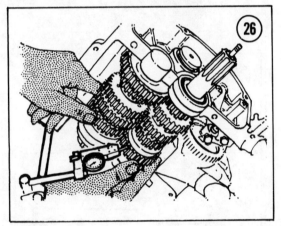

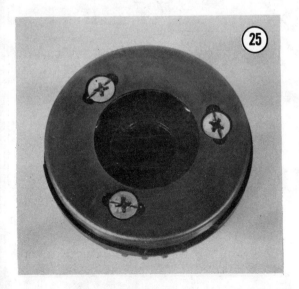

Assembly

Reassemble in reverse order of disassembly. Refer to Figures 16 through 20 and note the following points.

1. Assemble the outer clutch, coating the flat-head screws with a thread-locking compound. Stake the screw heads with a punch as shown in **Figure 27**.

2. Install the rubber dampers as shown in **Figure 28**.

3. Refer to **Figure 29** for the sequence of installing parts on the shaft. When it is fully assembled, install the shaft in the crankcase.

4a. *CB350/400:* Refer to **Figures 30 and 31** for proper positioning of the kickstarter spring.

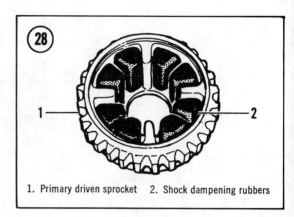

1. Primary driven sprocket   2. Shock dampening rubbers

4b. *CB500/550:* Refer to **Figure 32** for details of the kickstarter.

5a. *CB350/400:* Refer to **Figures 33 and 34** locations of the set rings and pins.

5b. *CB500/550:* Install bearing set rings and dowel pins in upper crankcase, **Figure 35**, before installing transmission.

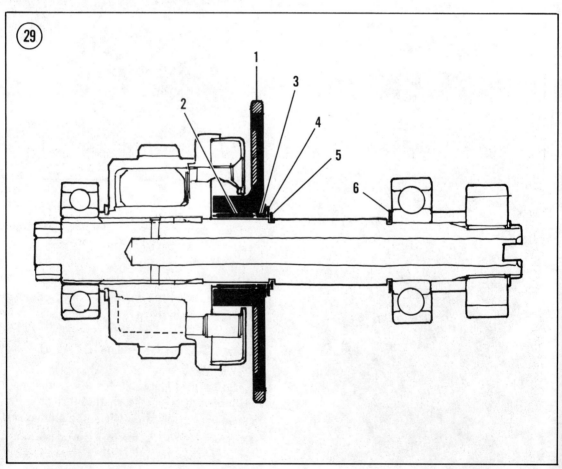

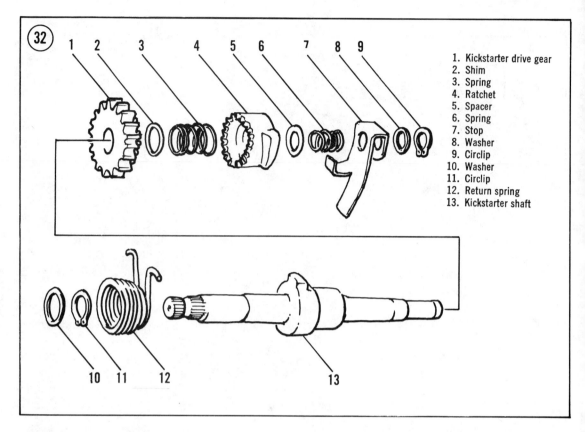

1. Kickstarter drive gear
2. Shim
3. Spring
4. Ratchet
5. Spacer
6. Spring
7. Stop
8. Washer
9. Circlip
10. Washer
11. Circlip
12. Return spring
13. Kickstarter shaft

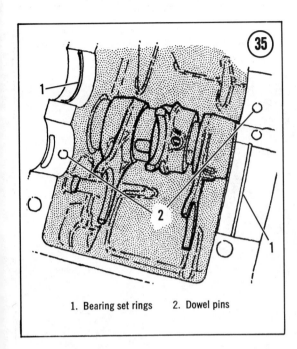

(35)

1. Bearing set rings   2. Dowel pins

GEARSHIFT MECHANISM

Refer to **Figures 36 and 37** for the following procedures.

Disassembly

1. Remove the clutch.
2. Remove the gearshift pedal.
3. Remove the gearshift arm, holding it down as shown in **Figure 38**.
4. Refer to **Figure 39** (CB500/550) and remove the stopper bolt, shift drum stopper, screw, and stopper cam plate.
5. Disassemble the transmission.
6. Remove the neutral stopper switch from the gearshift drum.
7. Remove the guide screw from the upper crankcase as shown in **Figure 40** and remove the spring cap and ball.

5

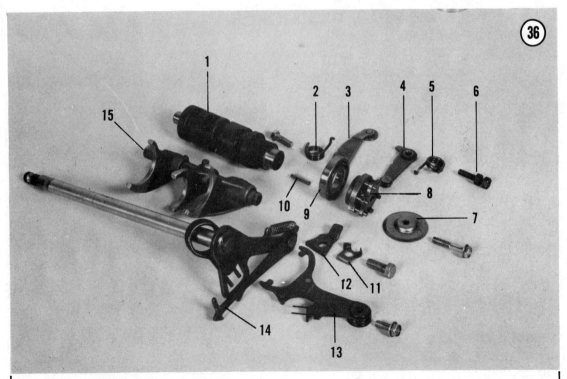

(36)

1. Shifter drum	5. Neutral stopper return spring	9. Bearing	13. Positive stopper
2. Drum stopper return spring	6. Lock bolt	10. Drum indexing pin	14. Gear selector ratchet and
3. Drum stopper roller	7. End plate	11. Bolt lock plate	shaft assembly
4. Neutral stopper roller	8. Drum stopper assembly	12. Guide plate	15. Shifting forks and shaft

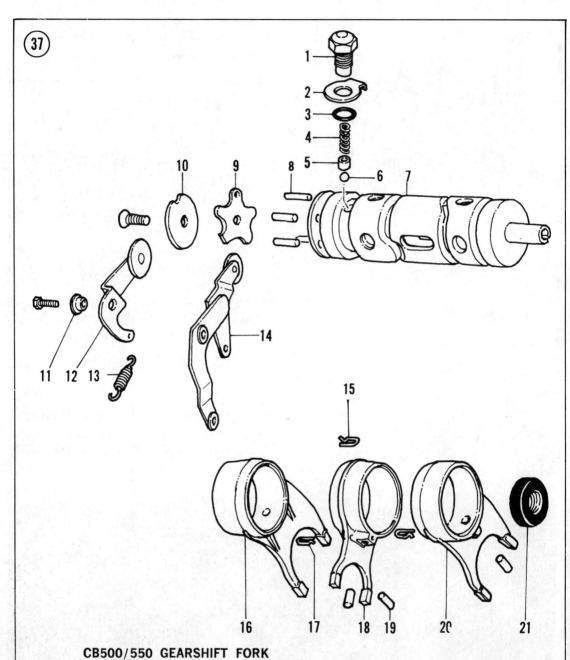

CB500/550 GEARSHIFT FORK AND SHIFT DRUM

1. Guide screw
2. Lockwasher
3. O-ring
4. Clutch damper spring
5. Guide screw collar
6. Steel ball
7. Gearshift drum
8. Gearshift drum pins
9. Cam plate
10. Stopper collar
11. Collar stopper
12. Shift drum stopper
13. Stopper spring
14. Drum stopper
15. Clip
16. Right gearshift fork
17. Clip
18. Gearshift fork
19. Guide pin
20. Gearshift fork
21. Oil seal

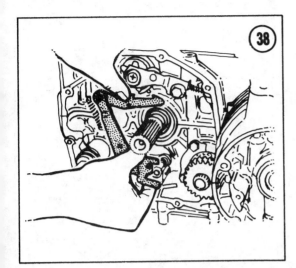

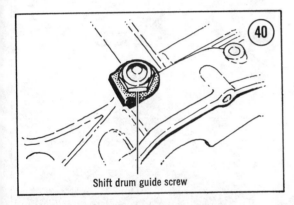

Shift drum guide screw

8. Remove the guide pin clips and guide pins (**Figure 41**) and then remove the gearshift drum from the crankcase.

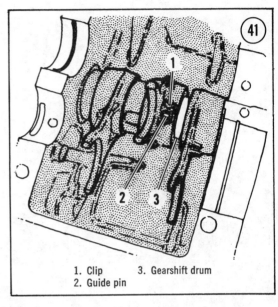

1. Clip   3. Gearshift drum
2. Guide pin

Inspection

1. *CB500/550:* Measure the outer diameter of the gearshift drum with a micrometer as shown in **Figure 42**. Replace if worn beyond 1.5709 in. (39.9mm).

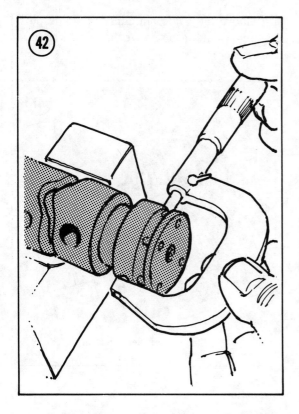

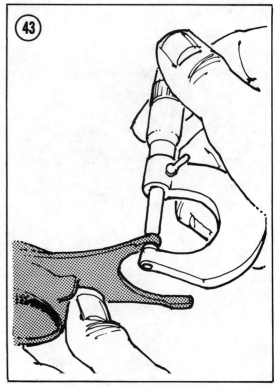

2. Measure the inner diameter of the gearshift forks with an inside micrometer. Replace the ones that are worn beyond the following limits:

CB350/400: 0.51 in. (12.95mm)
CB500/550: 1.58 in. (40.08mm)

3. Measure the width of the gearshift fork fingers (**Figure 43**) with a micrometer. Replace those that are worn beyond the following limits:

CB350: 0.22 in. (5.5mm)
CB400: 0.23 in. (5.9mm)
CB500/550: center 0.22 in. (5.6mm)
CB500/550: (right/left)
          0.181 in. (4.60mm)

Assembly (CB350/400)

Assemble in reverse order of disassembly. Refer to Figure 36 and note the following steps.

1. Install the gearshift drum and transmission gears in the neutral position.

2. After installing the guide set plate, bend the lug of the lockwasher against the 8mm bolt as shown in **Figure 44**.

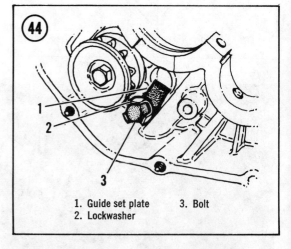

1. Guide set plate   3. Bolt
2. Lockwasher

3. The gearshift forks are marked with "R" (right), "C" (center), and "L" (left) so that their positions will not be confused.

Assembly (CB500/550)

Assembly is the reverse of disassembly. Refer to Figure 37 and note the following.

1. Set shift forks into crankcase (**Figure 45**) and then install the gearshift drum.

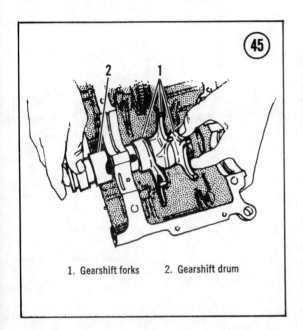

1. Gearshift forks   2. Gearshift drum

2. Insert the guide pin into the shift fork as shown in **Figure 46** and secure it with the guide pin clip. Make sure the clip is installed in the proper direction.

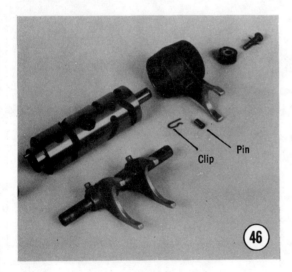

Pin

Clip

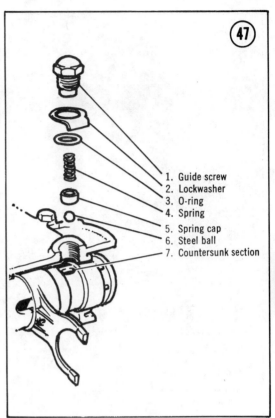

1. Guide screw
2. Lockwasher
3. O-ring
4. Spring
5. Spring cap
6. Steel ball
7. Countersunk section

3. Refer to **Figure 47** for the sequence of installing these parts. Lock the guide screw by bending up the tab on the lockwasher.

4. Align the neutral switch with the gearshift drum groove, as shown in **Figure 48**, and lock with the 6mm screw.

5. Assemble the transmission and the upper and lower crankcase.

6. Refer to **Figure 49** and align the pinhole in the cam plate with the pin on the gearshift drum. Secure with the 6mm screw, coating it with a thread-locking compound.

7. Place the spring on the shift drum stopper and insert the other end into the groove in the crankcase, as shown in **Figure 50**. Tighten the bolt and then ensure that the stopper operates smoothly. Replace the part if excessively loose.

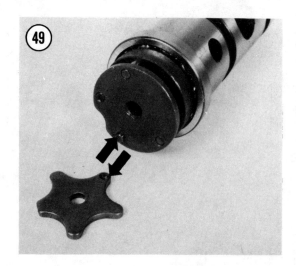

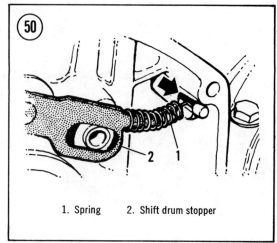

1. Spring   2. Shift drum stopper

CHAPTER SIX

FUEL SYSTEM

The fuel system consists of the fuel tank, fuel shut-off valve, and 4 carburetors.

CARBURETORS

The carburetors are accurately adjusted at the factory and rarely require adjustment. Before suspecting the fuel system, always make certain that valve clearance is proper and that the ignition system is accurately timed and in good condition.

Adjustment

The following adjustments should be performed in order:

a. Float level adjustment
b. Idle mixture
c. Idle speed
d. Synchronization (balance)
e. Throttle linkage

Honda sells a special float level gauge for each model. In addition, they sell a universal gauge (**Figure 1**) which is useful for any Honda and many other bikes.

Synchronization requires a special set of 4 gauges. Honda has a set with all necessary tubes and adapters. Is is relatively expensive, but makes the job very simple.

A simple manometer set described in this chapter can be built for about $2 and works as well as the Honda gauges.

Synchronization devices such as Uni-syn and other similar airflow measuring devices may also be used. However, they are inconvenient with a 4 carburetor setup as they must be moved back and forth from carburetor to carburetor several times to perform adjustment.

Float Level Adjustment

1. Close the fuel tank petcock.

2. Remove the float bowls by slipping the snap ring toward the front of the engine.

CAUTION
Remove the bowls carefully so as not to damage the floats or the valves. There may be gasoline in the bowls.

3. Flush any sediment from the bowls with solvent and dry.

4. Use a float level gauge to check the float height. The measurements should be taken when the float arm is just barely touching the valve, but not compressing the valve spring. See **Figure 2**.

The standard heights are:

    CB350/400: 21mm
    CB500/550: 22mm

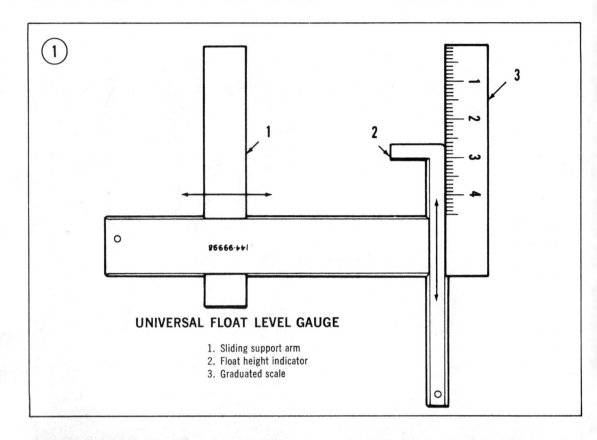

UNIVERSAL FLOAT LEVEL GAUGE

1. Sliding support arm
2. Float height indicator
3. Graduated scale

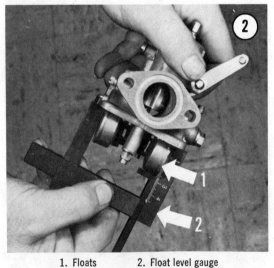

1. Floats   2. Float level gauge

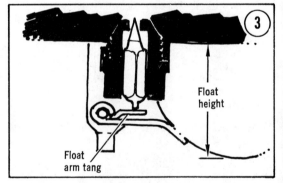

5. To adjust, carefully bend the float arm tang (**Figure 3**) toward or away from the valve. Correct any misalignment between the 2 floats by carefully twisting the float arm.

6. Install bowls and gaskets, making sure that the bowl lips seat properly and clips are secure.

Float Level External Check

1. Purchase a single carburetor drain plug screw from a dealer.

2. Drill the end of the screw to snugly accept a piece of brass tubing approximately one inch (25mm) long. See **Figure 4**.

3. Epoxy the tubing in place leaving enough exposed for a piece of clear tubing to be slipped over the end.

4. Clamp the plastic tubing to the piece of exposed brass tubing.

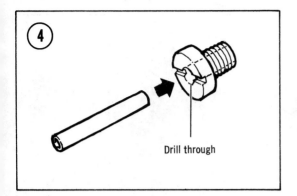

Drill through

5. Shut off the fuel petcock and drain the float bowl of one carburetor.

6. Remove the stock drain plug from the float bowl and install the modified drain plug.

7. Check and adjust the float level as previously described under *Float Level Adjustment*.

8. Install the bowl and hold the plastic tube as shown in **Figure 5**.

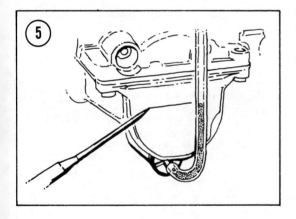

9. Turn on the fuel petcock and wait for the fuel to seek its level in the exposed tube. Record this level by scoring a mark on the float bowl. This mark can be used for adjusting the other 3 carburetors and all of them at any time in the future.

10. Make any necessary adjustments and re-install all of the float bowls.

Idle Mixture Adjustment

1. Warm up engine to normal operating temperature.

2. Remove the fuel tank to allow access to the carburetors.

3. Turn in the air screw on each carburetor (**Figure 6**) until they seat gently. Then back them out about 1½-2 turns.

Idle Speed

1. Adjust the engine idle speed with the throttle stop screw (**Figure 7**). Turn the screw clockwise, in the direction of "A", to increase the speed, and "B" to decrease.

Standard idle speeds:

    CB350/400: 1,200 rpm
    CB500/550: 1,000 rpm

Carburetor Synchronization (Honda Gauge Set)

1. Remove the fuel tank and reconnect it with a longer fuel line. Keep the tank higher than the carburetors.

2. Adjust throttle adjusting nut (**Figure 8**) to just take up any slack.

3. Remove the plugs from the intake manifolds (**Figure 9**) and screw in the adapters for the vacuum gauges. The longer adapters are used for the 2 inside carburetors.

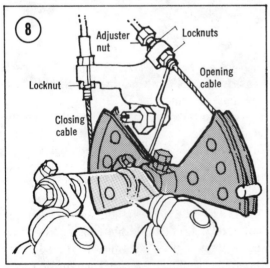

Adjuster nut — Locknuts

Locknut

Opening cable

Closing cable

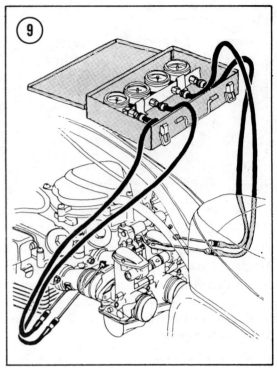

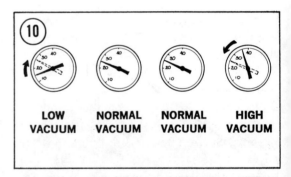

LOW VACUUM NORMAL VACUUM NORMAL VACUUM HIGH VACUUM

7. To adjust, refer to **Figure 11** and loosen the locknuts on the carburetor. Turn the adjusting screws clockwise to increase vacuum; counterclockwise to decrease it.

NOTE: *All 4 carburetors should be adjusted to register the same vacuum, regardless of the particular numbers on the gauges.*

8. When the carburetors are balanced, tighten the locknuts and rev the engine a couple of times. Recheck the vacuum readings and readjust if necessary. If the engine does not run properly, check for a loose or broken valve plate stud.

4. Close the damping valves on the vacuum gauge tubes and start the engine. Double-check to make sure it is idling at the correct rpm.

5. Slowly open the damping valves until the needles in each gauge flutter slightly but do not swing beyond one graduation.

6. Vacuum readings should be between 16 cm-hg and 24 cm-hg, with difference between carburetors not exceeding 3 cm-hg. **Figure 10** shows typical vacuum readings for four cylinders.

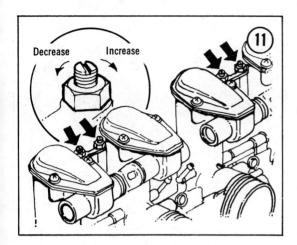

9. Remove the vacuum adapters and reinstall the plugs in the intake manifolds.

10. Adjust throttle linkage as described later.

Carburetor Synchronization (Do-It-Yourself Manometer)

> NOTE: *See procedure later in this chapter for constructing manometer.*

1. Remove the fuel tank and reconnect it with a longer fuel line. Keep the tank higher than the carburetors.

2. Adjust throttle adjusting nut (Figure 8) to take up slack.

3. Remove the air filter and connecting hoses.

4. Place an orifice plate over each carburetor opening. Small holes can be drilled near the edges and springs attached to hold the plate firmly against the carburetor.

5. Start the engine and allow it to warm up long enough for the idle to stabilize.

6. Loosen locknuts on carburetors (Figure 10).

7. Adjust each carburetor screw (Figure 11) until all 4 carburetors register the same level on the manometer. Turn the screw clockwise to increase level, counterclockwise to decrease level.

8. When carburetors are synchronized at the same level, tighten locknuts.

9. Rev the engine several times and recheck synchronization. Readjust if necessary.

10. Remove orifice plates.

11. Reinstall air filters and fuel tank.

12. Adjust throttle linkage as described later.

Throttle Linkage Adjustment

The throttle cable is looped around a bell-crank (**Figure 12**) mounted on the linkage shaft so that the throttles open and close in a positive, push-pull action. The twist grip should rotate smoothly to the full open or full closed position when the steering is on right or left lock.

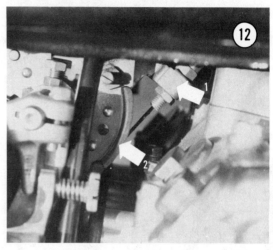

1. Adjuster   2. Walking beam

If the carburetors were just balanced, or if the cable seems to be binding, the throttle linkage must be adjusted.

Refer to the detail of the handlebar throttle grip in **Figure 13**. The amount of free play is a matter of personal preference, although the factory recommends between 10 and 15 degrees of the full rotation, or 0.13-0.16 in. (3-4mm) as measured around the circumference of the grip.

Major adjustments should be made at the carburetor end of the cable (**Figure 14**). Both the opening and closing sides of the adjusters should be changed by equal amounts. Leave about 0.12 in. (3mm) at the grip adjuster (**Figure 15**) for final micro-adjustment.

The eccentric link pin (**Figure 16**) limits over-travel of the cable crank when the throttle grip is forced past its normal closed position.

The clearance between the pin and throttle lever "H" (Figure 16) should be:

    CB350/400: 0.08-0.083 in. (2-2.1mm)
    CB500/550:   0.08-0.12 in. (2-3mm)

Adjust by loosening the locknut behind the eccentric pin, rotating the pin until the correct

6

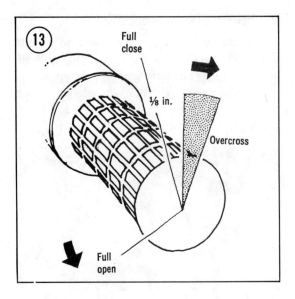

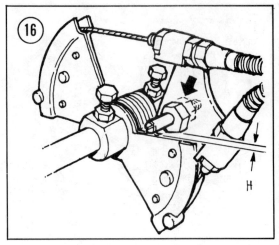

clearance is obtained, then retightening the locknut.

Removal/Installation

1. Remove the fuel tank.

2. Disconnect the throttle cables at the link lever. Loosen the air cleaner connecting and insulator bands, and then remove the carburetors as an assembly.

3. Reverse removal procedure for installation.

Disassembly

Refer to **Figures 17 and 18** for this procedure.

1. Remove the carburetors from the engine using procedure above.

2. Refer to **Figure 19** and unhook the throttle return spring from the link lever. Be careful not to damage the hook.

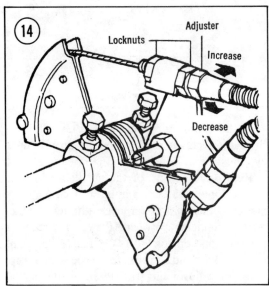

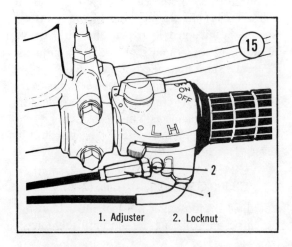

1. Adjuster   2. Locknut

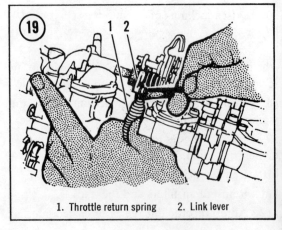

1. Throttle return spring   2. Link lever

⑰

⑱

CB350/400 CARBURETOR

CB500/550 CARBURETOR

1. Jet needle
2. Throttle valve
3. O-ring
4. Valve seat
5. Clip plate
6. Leaf spring
7. Float chamber body
8. Lockwasher
9. Drain screw
10. Float
11. Slow jet No. 40
12. Needle jet
13. Air screw spring
14. Adjuster screw
15. Bar clip
16. Spring seat A
17. Spring seat C
18. Lockwasher
19. Special bolt A
20. Tongued washer
21. Throttle shaft holder
22. Coil spring
23. Throttle shaft
24. Valve plate
25. Main jet No. 100

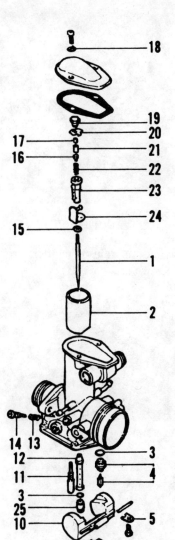

6

3. Refer to **Figure 20** and loosen the hex nuts so that dust plate B can be removed. Then remove the cap nuts.

1. Hex nuts   3. Cap nuts
2. Dust plate B

4. Separate the adjuster holders from the link arm as shown in **Figure 21**.

1. Link arm   2. Adjuster holder

5. Remove the 4 carburetors from the bracket by loosening the eight 6mm flathead screws.

6. Remove the tops from each carburetor (**Figure 22**) by unscrewing the 2 mounting screws.

Carburetor top

7. Straighten the tabs of the 2 lockwashers and remove the 4mm and 6mm bolts (**Figure 23**).

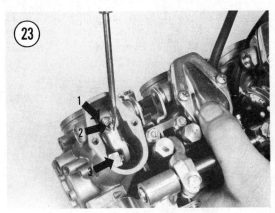

1. Lockwashers   3. 6mm bolt
2. 4mm bolt

8. Refer to **Figure 24** and pry the link arm free of the throttle shaft with a screwdriver.

9. Remove the valve plate (**Figure 25**) by loosening the two 3mm screws, then turn the plate 90 degrees in either direction so that the tap is aligned with the groove in the shaft.

10. Remove the needle from the throttle valve.

11. Remove the adjusting screw from the holder (**Figure 26**).

12. Remove the adjuster holder by setting the throttle valve in the halfway open position.

13. Remove the float chamber.

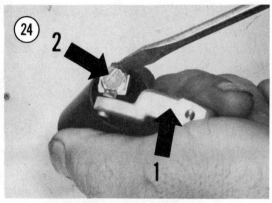

1. Link arm   2. Throttle shaft

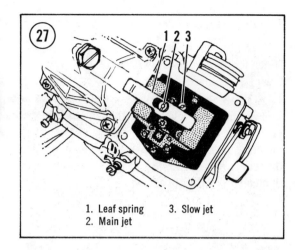

1. Leaf spring   3. Slow jet
2. Main jet

1. Screws   3. Throttle valve
2. Valve plate

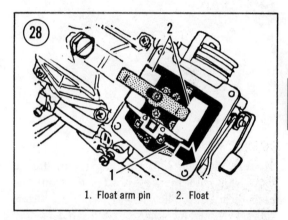

1. Float arm pin   2. Float

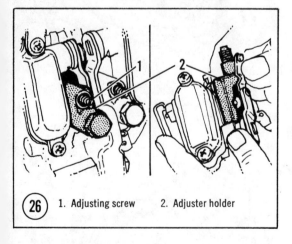

1. Adjusting screw   2. Adjuster holder

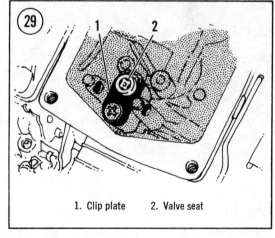

1. Clip plate   2. Valve seat

14. Refer to **Figure 27** and remove the leaf spring, main jet, and slow jet.

15. Extract the float arm pin (**Figure 28**) and remove the float.

16. Remove the clip plate (**Figure 29**) and then remove the valve seat.

Inspection

1. Blow out the jets with compressed air to remove any foreign matter.

2. Adjust the float level with a gauge made for the purpose as described in *Float Level*.

Assembly

Assemble in reverse order of disassembly. Refer to Figures 17 and 18 and note the following procedures.

1. Assemble the valve plate with its two 3mm screws and spring washers; then align the key protruding from the plate with the slot in the throttle valve (**Figure 30**). Turn the plate 90 degrees toward the link arm side and then tighten with the 3mm screws.

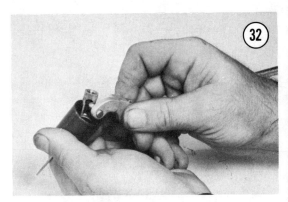

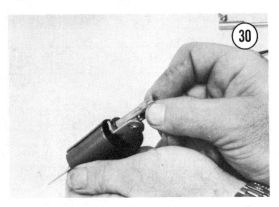

2. Refer to **Figure 31** and align the throttle valve slot with the key protruding from the carburetor body. The cutaway part of the throttle valve should face the side of the choke valve.

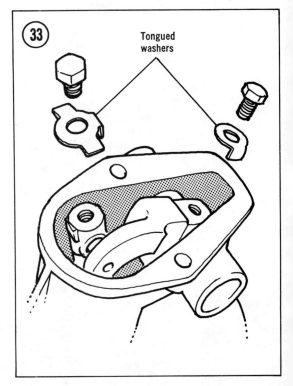

Tongued washers

3. Unscrew the 6mm bolt in the throttle shaft (**Figure 32**), then pull up on the shaft while simultaneously pushing the spherical end of the link arm into the opening.

4. Install the tongued lockwasher as shown in **Figure 33**. Tighten the bolts and then bend the tongues against the bolt head to lock them in place.

5. Route the fuel tubes as shown in **Figure 34**.

FUEL TANK

Removal/Installation

1. Drain fuel tank.

2. Disconnect one end of balance tube between left and right halves of tank.

3. Disconnect fuel lines from fuel petcock.

4. Unlatch seat and swing it out of the way.

5. Pull fuel tank clear of rear rubber mount.

6. Lift rear of tank and pull it out to the rear.

7. Installation is the reverse of these steps.

Inspection

1. Disassemble the fuel valve and check parts for wear, clogging, or damage.

2. Check the tank for leaks and the fuel tubes for age cracks or other damage.

3. Check rubber mounts for deterioration. Replace if necessary.

> NOTE: *Engine heat causes these to deteriorate fairly quickly.*

AIR CLEANER

Figures 35, 36, and 37 show details of the air cleaner systems.

"DO-IT-YOURSELF" MANOMETER

This do-it-yourself manometer costs less than $3 and works as well as the expensive Honda gauge set.

To build it, you will need:

   a. 40 ft. of ¼-in. clean surgical or aquarium tubing

   b. A ¼-in. thick sheet of 2 x 4 ft. plywood or masonite

   c. 4 large baby food jars with lids

   d. 4 tin cans (12 oz. or larger)

Manometer Construction

1. Build a stand for the board to keep it upright.

2. Attach the jars 6 in. from the bottom of the board.

3. Cut the tubing into four 4-ft. sections and four 6-ft. sections.

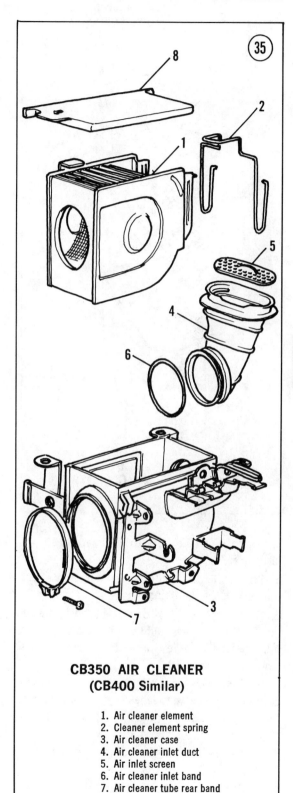

CB350 AIR CLEANER
(CB400 Similar)

1. Air cleaner element
2. Cleaner element spring
3. Air cleaner case
4. Air cleaner inlet duct
5. Air inlet screen
6. Air cleaner inlet band
7. Air cleaner tube rear band
8. Air cleaner case lid

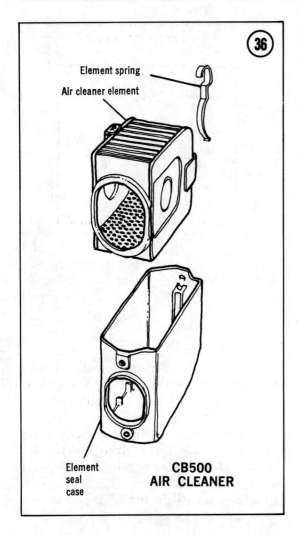

Element spring

Air cleaner element

Element
seal
case

**CB500
AIR CLEANER**

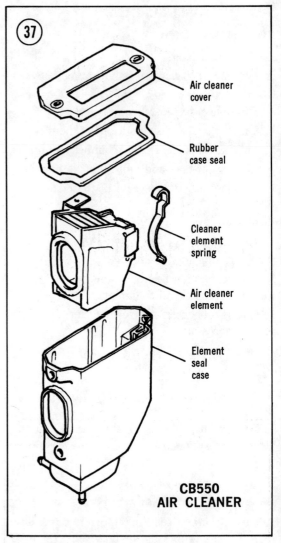

Air cleaner
cover

Rubber
case seal

Cleaner
element
spring

Air cleaner
element

Element
seal
case

**CB550
AIR CLEANER**

4. Affix the 4-ft. sections to the board as shown in **Figure 38**.

5. Scrape the paint off the center section of the top surface of the 4 jar lids.

6. Drill one ¼-in. and one ⅛-in. hole in each lid. The ¼-in. hole should be in the center of the lid. The smaller hole is a vent and can be anywhere. See **Figure 39**.

7. Solder a piece of tubing to the jar lids so the bottom edge nearly touches the jar and the top section protrudes at least ½ inch as shown in Figure 39.

8. Push the clean plastic tubing onto the brass tubing.

9. Drill four ¼-in. holes at the top of the plywood directly above each jar and insert four 2-in. lengths of brass tubing.

10. Connect the 4-ft. lengths of tubing to the four 2-in. tubes.

11. Fill the jars ¾ full of water. Tint with food coloring. Suck all air out of the U-shaped pieces of tubing.

12. Fabricate 4 plates of aluminum or steel to be ½-in. larger in diameter than the carburetor throat. Drill a hole ⅔ the size of the carburetor intake in the center of each plate and a ¼-in. hole just to the side. See **Figure 40**.

13. Epoxy a short piece of brass tubing in the ¼-in. plate hole for each unit.

14. Glue pieces of gasket material around each orifice plate to ensure a good seal against the carburetor.

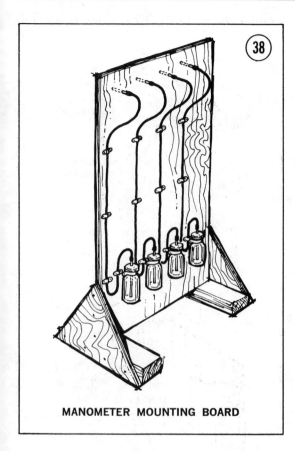

MANOMETER MOUNTING BOARD

③⑧

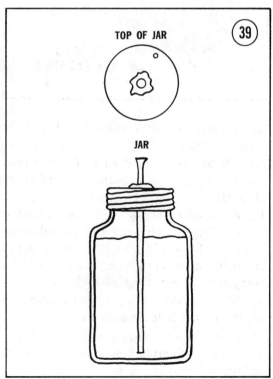

TOP OF JAR ③⑨

JAR

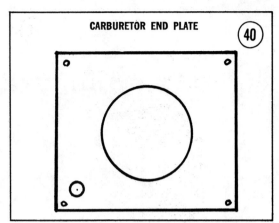

CARBURETOR END PLATE ④⓪

15. Connect each orifice plate to one of the 6-ft. sections of tubing and connect the other end to the brass tubing at the top of the manometer board.

Using the Manometer

Place orifice plates over carburetor throats. Make sure that plates seal well against throats. Adjust synchronization as described elsewhere in this chapter.

If the water levels fluctuate too widely, make stabilizers out of tin cans as shown in **Figure 41**. This set-up can be used with any multi-cylinder motorcycle or car. The orifice size is unimportant as long as it and the small tube hole are less than the carburetor intake.

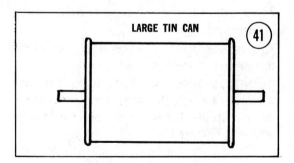

LARGE TIN CAN ④①

EMISSIONS CONTROL

A device has been installed on all 1975 and later Honda 350-550 fours to cut down on emissions. The device simply filters oil out of blow-by gases and recirculates these gases to burn unused fuel. The only maintenance is to clean the filter and tubing.

CHAPTER SEVEN

ELECTRICAL SYSTEM

This chapter covers maintenance and repair of the:

a. Starting system

b. Ignition system

c. Charging system

d. Lighting system

e. Horn

The ignition system consists of the battery, 2 coils, 2 sets of contact breaker points, spark advancer, and 4 spark plugs.

One set of points supplies current to the No. 1 and No. 4 cylinders and the other to the No. 2 and No. 3 cylinders. There is no distributor.

The spark advancer is mounted on the crankshaft inboard of the breaker point assembly. As engine speed increases, the device advances point opening to cause earlier ignition.

The charging system consists of the alternator, rectifier, voltage regulator, and a fuse. **Figure 1** shows the system.

If battery voltage is low, current flows from the battery through the voltage regulator's upper contact (5) to the field coil. The high field current produces high generator output.

When battery voltage exceeds 14.5 volts, a coil in the regulator pulls the armature away from the upper contact, breaking that circuit, and closes the lower contact (7). A 10 ohm resistance is incorporated in the new circuit which limits current reaching the field coil. This produces a lower generator output than in the first operating mode.

STARTER

Removal/Installation

When the pushbutton starter switch on the handlebar is pressed, it energizes the magnetic switch which closes the starting circuit. About 120 amperes flow from the battery to operate the starting motor.

Refer to **Figures 2 and 3** for exploded views of all starters.

1. Disconnect the starter motor cable at the solenoid switch, shown in **Figure 4**.

2. Remove the motor cover and the left crankcase cover.

3. Remove the motor by unscrewing the 2 mounting bolts. See **Figure 5**.

4. Installation is the reverse of these steps.

Inspection and Adjustment

Overhaul of the starter is best left to an expert. This section shows how to determine if the unit is defective. Refer to Figures 2 and 3.

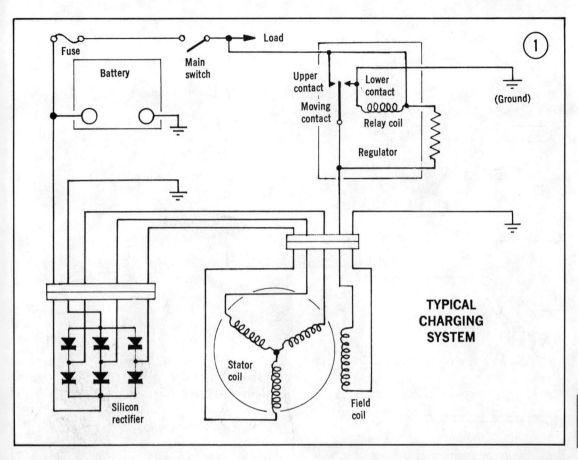

Fuse

Battery

Main switch

Load

Upper contact

Moving contact

Lower contact

Relay coil

(Ground)

Regulator

Silicon rectifier

Stator coil

Field coil

TYPICAL CHARGING SYSTEM

7

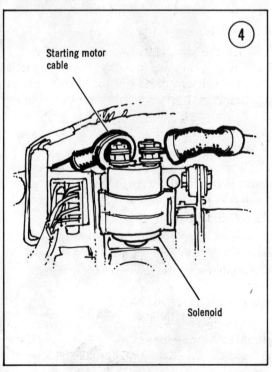

Starting motor cable

Solenoid

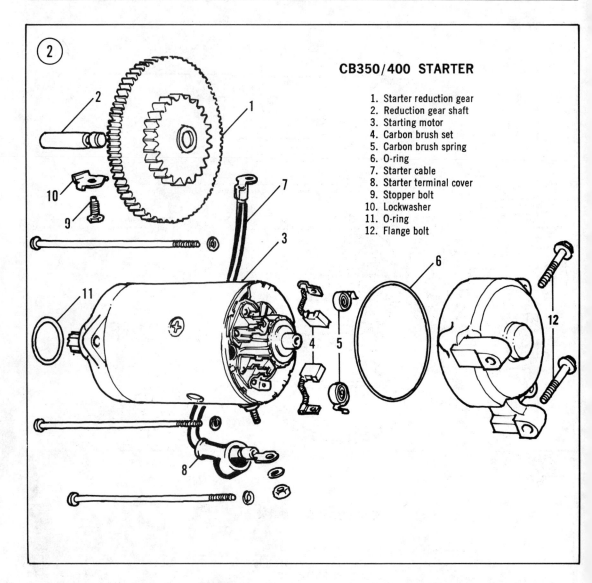

② **CB350/400 STARTER**

1. Starter reduction gear
2. Reduction gear shaft
3. Starting motor
4. Carbon brush set
5. Carbon brush spring
6. O-ring
7. Starter cable
8. Starter terminal cover
9. Stopper bolt
10. Lockwasher
11. O-ring
12. Flange bolt

1. Inspect the carbon brushes. They should be replaced if they are worn or pitted.

2. Measure the length of the brushes with a vernier caliper. The length should be not less than 0.22 in. (5.5mm).

3. Check the electrical continuity between the armature and the core. If there is a short, replace the armature.

4. Measure the amount of mica undercut (the depth of the grooves); if it is less than 0.012 in. (0.3mm), replace the commutator.

5. Check continuity between the brush wired to the stator coil and the starter motor cable. If there is no continuity, the coil is open and it should be replaced.

STARTER SOLENOID

Testing

1. While the switch is still wired to the cycle, push the button and listen for the click of the iron core striking the coil, signifying the device is operating.

2. Check the condition of the contact points and dress them with a point file if they are pitted or burned.

IGNITION COIL

Removal/Installation

1. Raise the seat and remove the fuel tank.

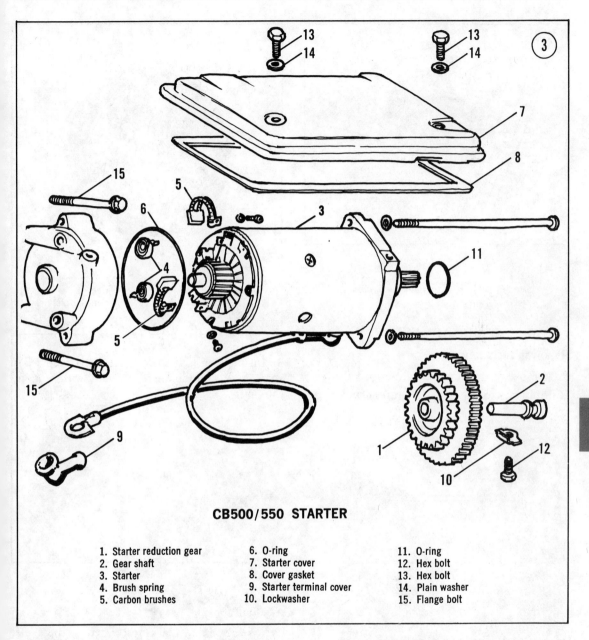

CB500/550 STARTER

1. Starter reduction gear
2. Gear shaft
3. Starter
4. Brush spring
5. Carbon brushes
6. O-ring
7. Starter cover
8. Cover gasket
9. Starter terminal cover
10. Lockwasher
11. O-ring
12. Hex bolt
13. Hex bolt
14. Plain washer
15. Flange bolt

2. Disconnect the 3 ignition coil leads which are color-coded yellow, blue, and black/white.

3. Unscrew the 2 mounting bolts (**Figure 6**) and remove the coils from the frame.

Testing

Electrical testers are available at many service shops to bench test ignition coil. If one is available, use it. However, one easy way to test for a defective coil is to substitute a known good one.

BREAKER POINTS

Breaker point maintenance is covered fully in Chapter Two.

Breaker Plate Removal/Installation

1. Remove point cover.

2. Disconnect the yellow and blue leads at the junction point at the center of the frame.

3. Refer to **Figure 7** and unscrew the 6mm bolt, remove the special washer, loosen the base plate mounting screws, and lift out the unit.

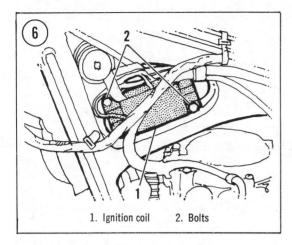

1. Ignition coil   2. Bolts

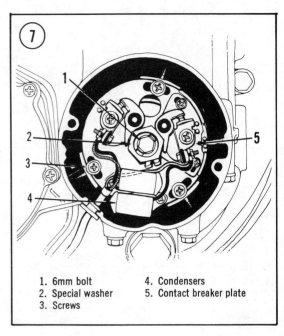

1. 6mm bolt   4. Condensers
2. Special washer   5. Contact breaker plate
3. Screws

NOTE: *Do not reassemble breaker point if the spark advance mechanism is to be serviced.*

SPARK ADVANCER

Removal/Installation

1. Remove the breaker plate described above.
2. Pull spark advancer off (**Figures 8 and 9**).

3. Installation is the reverse of these steps. Be sure that dowel pin aligns properly with hole in the shaft.

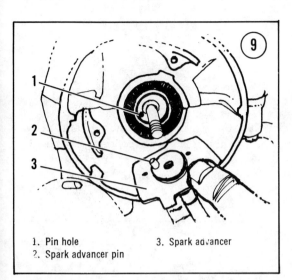

1. Pin hole
2. Spark advancer pin
3. Spark advancer

Inspection

1. Clean the advancer with solvent and make sure the weights pivot smoothly.

2. Check the tension of the springs and the wear of the shaft.

ALTERNATOR

Removal/Installation

Refer to **Figure 10**.

1. Remove the alternator cover.

2. Remove the rotor (**Figure 11**) with a special puller.

3. Remove the stator coil from inside the alternator cover by removing the three 6mm screws.

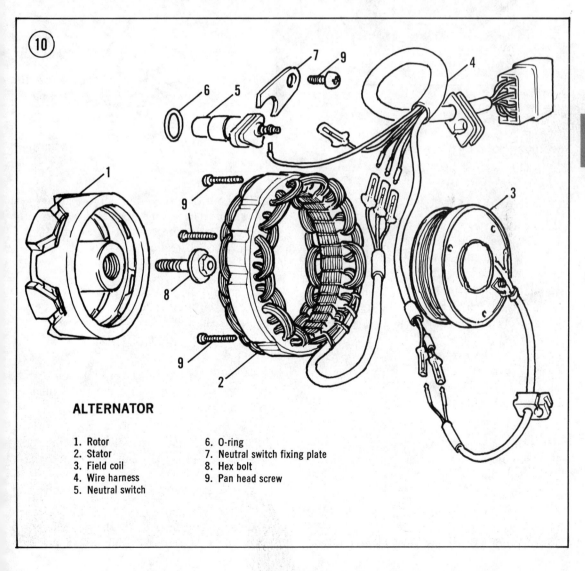

ALTERNATOR

1. Rotor
2. Stator
3. Field coil
4. Wire harness
5. Neutral switch
6. O-ring
7. Neutral switch fixing plate
8. Hex bolt
9. Pan head screw

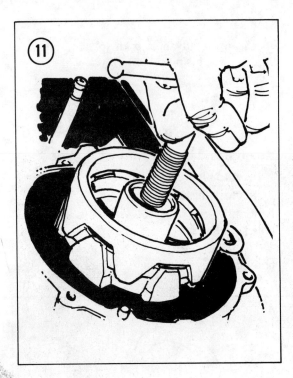

4. Remove the field coil from the outside of the alternator cover by removing the 3 screws.

5. Installation is the reverse of these steps.

VOLTAGE REGULATOR

Adjusting the alternator voltage regulator requires special equipment not ordinarily available to a home mechanic. If trouble appears to be in the voltage regulator, take the job to a dealer or competent repair shop.

Consider also replacing the regulator as repair costs may be many times that of buying a new one. There is even a chance the old regulator cannot be readjusted, so you will need a new regulator anyway.

Removal/Installation

Refer to Figure 1 for location of the voltage regulator.

1. Disconnect the leads at the junction and detach the unit by unscrewing the two 6mm mounting bolts.

2. Remove regulator cover by loosening the 2 screws.

3. Installation is the reverse of these steps.

SILICON RECTIFIER

Testing

CAUTION
The rectifier can be damaged by surges of high voltage.

Test the continuity of the rectifier in both normal and reverse directions as shown in **Figure 12**. Use an ohmmeter or other continuity tester with no more than 12 volts as a test source.

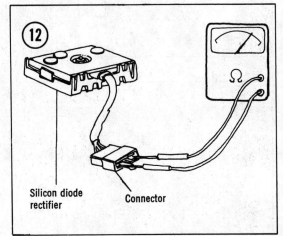

Silicon diode rectifier   Connector

The rectifier is in good condition if the test shows continuity in the normal direction only. The rectifier is defective if the test shows continuity in both directions.

BATTERY

Battery electrolyte level should be checked regularly, especially in hot weather.

Removal

1. Remove the retaining strap. Disconnect the ground, or negative (−) cable first, then the positive (+) cable.

2. Lift the battery from the mounting, noting the location of the terminal covers, mounting pads, and vent tube for reinstallation later.

Inspection and Testing

1. Corrosion on the battery terminals causes leakage of current. Clean them with a wire brush and a solution of baking soda and water.

2. The electrolyte level should be between the upper and lower marks (**Figure 13**). Top up the low cells with distilled water only.

3. Measure the specific gravity of the electrolyte with a bulb hydrometer, reading it as shown in **Figure 14**. Generally, the reading should be between 1.26 and 1.28. If the value is less than 1.189 at 68°F (20°C), the battery is in poor condition and should be charged. **Figure 15** shows the relationship between specific gravity and residual battery capacity.

Charging

A "trickle" charger is recommended for restoring a low voltage battery to normal. Most such inexpensive chargers have outputs ranging from 1-6 amps.

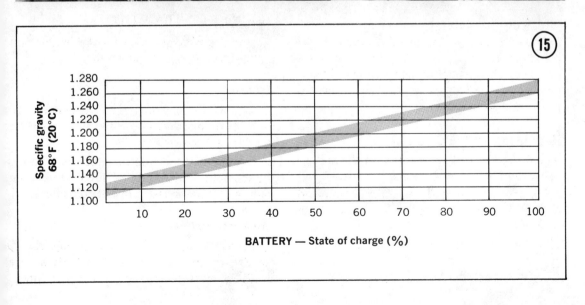

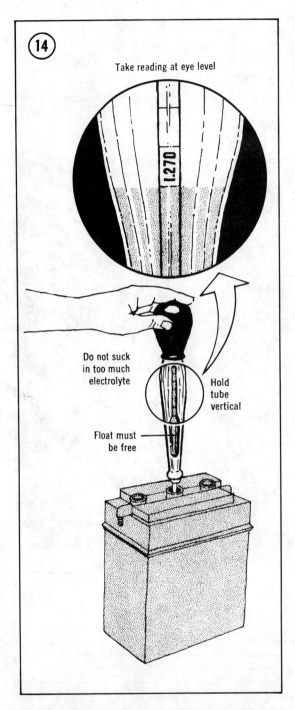

Take reading at eye level

1.270

Do not suck
in too much
electrolyte

Hold
tube
vertical

Float must
be free

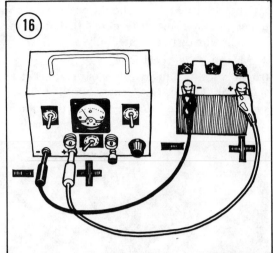

2. The electrolyte will begin bubbling, signifying that explosive hydrogen gas is being released. Make sure the area is adequately ventilated and there are no open flames.

3. It will take at least 8 hours to bring the battery to full charge. Test the electrolyte periodically with a hydrometer to see if the specific gravity is within the standard range of 1.26-1.28. If the reading remains constant for more than an hour, the battery is charged.

Installation

1. Make sure battery terminals, cable clamps, and case are free of corrosion. Silicone spray or petroleum jelly can be applied to the terminals to retard the process.

2. When replacing the battery, be careful to route the vent tube so that it is not crimped. Connect the positive terminal first, then the negative one. Do not overtighten the clamps.

SWITCHES

The following procedures may be used to test for defective switches.

1. Disconnect the switch leads at their junctions and test the circuits for continuity.

2. Refer to the wiring diagrams. There should be continuity in each circuit (designated by infinity). If there is no continuity where there should be, or if there is continuity where there should not be, switch is defective and should be replaced.

The so-called "quick" chargers at gas stations drastically shorten battery life by overheating which causes plate warpage.

1. **Figure 16** shows the connection of a charger. Note that the positive lead must be clipped to the positive terminal and the negative lead to the negative terminal or damage will result.

WIRING DIAGRAMS

7

WIRING DIAGRAM — CB350F/CB400

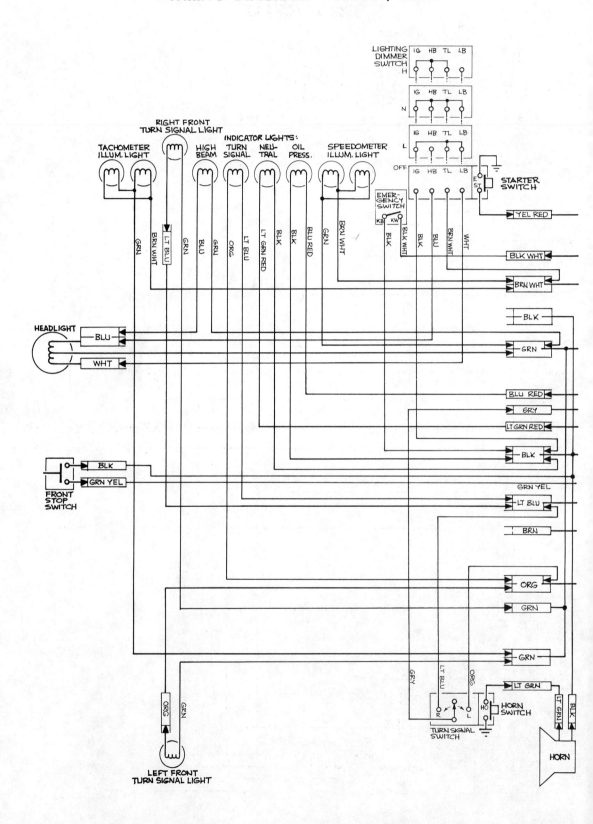

WIRING DIAGRAM
CB350F/CB400

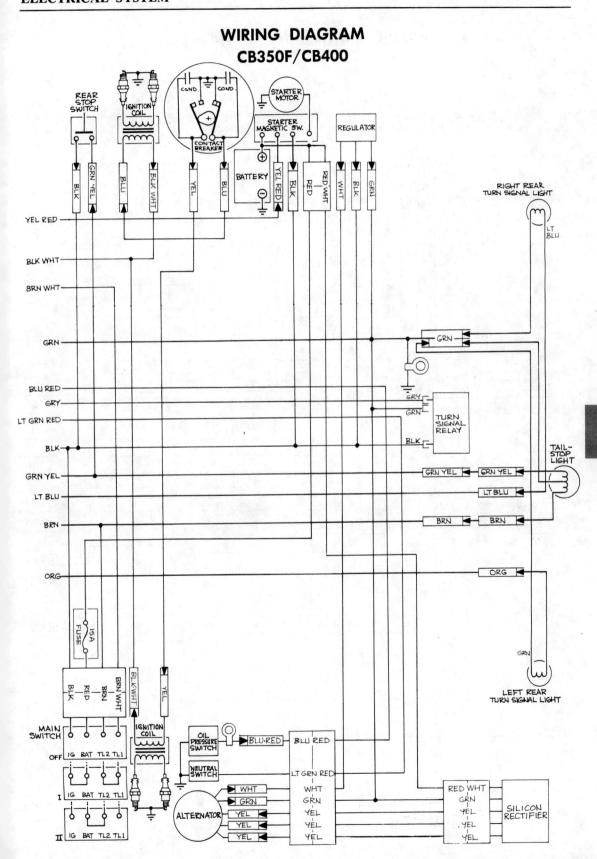

WIRING DIAGRAM — CB500

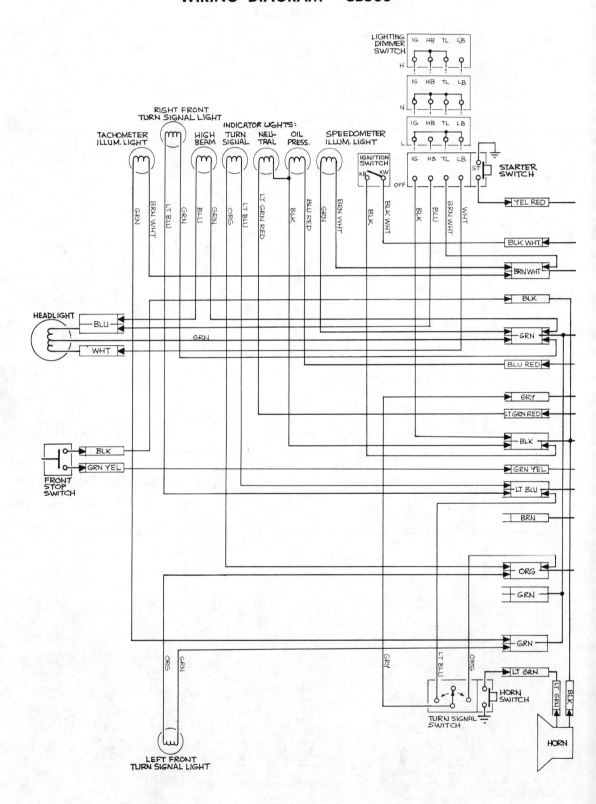

WIRING DIAGRAM
CB500

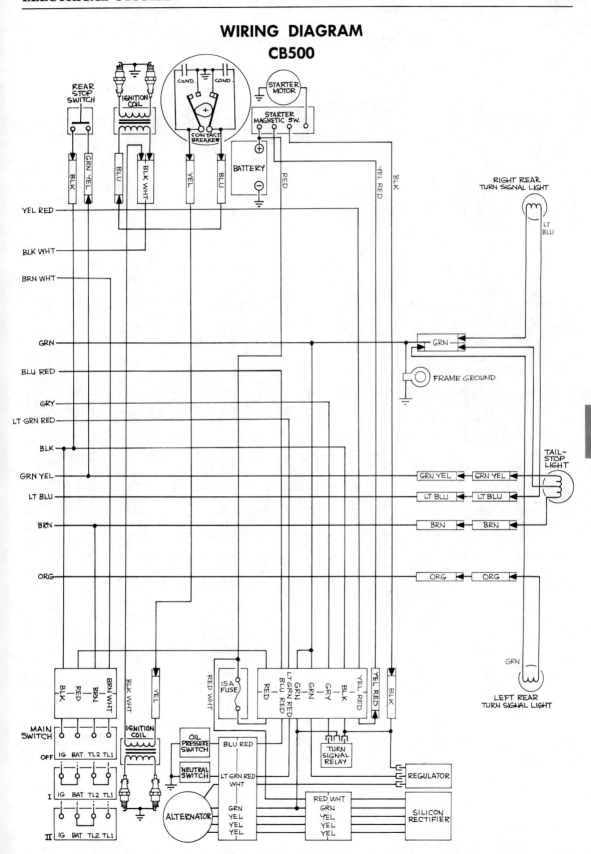

WIRING DIAGRAM — CB550

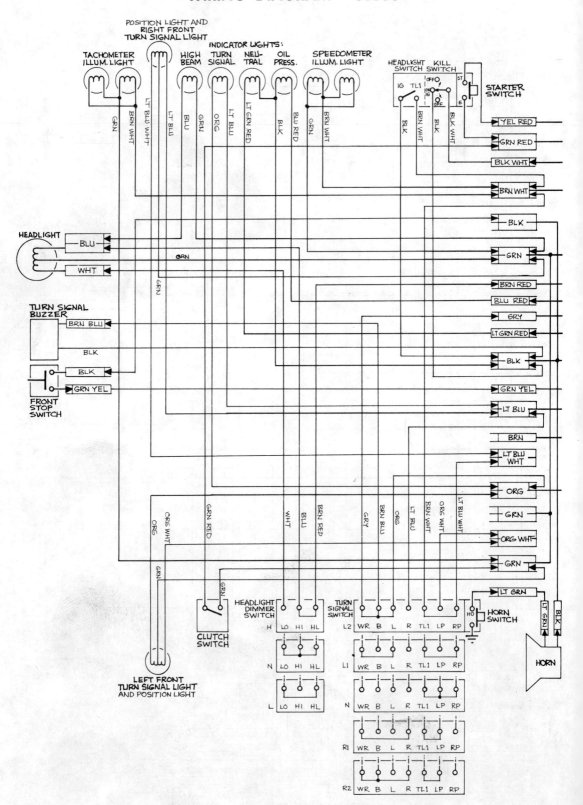

WIRING DIAGRAM — CB550

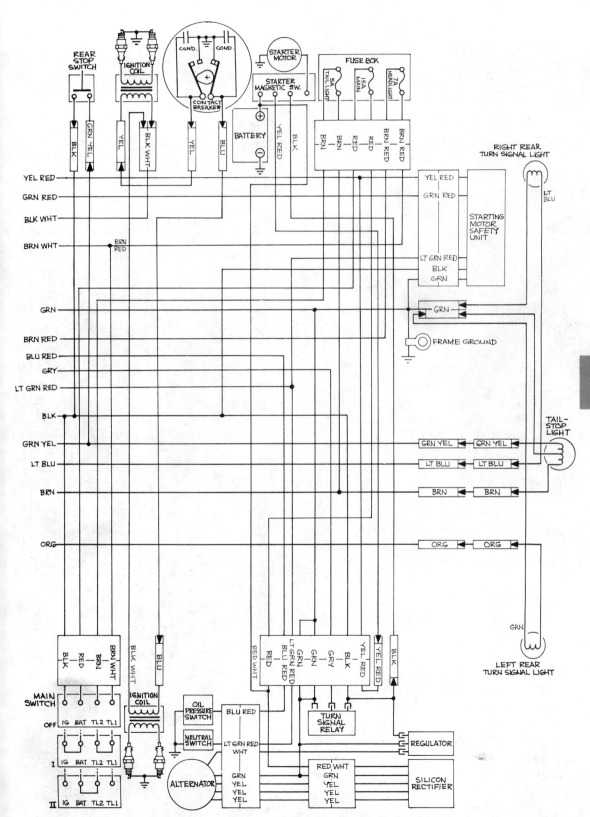

CHAPTER EIGHT

FRONT WHEEL AND BRAKE

The front wheel and brake are very critical components on any motorcycle. No matter how well the bike is running, if it cannot be ridden safely it is useless.

The front brake must supply more braking effort than the rear to stop in the shortest possible distance. Therefore, Honda fits these bikes with a disc brake. Proper maintenance will assure that these operate safely.

Balance and shimmy are more critical on the front wheel than the rear. The front wheel affects all other handling aspects of the bike. The front wheel should be checked for balance, shimmy (side-to-side play), wobble (out-of-round), runout, and proper tire inflation. Many of these problems go unnoticed at low speeds but become dangerous at highway speeds.

FRONT WHEEL

Refer to **Figures 1 and 2** for details of the front wheel assembly.

Removal

1. Raise the front wheel clear of the ground by placing a block under the engine.

2. Refer to **Figure 3** and disconnect the speedometer cable at the hub.

3. Loosen the axle holding nuts and remove the wheel from the fork.

NOTE: *Do not operate the brake lever when the wheel is off the frame. The caliper piston will pop out of the cylinder.*

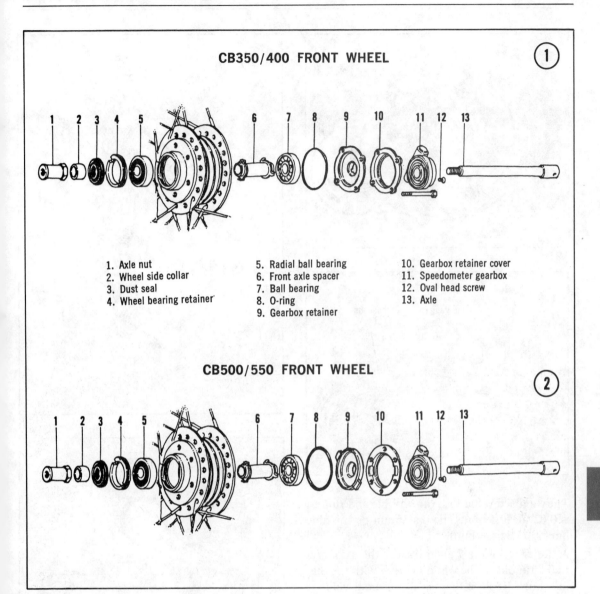

CB350/400 FRONT WHEEL   ①

1. Axle nut
2. Wheel side collar
3. Dust seal
4. Wheel bearing retainer
5. Radial ball bearing
6. Front axle spacer
7. Ball bearing
8. O-ring
9. Gearbox retainer
10. Gearbox retainer cover
11. Speedometer gearbox
12. Oval head screw
13. Axle

CB500/550 FRONT WHEEL   ②

8

4. Unscrew the axle nut, and remove the axle.

5. Refer to **Figure 4** to remove the bearing retainer from the hub. Extract the dust seal from the retainer.

6. Refer to **Figure 5** and straighten the tongues on the washers; then unscrew the mounting bolts. Remove the brake disc.

7. Remove the speedometer gearbox and the retainer cover from the other side of the hub.

8. Remove the wheel bearing.

Inspection

1. Measure the wobble and runout of the wheel rim with a dial indicator as shown in **Figure 6**.

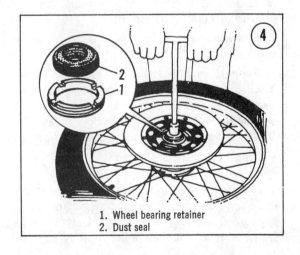

④

1. Wheel bearing retainer
2. Dust seal

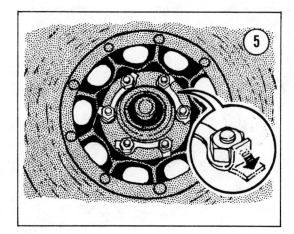

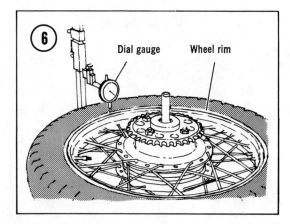

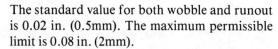

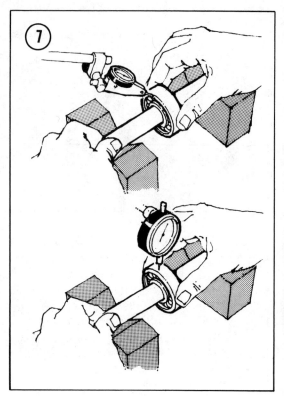

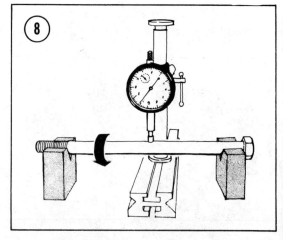

The standard value for both wobble and runout is 0.02 in. (0.5mm). The maximum permissible limit is 0.08 in. (2mm).

2. Refer to **Figure 7** and measure the axial and radial runout of the wheel bearing with the dial indicator. Replace the bearing if axial value is more than 0.004 in. (0.1mm) or radial value is more than 0.002 in. (0.05mm).

3. Straighten or replace any bent or loose spokes.

4. Support each wheel shaft in a lathe, V-blocks, or other suitable centering device as shown in **Figure 8**. Rotate the shaft through a complete revolution. Straighten or replace the shaft if it is bent more than 0.028 in. (0.7mm).

Spokes

The spokes support the weight of the motorcycle and rider, and transmit tractive and braking forces, as shown in **Figure 9**. Diagram A illustrates action of the spokes as they support

the machine. Tractive forces are shown in Diagram B. Braking forces are shown in Diagram C.

Check the spokes periodically for looseness or binding. A bent or otherwise faulty spoke will adversely affect neighboring spokes, and should therefore be replaced immediately. To remove the spoke, completely unscrew the threaded portion, then remove the bent end from the hub.

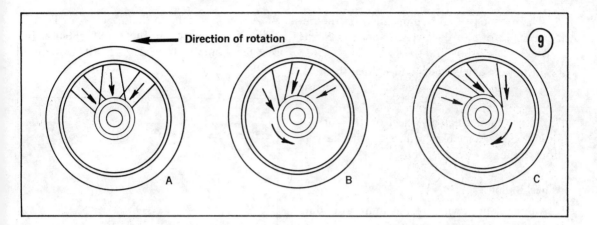

Spokes tend to loosen as the machine is used. Retighten each spoke one turn, beginning with those on one side of the hub, then those on the other side. Tighten the spokes on a new machine after the first 50 miles of operation, then at 50-mile intervals until they no longer loosen.

If the machine is subjected to particularly severe service, as in off-road or competition riding, check the spokes frequently.

Installation

1. Refer to **Figure 10** and use a driver to install the wheel bearing.

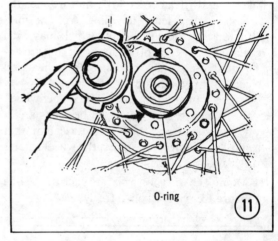

O-ring

2. Mount the dust seal on the bearing retainer and then install the unit into the hub with the O-ring.

3. Align the gearbox retainer with the corresponding flat cutouts on the bearing retainer and install as shown in **Figure 11**.

8

4. Install the brake disc with the mounting bolts and nuts, using new tongued washers. Torque to 13-16.6 ft.-lb. (1.8-2.3 mkg). Then bend the washer tabs, as in **Figure 12**, so they will lock the nuts in place.

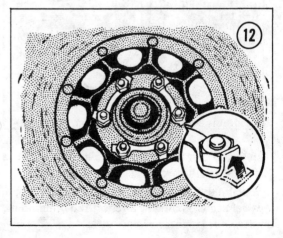

5. The gearbox should be installed on the opposite side of the disc. Then insert the axle through the gearbox into the hub.

6. Install the axle holders and tighten the nuts, first on the brake disc side and then on the other.

7. Before mounting the wheel on the fork, it should be balanced according to the instructions in the following section.

Wheel Balance

An unbalanced wheel results in unsafe riding conditions. Depending on the degree of unbalance and the speed of the motorcycle, the rider may experience anything from a mild vibration to a violent shimmy which may even result in loss of control. Balance weights are applied to the spokes on the light side of the wheel to correct this condition.

Before you attempt to balance the wheel, check to be sure that the wheel bearings are in good condition and properly lubricated, that the brakes do not drag, so that the wheel rotates freely, and that the rim is true.

1. Mount the wheel on a fixture such as the one in **Figure 13** so it can rotate freely.

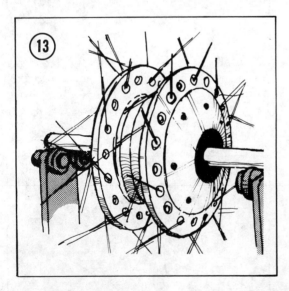

2. Give the wheel a spin and let it coast to a stop. Mark the tire at the lowest point.

3. Spin the wheel several more times. If the wheel keeps coming to a rest at the same point, it is out of balance.

4. Attach a weight to the upper — or light — side of the wheel at the spoke (**Figure 14**). Weights come in four sizes: 5, 10, 15, and 20 grams.

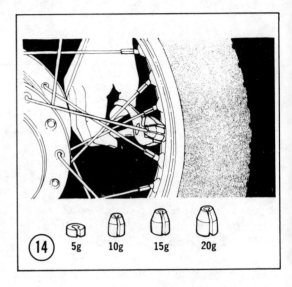

5g   10g   15g   20g

5. Experiment with different weights until the wheel, when spun, comes to rest at a different position each time.

BRAKES

Figure 15 shows the elements of the front disc brake system.

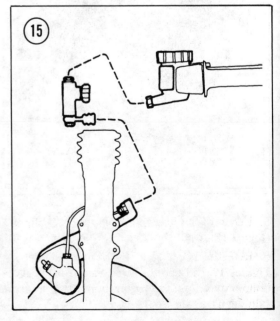

Removal

1. Remove the front wheel as described earlier.

2. Drain the brake fluid from the system.

3. Disconnect the brake hose (**Figure 16**) by unscrewing the oil joint bolt.

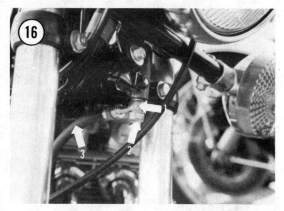

1. Connector   2. Bolt   3. Brake hose

4. Refer to **Figure 17** for details of the caliper assembly. Remove the 3 mounting bolts, the adjusting bolt, and the 2 set bolts. Then separate the 2 calipers.

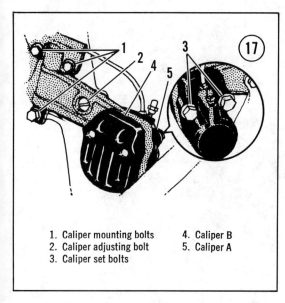

1. Caliper mounting bolts   4. Caliper B
2. Caliper adjusting bolt   5. Caliper A
3. Caliper set bolts

5. Remove the pistons from the 2 calipers (**Figure 18**).

6. Refer to the views of the master cylinder in **Figures 19 and 20**. In order, remove the joint bolt, brake hose, mounting bolts, and master cylinder unit.

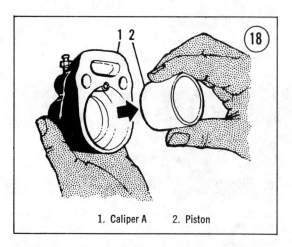

1. Caliper A   2. Piston

1. Bolt   2. Master cylinder

7. To disassemble the master cylinder, refer to **Figure 21** and also the exploded view. Remove the snap rings, the 10.5mm washer, piston, secondary cup, spring, and check valve.

Inspection

1. Red grooves in both pads (inset, **Figure 22**) mark the wear limit. When the pad is worn down to the red groove it should be replaced.

2. Measure the inner diameter of the caliper cylinder with a dial indicator (**Figure 23**) and the outer diameter of the piston with a micrometer. Compute the clearance by subtraction. If the difference is greater than 0.004 in. (0.1mm), the parts should be replaced.

3. Take the same measurements of the master cylinder and its piston (**Figure 24**). Replace if the clearance is more than 0.004 in. (0.1mm).

4. Check the caliper piston seal and the brake hose for damage and replace if required.

8

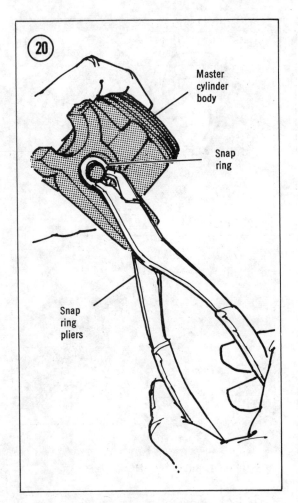

⑳

Master
cylinder
body

Snap
ring

Snap
ring
pliers

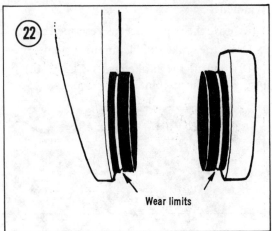

㉒

Wear limits

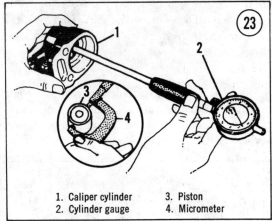

㉓

1
2
3
4

1. Caliper cylinder   3. Piston
2. Cylinder gauge   4. Micrometer

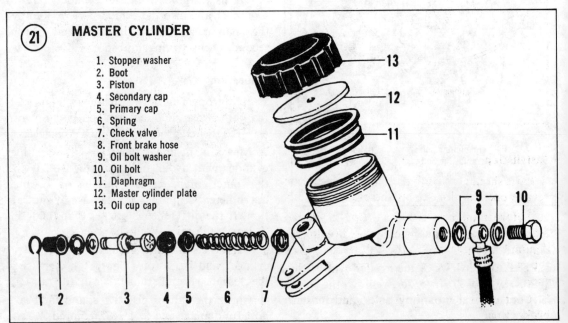

㉑   **MASTER CYLINDER**

1. Stopper washer
2. Boot
3. Piston
4. Secondary cap
5. Primary cap
6. Spring
7. Check valve
8. Front brake hose
9. Oil bolt washer
10. Oil bolt
11. Diaphragm
12. Master cylinder plate
13. Oil cup cap

13
12
11

9
8
10

1   2   3   4   5   6   7

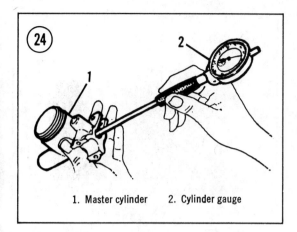

1. Master cylinder   2. Cylinder gauge

5. Check the flatness of the brake disc with a dial indicator, as shown in **Figure 25**, with the disc lying on a perfectly flat surface. If the disc is distorted by more than 0.012 in. (0.3mm), the disc should be replaced. Usually this much distortion is evident by spinning the wheel and sighting along the disc.

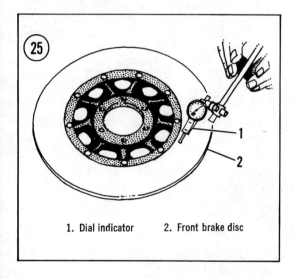

1. Dial indicator   2. Front brake disc

Installation

Parts should be absolutely clean. Assemble in reverse order of disassembly; note the following.

1. Before mounting the pads, apply a small amount of silicone sealing grease — not molybdenum brake grease — to the sliding surfaces of the calipers. Do not get any on the pad surfaces.

2. Coat the inside of the master cylinder with brake fluid.

3. Refer to **Figure 26** and install the check valve with its return spring.

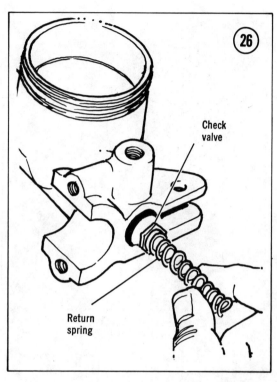

Check valve

Return spring

4. Coat the primary cup with brake fluid and install as shown in **Figure 27**.

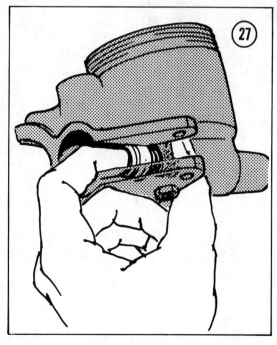

8

5. Replenish brake fluid (**Figure 28**) using only fresh, heavy duty fluid. Painted surfaces will be permanently etched if the corrosive brake fluid is spilled on them. Wash off any spillage immediately.

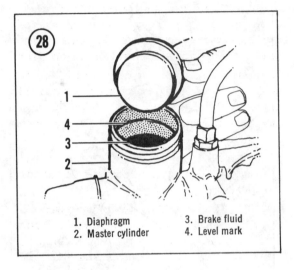

1. Diaphragm   3. Brake fluid
2. Master cylinder   4. Level mark

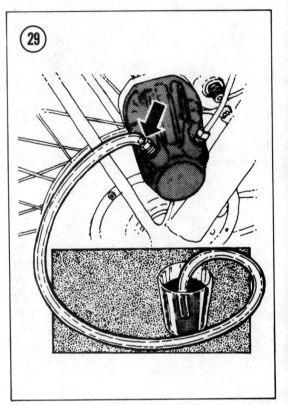

Bleeding Front Brake System

Air should be bled off from the brake system after it has been serviced or whenever the travel of the brake lever increases markedly or if the action is spongy.

The bleeding operation itself is best performed by 2 persons, one pumping the brake lever and the other monitoring the bleed valve.

1. Remove the cap and diaphragm from the master cylinder reservoir and fill with brake fluid.

2. Attach a tube to the bleeder valve (**Figure 29**) and immerse the other end in a cup of brake fluid. This is to prevent suction of air back into the system.

3. Open the bleeder valve ½ turn, squeeze the brake lever until it bottoms, close the bleeder valve, then release the brake lever. Top up the reservoir with brake fluid if necessary. No air should enter the system from either end.

4. Repeat the bleeding steps until no air bubbles issue from the tip of the hose.

5. Replace the master cylinder reservoir cap and diaphragm and squeeze the brake lever several times. Check for seepage.

6. If the brakes continue to feel spongy or low at the lever, there may be an air lock where air

is trapped in the line and moving in and out with the fluid. To correct this, remove the brake line at the master cylinder. Fill a clean oil can with brake fluid and pump it into the line. Loosen the bleeder valve and continue pumping to expel air. Tighten the bleeder valve after nothing but fluid comes from the line for a few pumps and hook up the brake line. Continue bleeding in the standard manner.

Front Brake Adjustment

1. Prop the bike so the front wheel is clear of the ground.

2. Refer to **Figure 30** and loosen the stopper bolt locknut.

3. With a screwdriver, turn the stopper bolt clockwise until the brake pad touches the disc. The wheel should drag slightly when it is turned.

4. Rotate the wheel and slowly back off the stopper bolt counterclockwise until the wheel turns freely without drag.

5. Back off the bolt ½ turn more and tighten down the locknut.

TIRE CHANGING AND REPAIR

1. Remove the valve core to deflate the tire.

2. Press the entire bead on both sides of the tire into the center of the rim.

3. Lubricate the beads with soapy water.

4. Insert the tire iron under the bead next to the valve. Force the bead on the opposite side of the tire into the center of the rim and pry the bead over the rim with the tire iron (**Figure 31**).

5. Insert a second tire iron next to the first to hold the bead over the rim. Then work around the tire with the first tire iron, prying the bead over the rim (**Figure 32**). Be careful not to pinch the inner tube with the tire irons.

6. Remove the valve from the hole in the rim and remove the tube from the tire. Lift out and lay aside.

7. Stand the tire upright. Insert a tire iron between the second bead and the side of the rim that the first bead was pried over (**Figure 33**). Force the bead on the opposite side from the tire iron into the center of the rim. Pry the second bead off the rim, working around as with the first.

8

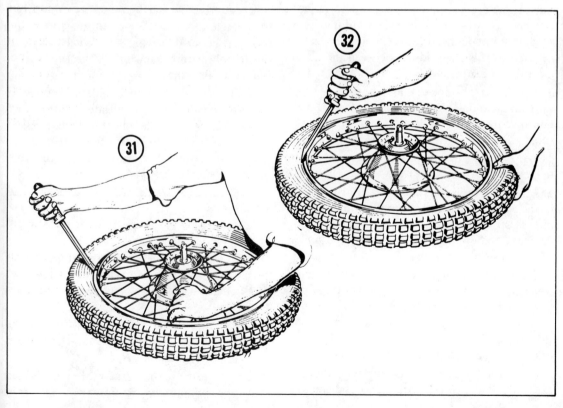

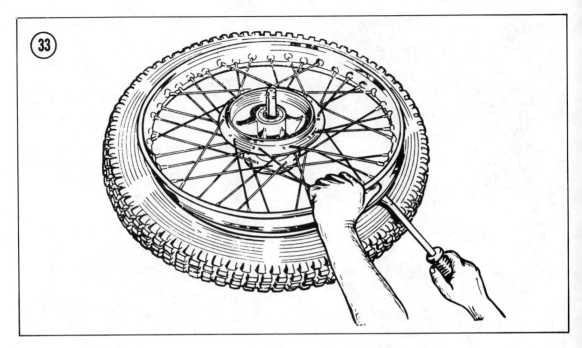

Tire Replacement

1. Carefully check the tire for any damage, especially inside.

2. A new tire may have balancing rubbers inside. These are not patches and should not be disturbed. A white spot near the bead indicates a lighter point on the tire. This should be placed next to the valve or midway between the 2 rim locks if they are installed.

3. Check that the spoke ends do not protrude through the nipples into the center of the rim to puncture the tube. File off any protruding spoke ends.

4. Be sure the rim rubber tape is in place with the rough side toward the rim.

5. Put the core in the tube valve. Put the tube in the tire and inflate just enough to round it out. Too much air will make installing the tire difficult, and too little will increase the chances of pinching the tube with the tire irons.

6. Lubricate the tire beads and rim with soapy water. Pull the tube partly out of the tire at the valve. Squeeze the beads together to hold the tube and insert the valve into the hole in the rim (**Figure 34**). The lower bead should go into the center of the rim with the upper bead outside it.

7. Press the lower bead into the rim center on each side of the valve, working around the tire

in both directions. See **Figure 35**. Use a tire iron for the last few inches of bead (**Figure 36**).

8. Press the upper bead into the rim opposite the valve. Pry the bead into the rim on both sides of the initial point with a tire iron, working around the rim to the valve. See **Figure 37**.

9. Wiggle the valve to be sure the tube is not trapped under the bead. Set the valve squarely in its hole before screwing on the valve nut to hold it against the rim.

10. Check the bead on both sides of the tire for even fit around the rim. Inflate the tire slowly to seat the beads in the rim. It may be necessary to bounce the tire to complete the seating. Inflate to the required pressure. Balance the wheel as described previously.

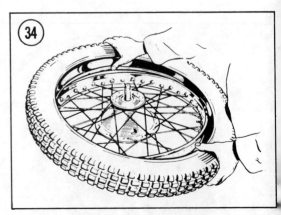

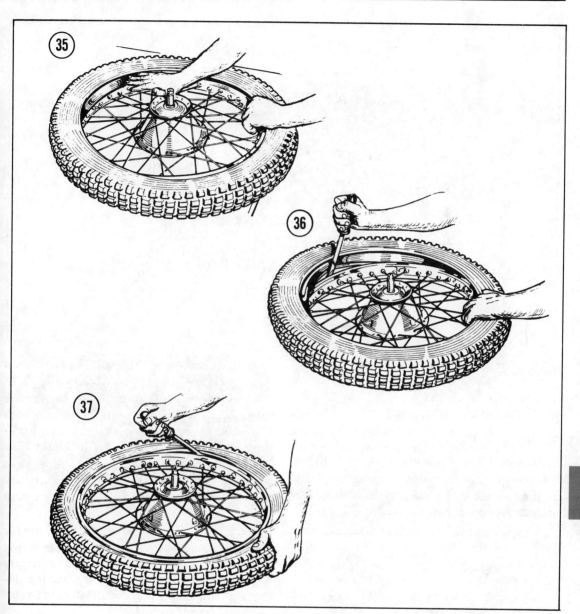

8

CHAPTER NINE

REAR WHEEL AND BRAKE

This chapter provides maintenance and repair procedures for the rear wheel and brake.

REAR WHEEL

Removal/Installation

Refer to **Figures 1 and 2** for details of the rear wheel.

1. Remove the brake rod and bolt, then disconnect the stopper arm, **Figure 3**.

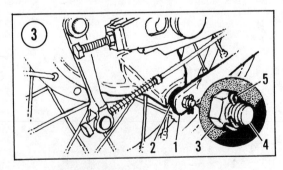

1. Hub stopper arm
2. Stopper arm cushion rubber
3. 8mm nut
4. Bolt
5. Lock pin

2. Remove muffler(s) and exhaust pipes if necessary.

3. Refer to **Figure 4**. Loosen the chain adjusting bolt on both sides, pull out the cotter pin, and loosen the axle nut.

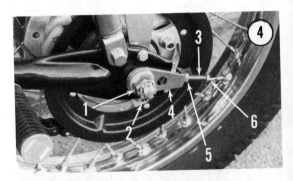

1. Axle nut
2. Cotter pin
3. Drive chain adjuster
4. Chain adjuster stopper
5. Lock nut
6. Chain adjusting bolt

4. Push the wheel forward so that the chain can be lifted free of the sprocket. Referring again to Figure 4, remove the lock bolts and adjusting stoppers.

5. Remove the wheel and its axle by pulling the assembly to the rear of the cycle.

6. Installation is the reverse of these steps. Adjust drive chain slack and brake pedal free play as described in Chapter Two.

Sprocket Removal/Installation

Remove the sprocket by straightening the tongues on the washers, unscrewing the 4 mounting bolts (3), **Figure 5**. Referring to **Figure 6**, tap the sprocket (1) free with a wood block (2).

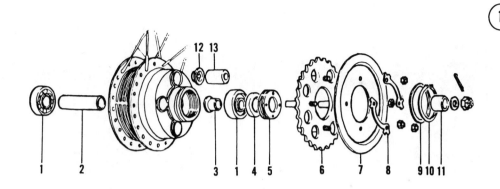

CB350 REAR WHEEL
(CB400 Similar)

1. Radial ball bearing
2. Axle spacer A
3. Axle spacer B
4. Dust seal
5. Wheel bearing retainer
6. Sprocket
7. Sprocket side plate
8. Tongued washer
9. Washer
10. External circlip
11. Wheel side collar
12. Wheel hub plug
13. Wheel damper bushing

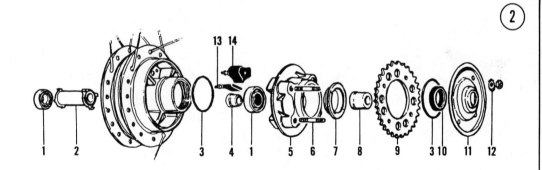

CB500/550 REAR WHEEL

1. Ball bearing
2. Axle spacer
3. O-ring
4. Axle spacer B
5. Final driven flange
6. Stud bolt
7. Bearing retainer
8. Wheel side collar
9. Final driven sprocket
10. Oil seal
11. Sprocket side plate
12. Tongued washer
13. Wheel damper B
14. Wheel damper A

9

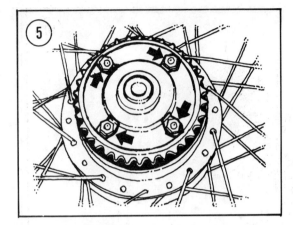

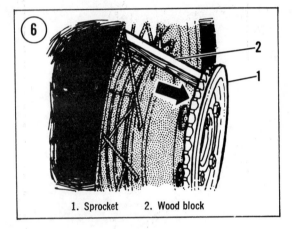

1. Sprocket   2. Wood block

Bearing Removal/Installation

1. Remove wheel and sprocket.

2. Drill out stake marks with a 0.25 in. (6mm) drill bit.

3. Remove the bearing retainer (**Figure 7**) and drive the bearing out of the hub. The retainer has a left-hand thread.

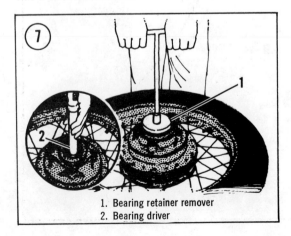

1. Bearing retainer remover
2. Bearing driver

4. Installation is the reverse of these steps. Use Loctite or a similar thread-locking compound on the bearing retainer. On the CB350/400, stake the retainer with a punch as shown in **Figure 8** in an area apart from the original stake mark locations.

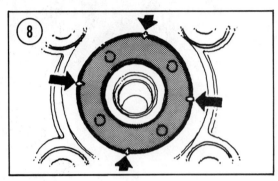

Wheel Inspection

1. Check runout and wobble of the wheel rim and the condition of the bearing as described for the front wheel in Chapter Eight.

2. Check the final driven sprocket for excessive wear. Compare with **Figure 9**.

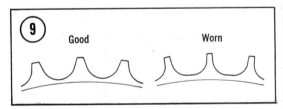

Good   Worn

3. Check the final drive chain for wear and stretch. See Chapter Two for routine maintenance and repair.

Spokes

See Chapter Eight.

Wheel Balance

See Chapter Eight.

BRAKE

Disassembly/Assembly

Refer to **Figures 10 and 11** for the following procedure.

1. Remove rear wheel.

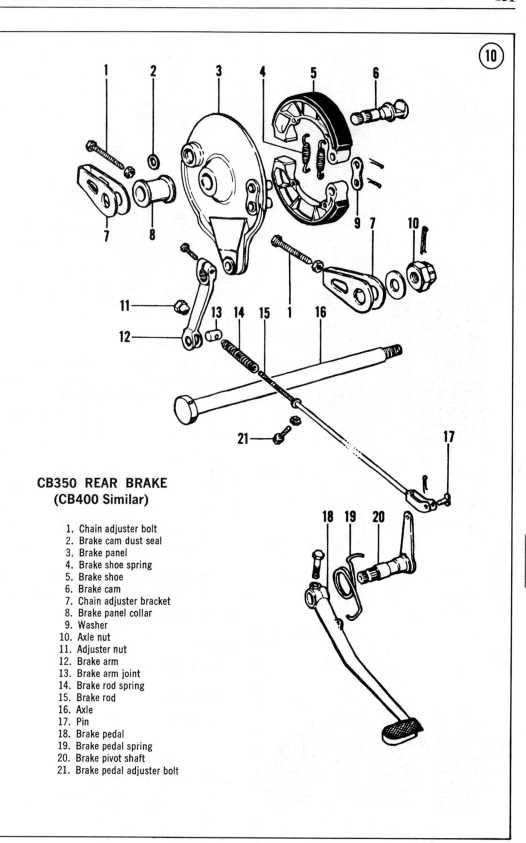

**CB350 REAR BRAKE
(CB400 Similar)**

1. Chain adjuster bolt
2. Brake cam dust seal
3. Brake panel
4. Brake shoe spring
5. Brake shoe
6. Brake cam
7. Chain adjuster bracket
8. Brake panel collar
9. Washer
10. Axle nut
11. Adjuster nut
12. Brake arm
13. Brake arm joint
14. Brake rod spring
15. Brake rod
16. Axle
17. Pin
18. Brake pedal
19. Brake pedal spring
20. Brake pivot shaft
21. Brake pedal adjuster bolt

9

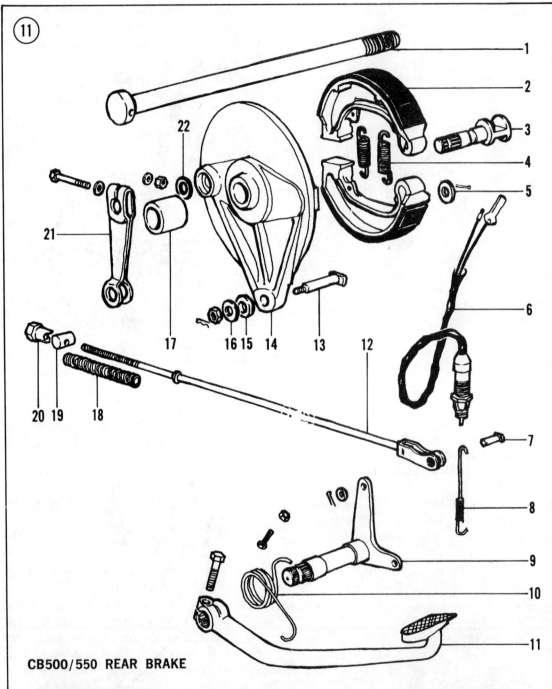

⑪

1 — Rear axle

CB500/550 REAR BRAKE

1. Rear axle
2. Rear brake shoe
3. Rear brake cam
4. Front brake shoe spring
5. Handle holder setting washer
6. Stoplight switch assembly
7. Pin
8. Switch spring

9. Pivot shaft
10. Pedal spring
11. Brake pedal
12. Rear brake rod
13. Brake stopper arm bolt
14. Rear brake panel
15. Stopper arm cushion rubber

16. Handle holder setting washer
17. Brake panel side collar
18. Brake rod spring
19. Brake arm joint
20. Adjuster nut
21. Rear brake arm
22. Brake cam dust seal

2. Remove brake panel from wheel.

3. Remove cotter pins and washer (**Figure 12**), and remove brake shoes.

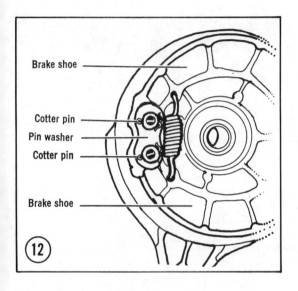

4. Inspect as described below. Replace parts as necessary.

5. Assembly is the reverse of these steps.

CAUTION
Do not get grease or oil on brake linings.

Inspection

1. Measure the thickness of the brake shoes with a vernier caliper as shown in **Figure 13**. Replace if worn beyond the following limits:

CB350/400: 0.1 in. (2.5mm)
CB500/550: 0.08 in. (2mm)

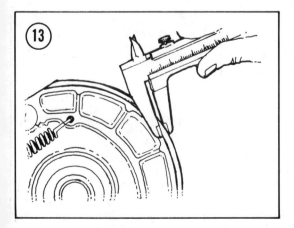

2. Measure the inside diameter of the drum with a vernier caliper as shown in **Figure 14**. Replace if the distance is greater than the following limits:

CB350/400: 6.339 in. (161mm)
CB500/550: 7.125 in. (181mm)

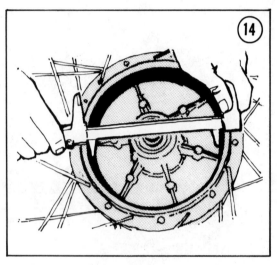

TIRES

Refer to Chapter Eight for tire changing and repair procedures.

WHEEL ALIGNMENT

1. Measure the width of the 2 tires at their widest points.

2. Subtract the smaller dimension from the larger.

3. Nail a piece of wood, equal to ½ the figure obtained in Step 2, to a straight piece of wood approximately 7 feet long. See (D), **Figure 15**.

4. Lay the straight edge on blocks 6 inches high and place against the tires. If the wheels are aligned, the board will touch each wheel at 2 points as shown in (B), Figure 15.

5. If the wheels are not aligned as in (A) and (C), Figure 15, the rear wheel must be shifted to correct the situation. The chain adjuster must cause the wheel to move toward the rear on the side shown for the error indicated in Figure 15.

6. If the frame has been bent, this may not correct the misalignment. Replace the frame or have it aligned by an expert.

9

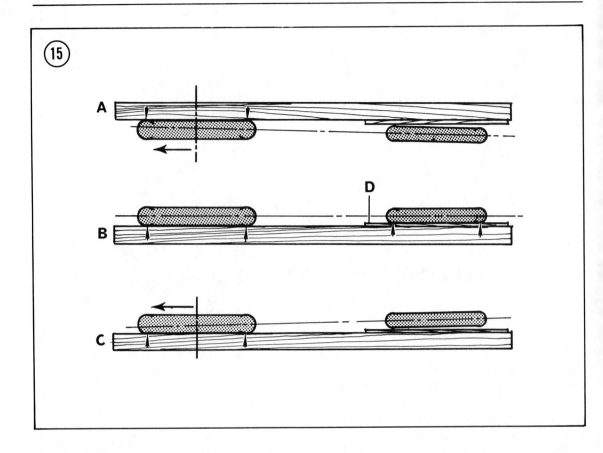

CHAPTER TEN

STEERING, SUSPENSION, AND FRAME

The front suspension is a critical part of the motorcycle for the rider's safety. A loose fork stem, worn steering bearings, or bent fork tubes can cause serious steering and handling problems at high speeds. Follow the chart and directions on periodic maintenance outlined in Chapter Two. Refer any problems to the troubleshooting section in Chapter Three.

The frame should never require any type of periodic maintenance other than an occasional spot check near tube junctures for signs of cracking or metal fatigue. If the motorcycle has been involved in an accident, regardless of severity, it should be checked by a shop for bends or fractures. Some damage can be so slight as to escape visual inspection. The only positive method, in some cases, may be magnafluxing (a process using magnetic force fields and iron particles to detect hairline fractures).

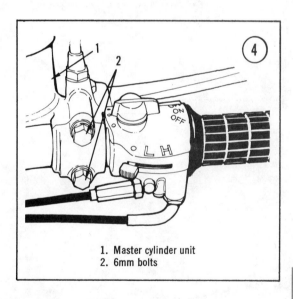

1. Master cylinder unit
2. 6mm bolts

STEERING

Disassembly

See **Figures 1 through 3** for this procedure.

1. Remove the master brake cylinder, **Figure 4**, by unscrewing the two 6mm bolts.

2. Disconnect the clutch and throttle cables. Remove the light switch.

3. Remove the headlight from its case and disconnect the electrical leads.

4. Refer to **Figure 5** and remove the upper handlebar holder by unscrewing the 4 bolts. Disconnect the wire harness.

5. Remove the speedometer and tachometer by unscrewing the mounting bolts.

6. Remove the front wheel (Chapter Eight).

7. Disconnect the brake hose at the 3-way joint at the stem.

8. Remove the front fork (see *Front Suspension Disassembly* section of this chapter).

9. Refer to **Figure 6** and unscrew the stem nut and the 8mm bolts. Remove the top fork bridge.

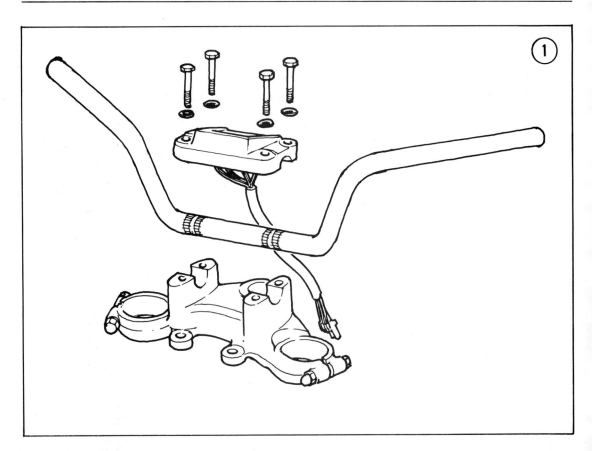

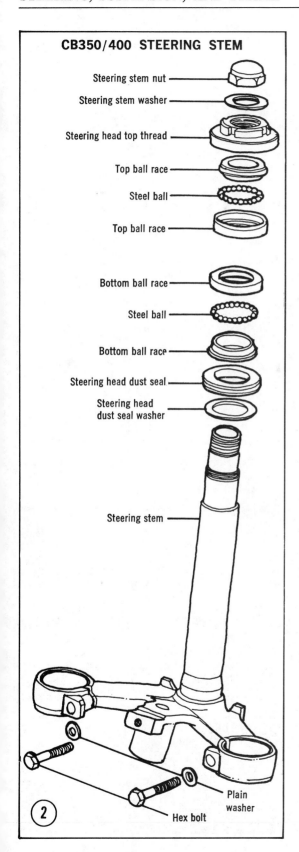

CB350/400 STEERING STEM

Steering stem nut
Steering stem washer
Steering head top thread
Top ball race
Steel ball
Top ball race
Bottom ball race
Steel ball
Bottom ball race
Steering head dust seal
Steering head dust seal washer
Steering stem
Plain washer
Hex bolt

②

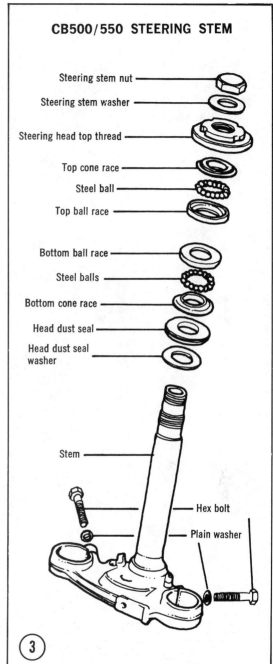

CB500/550 STEERING STEM

Steering stem nut
Steering stem washer
Steering head top thread
Top cone race
Steel ball
Top ball race
Bottom ball race
Steel balls
Bottom cone race
Head dust seal
Head dust seal washer
Stem
Hex bolt
Plain washer

③

10. Use a special wrench, **Figure 7**, to unscrew the stem head nut.

11. Pull the stem head out from the bottom.

> NOTE: *A total of 37 steel balls form the 2 stem bearings. Some will drop free when the stem is removed. Be careful not to lose them.*

10

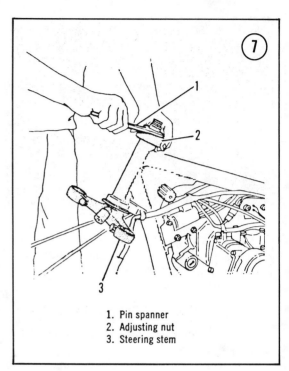

1. Pin spanner
2. Adjusting nut
3. Steering stem

1. Clean the cone races, ball races, and steel balls; and then coat with chilled grease to hold the bearings in place.

2. Install the correct number of steel balls, **Figure 8**.

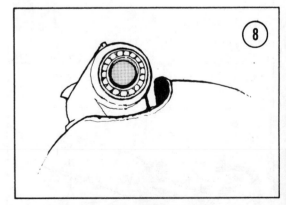

All models: 18 balls upper race
19 balls lower race

3. When installing the handlebar, ensure that punch marks (**Figure 9**) are aligned with the mating edges of the holders and top bridge. Tighten the bolts at the front first, then those at the rear.

Inspection

1. Inspect the handlebar and stem for bending, twisting, cracking, or damage.

2. Check the wiring and cables for damage.

3. Check the steel balls for wear. Clean them in solvent.

4. Check bearing races on the stem for wear.

5. Check the steering head dust seal for wear.

Assembly

Refer to Figures 1 through 3 and note the following when reassembling.

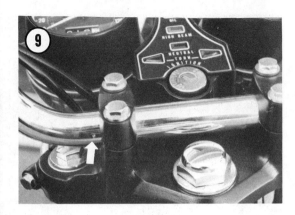

4. When the wiring and cables are hooked up, turn the steering fully from side to side and check for binding.

FRONT SUSPENSION

Refer to **Figures 10 and 11** for views of the front suspension.

Disassembly (CB350/400)

1. Remove the front wheel (Chapter Eight).

2. Remove the brake caliper assembly and the front fender.

3. Refer to **Figure 12** and loosen the bolts at the fork top bridge and stem bottom bridge, freeing the front fork assembly which can then be removed from below.

4. Drain the oil from the forks.

5. Loosen the 8mm bolt (**Figure 13**), and then remove the fork tube and damper unit.

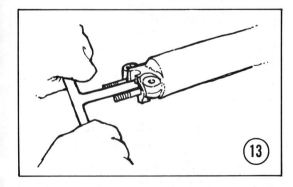

6. Remove the front fork bolt from the top of the fork tube so the cushion springs and seat can be removed.

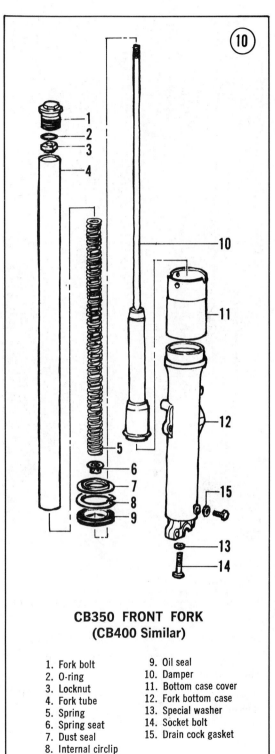

**CB350 FRONT FORK
(CB400 Similar)**

1. Fork bolt	9. Oil seal
2. O-ring	10. Damper
3. Locknut	11. Bottom case cover
4. Fork tube	12. Fork bottom case
5. Spring	13. Special washer
6. Spring seat	14. Socket bolt
7. Dust seal	15. Drain cock gasket
8. Internal circlip	

10

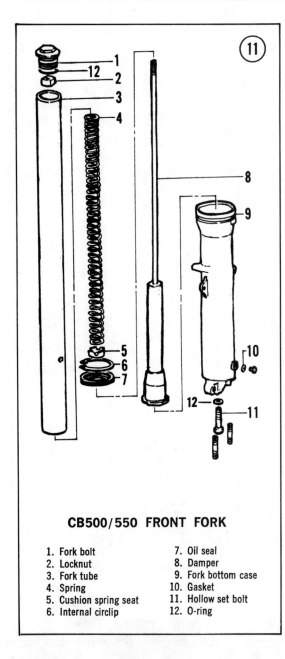

CB500/550 FRONT FORK

1. Fork bolt
2. Locknut
3. Fork tube
4. Spring
5. Cushion spring seat
6. Internal circlip
7. Oil seal
8. Damper
9. Fork bottom case
10. Gasket
11. Hollow set bolt
12. O-ring

7. Remove the circlip (**Figure 14**) to remove the oil seal.

Disassembly (CB500/550)

1. Loosen the fork bolt and drain the damper oil by removing the plug.

2. Remove the front wheel (Chapter Eight).

3. Refer to **Figure 15** and remove the brake caliper from the left fork by unscrewing the 3 mounting bolts.

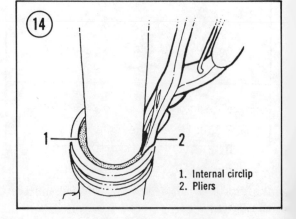

1. Internal circlip
2. Pliers

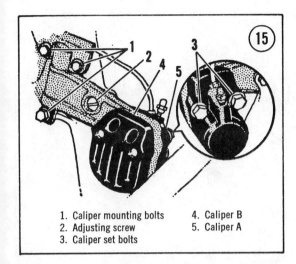

1. Caliper mounting bolts   4. Caliper B
2. Adjusting screw   5. Caliper A
3. Caliper set bolts

4. Remove the 4 bolts and pull the forks off from the bottom.

5. Refer to Figures 10 and 11 and disassemble the fork by unscrewing the front fork bolt, loosening the locknut, and removing the spring and the spring seat. A special tool is needed to remove the 8mm bottom case bolt so the damper can be removed.

Inspection

1. Measure the uncompressed length of the front spring as shown in **Figure 16**.

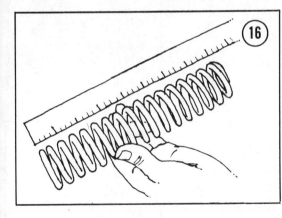

Replace if shorter than the following limit:

    CB 350: 16.38 in. (416mm)
    CB400: 18.84 in. (479mm)
    CB500/550: 16.73 in. (425mm)

2. Inspect the fork tube and bottom case for damage or wear.

3. Inspect the oil seal for damage or scratches.

4. Check for wear in the shock absorber piston and cylinder.

Assembly

Assemble in reverse order of disassembly, referring to the exploded drawings and noting the following.

1. Coat the piston rod thread with Loctite or a similar thread-locking compound before installing the locknut.

2. Use a new oil seal, press-fitting it with a special tool (**Figure 17**).

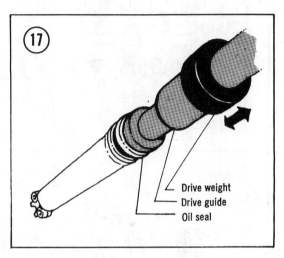

Drive weight
Drive guide
Oil seal

3. Adjust the front disc brake according to the instructions in Chapter Eight.

4. Fill the forks with fluid:

    CB350: 4.2 oz. (125cc)
        Automatic Transmission Fluid (ATF)
    CB400/500/550: 5.4 oz. (160cc)
        SAE 10W-30 oil

REAR SUSPENSION

Refer to **Figures 18 and 19** for the following procedures.

Disassembly (CB350/400)

1. Remove the sissy bar by loosening the 8mm bolts and upper nuts, as shown in **Figure 20**.

2. Remove the suspension by unscrewing the 10mm bolts.

10

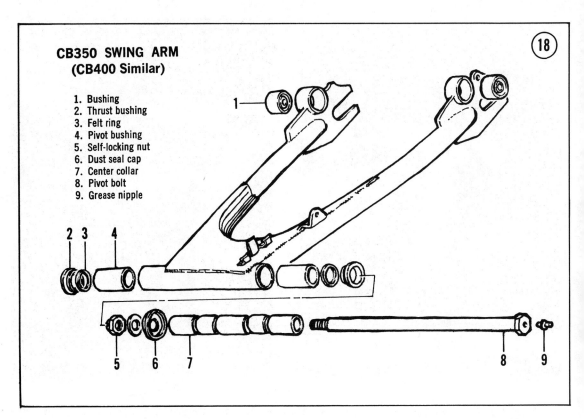

CB350 SWING ARM
(CB400 Similar)

1. Bushing
2. Thrust bushing
3. Felt ring
4. Pivot bushing
5. Self-locking nut
6. Dust seal cap
7. Center collar
8. Pivot bolt
9. Grease nipple

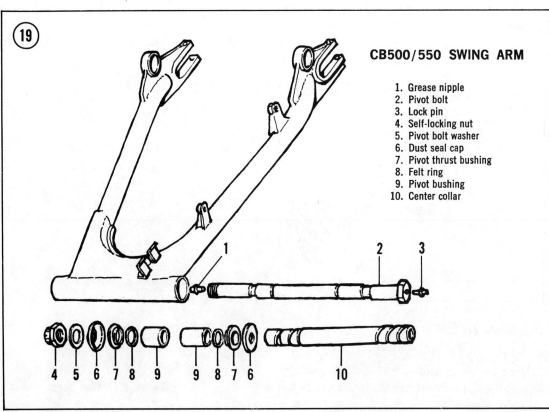

CB500/550 SWING ARM

1. Grease nipple
2. Pivot bolt
3. Lock pin
4. Self-locking nut
5. Pivot bolt washer
6. Dust seal cap
7. Pivot thrust bushing
8. Felt ring
9. Pivot bushing
10. Center collar

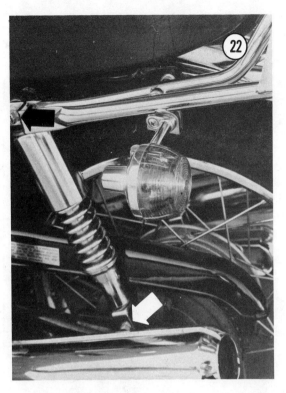

3. Compress the suspension units with special tool No. 07035-32901 (**Figure 21**). Remove the spring seat stoppers and the rear spring.

3. Refer to **Figure 23** and compress the suspension unit with the special tool, and disassemble the unit.

4. Remove the swing arm pivot nut (**Figure 24**), and remove the fork from the frame.

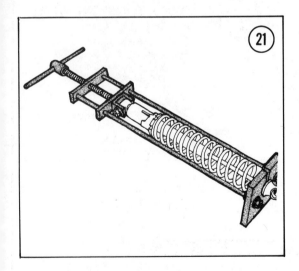

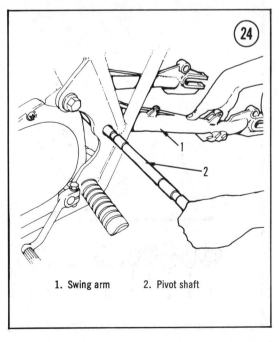

1. Swing arm   2. Pivot shaft

Disassembly (CB500/550)

1. Remove the muffler(s) and the rear wheel.

2. Remove the mounting nut and bolt and disengage the suspension from the frame and swing arm. See **Figure 22**.

10

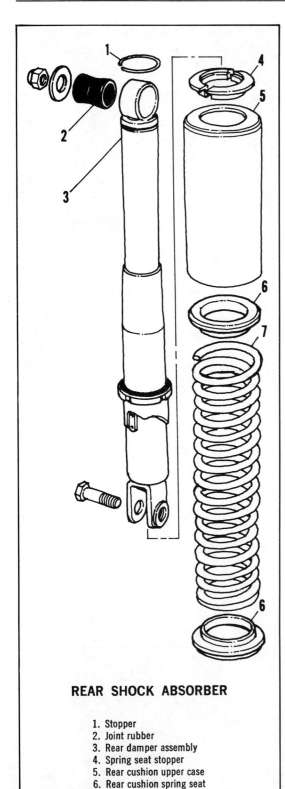

REAR SHOCK ABSORBER

1. Stopper
2. Joint rubber
3. Rear damper assembly
4. Spring seat stopper
5. Rear cushion upper case
6. Rear cushion spring seat
7. Rear cushion spring

(23)

Inspection

1. Measure the uncompressed length of the spring. Replace if less than the following limit:

> CB350: 8.07 in. (205mm)
> CB400: 8.28 in. (210mm)
> CB500/550: 7.48 in. (190mm)

2. Measure the inner diameter of the swing arm bushing with an inside dial indicator as shown in **Figure 25**. Serviceable limit of wear is:

> CB350: 0.855 in. (21.7mm)
> CB400: 0.849 in. (21.5mm)
> CB500/550: 0.859 in. (21.8mm)

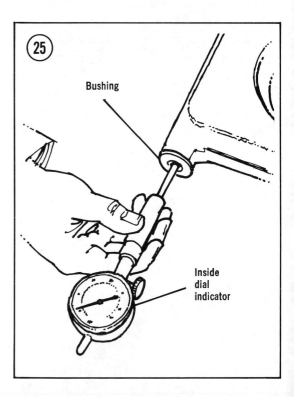

(25)

Bushing

Inside dial indicator

3. Measure the outer diameter of the center collar. The serviceable limit of wear is:

> CB350: 0.844 in. (21.35mm)
> CB400/500/550: 0.843 in. (21.4mm)

4. Measure the rear fork pivot bushing and its shaft. The clearance, calculated by subtraction, should not exceed 0.02 in. (0.5mm).

5. Check the various suspension members for bending or damage.

6. Inspect the damper for oil leaks.

Assembly

Assemble in reverse order of disassembly, referring to the exploded drawings and noting the following.

1. Grease the center collar and pivot bushing before assembling.

2. Adjust the rear brake and drive chain slack (Chapter Nine) when the suspension assembly is completed.

STRIPPING THE FRAME

1. Remove the fuel tank, seat, and battery. Be sure to disconnect ground cable at the negative (—) terminal first.

2. Remove the mufflers; dismount the engine.

3. Remove the front wheel, steering, and suspension.

4. Remove the rear wheel and suspension.

5. Remove electrical equipment, disconnecting the wiring at the couplings.

6. Remove the main and side stands.

7. Remove the bearing races from the steering head pipe with a wooden drift as shown in **Figure 26**.

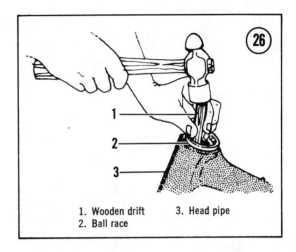

1. Wooden drift   3. Head pipe
2. Ball race

8. Check the frame for bending, cracks, distortion, or other damage, especially around welded joints.

9. Assembly is the reverse of these steps.

10

CHAPTER ELEVEN

PERFORMANCE IMPROVEMENT

While most of the publicity in motorcycling goes to the large-displacement, super-power multi-cylinder bikes, many owners have discovered that the smaller-displacement fours, marketed by most of the Japanese companies, are in many ways superior machines.

Almost without exception they're less expensive, more economical to operate (although about the same cost to maintain and rebuild), and offer vastly superior handling with only a slight loss in performance.

This is particularly true of the Honda 350-400-500-550 Fours — bikes which get far less praise than they deserve.

In addition to the already-mentioned virtues of a small multi-cylinder bike, the Hondas also accept performance increases with the same ease that their larger brother, the 750 Four, does. In fact, power can be increased amazingly — a built-up CB400 Four can offer acceleration almost equivalent to the superclass Kawasaki 900/1000, yet run rings around the bigger bike on a tight course.

There are many reasons to want more performance than just the desire to go racing.

Many owners of 350-550 Fours frequently ride with owners of bigger bikes. While the top end difference between a 750 and a 550 may not be much, the time it takes to get to that speed (or even to cruising speed) is significantly different.

For long distance riding, more power enables the rider to carry more gear with less strain on the engine, at better speeds.

For commuting on high speed throughways, instant power can spell the difference between getting out of someone's way and becoming a casualty.

With most motorcycles, particularly those of Japanese manufacture, horsepower increases should not be considered until the handling has been improved. All too many of these bikes have stock power far in excess of their stock handling capabilities. A machine with still greater horsepower may become actively hazardous to the unwary or full-tilt-boogie rider.

Fortunately, this is not the case with the smaller Honda Fours. Minor handling improvements should be made before power is increased — but these changes can be scheduled as normal replacement of worn-out OEM parts. **Table 1** at the end of the chapter lists manufacturers and services available for Honda 350-550 performance improvement.

Performance building should best be done on a step-by-step, month-by-month program, for two reasons:

1. With a planned program, the owner/builder will get the full benefits of each change when he makes it, not after further changes are made.

2. Planning keeps the budget reasonable and minimizes overbuilding the bike. A bike which

has twice the horsepower as stock, but develops it at 12,000 rpm is considerably less than fun. The owner will most likely find in such a case that he spends far less time riding his pride-and-joy hot rod than he did on the stock machine.

Caution should be used in building any of the small Fours. Performance costs money, and the more performance desired the more money must be spent. In many cases, it would be far more sensible to make minor improvements to a small Four, and then save money for the purchase of a larger-displacement Honda in the future.

Very little of the money invested in performance will be recovered when the bike is sold. Most used-bike purchasers are looking for a well-maintained stocker. They assume that a modified bike is flogged-out and too radical.

Performance improvements will be outlined in a step-by-step, model-by-model manner in this chapter. The suggestions are oriented toward the rider who wants a streetable machine though it may have minor, amateur competition possibilities.

TO BUILD OR
NOT TO BUILD

It is stongly suggested that one model of the Honda small Four line be left stock, and that the owner trade up to a larger machine if he wishes more performance.

This model is the Honda 350 Four. Even though all of the small Fours have been discontinued, the 350 was dropped quite a few years back. As a result, owners of this particular model may well have problems finding stock parts at their local dealers. Since performance, or more correctly, performance riding, is more likely to strain a bike than normal riding styles, there is little point in building up a machine that may have high downtime when it does break. In addition, since the 350 was not exactly Honda's biggest-selling bike, performance parts for the machine are hard to come by.

Owners of 350 Fours who absolutely must build their existing machine up would be advised to begin by upping the displacement to 400cc's. This may be done by removing the cylinder, and reboring the liner to accept stock Honda 400 pistons.

At significant expense, the 400 Four barrel may be fitted to the 350 engine. The engine may then be further built using top end components intended for the 400 Four. But, since conversion requires complete disassembly of the engine and hogging out the top case to accept the larger cylinder spigots, it's not recommended.

Any of the Honda Fours with 25,000 or more miles on them should be closely inspected and probably rebuilt before performance modifications are made.

Worn parts which are subjected to the increased stress of hotrod parts will break very rapidly. It is suggested that the owner of such a machine use high-quality performance parts rather than OEM parts whenever possible (such as clutch, valve springs, etc.). This will not only increase the lifespan of the engine in stock trim, but cut the cost of the later performance modifications.

MORE PERFORMANCE
WITH LESS DOLLARS

Gearing—All Models

For some reason, all of the Honda small Fours are highly overgeared. None of them can pull peak rpm in fifth (or sixth) gear in stock configuration. Since even if they could pull redline, that would be at a speed well over 100mph, regearing the bike for more low end power is sensible — an almost something-for-nothing performance boost.

The stock countershaft sprocket should be replaced with a one-tooth-smaller sprocket. This gives better off-the-line performance and acceleration. It also reduces the amount of clutch slipping necessary to get the bike underway, and reduces the strain on an already highly-stressed part of the drive train.

The only cost such a change will have (besides that of the sprocket itself) is that the bike will be pulling about 300 more rpm at a given speed than previously. Vibration will be slightly higher as will engine noise — neither significantly.

It is possible to use a still-smaller countershaft sprocket for greater low end performance, but this change is not recommended, due to the probability of creating too small a chain

11

travel circle around the sprocket, and causing drive chain kinking and damage. See **Figure 1**.

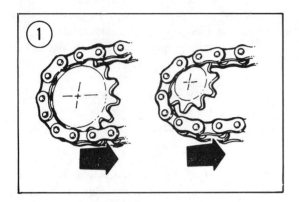

Oil Cooler—All Models

Heat is the enemy of engine longevity. Since all of the Honda small Fours normally run at fairly high temperatures, installation of an oil cooler is recommended on any of the Fours. This is particularly true if the bike is used for long distance riding. An oil cooler will generally reduce oil temperature 20-40 degrees — a significant amount.

When horsepower increases are made, an oil cooler is absolutely necessary. Increased compression and rpm make the engine run hotter. Furthermore, a performance-oriented rider will generally ride the bike harder than a casual commuting rider.

For normal riding, use the standard Lockhart Industries oil cooler. For competition riding, use a YRS oil cooler (**Figure 2**) on 350 or 400 Fours. On the 500 or 550's, use the large-capacity Lockhart cooler. This comes equipped with a thermostat (**Figure 3**) to prevent over-cooling of the oil in winter or when starting out.

Either of these kits can be bolted on in about fifteen minutes on any model.

Clutch — All Models

The weak point common to all of the Honda small Fours is the clutch. The problem is not so much that they're failure-prone as that they fail to hook up properly. Obviously when subjected to the strains of competition, hard street riding, or touring starts/stops in heavy traffic, they'll wear out very, very quickly.

Most of the problem lies in the overly-weak springs. The least expensive of the solutions to this problem is to install ⅛ inch thick shims below each clutch spring, to slightly preload it.

However, shimming springs can present an even more serious problem — the springs may bind when the clutch lever is fully depressed. In that case, the plates would remain in contact with each other, accelerating wear.

For most riding conditions, a better solution is to install Yoshima or S&W heavy-duty springs on 350 or 400 Fours, and Action Fours' springs on 500's and 550's.

These are easily installed using the procedure for stock clutch disassembly and assembly in Chapter Five.

When the clutch is disassembled, the stock fiber plates should be roughened with sandpaper, to remove surface glazing.

For drag-racing 500's or 550's, it is strongly suggested that the entire stock clutch pack be replaced with an Action Fours' kit (which includes replacement heavy-duty springs). See **Figure 4**.

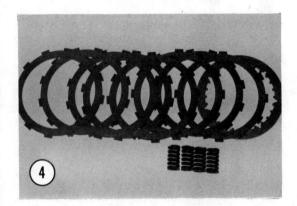

Still another solution is to install a heavy-duty clutch kit intended for use on Honda 350 twins, manufactured by Barnett Tool & Engineering. This will, indeed, give very positive hookups. However, it will be almost impossible to disengage the clutch when starting the engine cold, and the wear rate is very rapid. This kit is suggested for racing only.

Installation of heavy-duty springs will increase the clutch lever pressure. To reduce this slightly, and also increase cable life, a nylon-lined cable from Barnett Tool & Engineering should be used to replace the stock cable.

Clutch Actuating Rod—CB500

A frequent cause of sticky or occasionally-malfunctioning clutches on CB500's is a bent clutch actuating rod.

This rod should be removed from the bike and checked for straightness. The easiest way to do this is to roll it across a smooth glass plate. Any distortion will be readily apparent.

If bent, the dual-metal rod should be replaced with a late-model Honda 550K or CB350 twin rod, to prevent recurrence of the problem.

Rear Shocks—All Models

A major limiting factor in the handling of all of the Honda Fours is the stock rear shocks. They're under-sprung, provide inadequate damping, and have an extremely limited life-span (5,000 miles maximum).

The least expensive, and one of the best, replacement set of shocks to use is from S&W (**Figure 5**). These have better damping, are better made, and have longer life expectancy (in excess of 50,000 miles) than OEM shocks. This

modification will noticeably improve the handling and ride of *any* CB350-400-500-550.

The stock Honda rear springs should be replaced with 70-100 dual-rate S&W springs for solo riding, or 85-115 dual-rate S&W springs for two-up, touring, canyon, or competition riding.

Other, more expensive, conventional shocks are available from Koni or Girling.

For touring use, the S&W Airshocks (**Figure 6**), with their highly variable "spring" (actually a pressurized air reservoir) rate should be considered.

On the 500 and 550's, the S&W's will reduce the rear end height by approximately one inch. To keep front end rake and trail at stock figures, the triple clamp pinch bolts should be loosened and the front forks lowered an equivalent amount (**Figure 7**).

Air Filter—All Models

The better an engine breathes, the more power it can develop. The stock, restrictive air

11

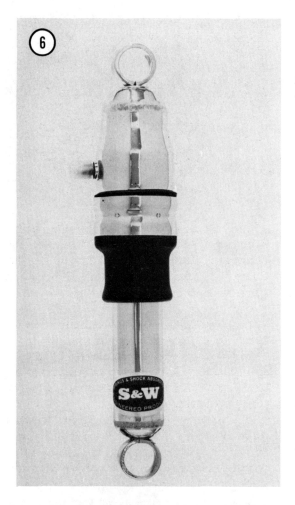

the oil directly into the air. However, this increases the possibility of contaminating the oil supply, and should not be done.

Under no circumstances should you ride a bike on the street without an air filter. This increases the probability of contaminants being sucked directly into the engine, which, at the very least, will radically shorten engine life.

Replacement of the stock air cleaner assembly with four small filters mounted directly to the carburetor bellmouth will not increase airflow, contrary to many people's beliefs. This modification should only be done when absolutely necessary, such as when changing the Honda 500-550 carburetors for a larger size (see *Carburetor Change—Honda 500 and 550*).

Swing Arm Bushing—All Models

A frequent cause of handling problems is a worn-out swing arm bushing.

This may be checked by removing the shocks at their lower mounts, and moving the rear wheel from side to side. If there is *any* perceptable movement, the bushing is worn out and should be replaced.

Rather than replace the bushing with an OEM part, use the Target Industries bushing kit. This consists of a replacement through shaft, fitted with a lube fitting, and two large plain bearings closely machined to the through shaft.

According to instructions, this part may be fitted to the bike with hand tools only. However, a power drill fitted with a grinding tip might be required, since the swing arm may need a slight amount of grinding to accept the new bushings.

With this bushing fitted, swing arm play will be reduced to nil. In addition, life expectancy of the bushing, with hard riding, will be well in excess of 20,000 miles.

cleaner should be removed, and replaced with a K&N model.

This OEM-sized part consists of two components — the filter and a replacement filter plate which contains a fitting for the oil vent line. Many riders simply cut the line, and vent

Tire—All Models

When the stock tires are worn out, replace them with stock-dimensioned Goodyear A/T tires.

These will provide greatly increased adhesion — well beyond the cornering limitations of the frames themselves — and acceptable lifespan.

Other excellent tires for the small Fours are available from Continental and Pirelli.

A swap to the large 16 inch rear tire (generally favored by chopper builders or touring riders) should be avoided by the performance-oriented rider, since all tires available in this size are built for maximum mileage rather than adhesion.

Overall

With the above-outlined modifications, any of the Honda multi-cylinder bikes will be far easier to ride, quicker and better-handling, even though no major modifications to the power-band have been made. For many riders, these modifications will make their bikes better enough machines for no further expensive improvements to be made.

Further modifications, of course, are not only possible but very practical — no reduction of the bike's rideability or reliability will be made, but power will be heavily increased.

At this point, although this has no effect on performance, the competition or performance rider may wish to fit rear-set pegs, clip-on, clubman or drag bars to improve his performance riding position (although these make riding excruciatingly uncomfortable over medium to long distances).

ENGINE

Big Bore Kit-CB400

Increasing an engine's displacement is the quickest, best and least expensive way to increase power throughout the rpm range, assuming of course that this increased size doesn't overstrain the engine.

The basic street big bore kit for the CB400 consists of a set of four cast pistons, plus rings, wrist pins, retainers, and new head gasket (**Figure 8**).

This increases displacement to 458cc's — the new piston diameter is 3mm oversize (54mm, with 54.5mm pistons available for overbore). The basic kit is available from Yoshimura R&D, a firm which has amassed an enviable reputation in production racing multi-cylinder machines over the past few years.

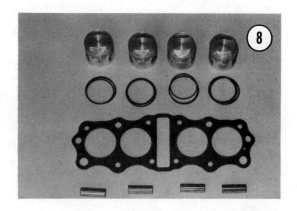

The second kit comes from Yoshima Racing, a new and small firm which has been phenomenally successful specializing in the 400 Fours. The Yoshima kit basically consists of a specially-modified version of the Yoshimura pistons.

Both work exceptionally well for street or street/track competition.

Installation consists of removal of the head and cylinder, reboring of the stock liners to the new dimensions, and reassembly of the engine with the kit parts.

It is strongly suggested that a performance camshaft be installed at this time, since most big bore kits are designed to work best with a specified performance shaft rather than the stock shaft (see *Camshaft* section).

Big Bore Kit—CB500

Two big bore kits may be installed on the CB500. Both of these will radically improve performance, and are ideal for the street. One kit, from Yoshimura R&D, increases compression ratio to 10:1, and displacement to 553cc's. The bore increases 3mm to 59mm (a 0.5mm set of pistons is available for overbore).

The second kit (**Figure 9**), from the famous drag-racing firm, Action Fours, also uses cast pistons. Compression ratio on this kit goes up to 11:1, and total displacement to 570cc's.

Both of these kits are designed to be used in bored-out stock liners, and both of them *must* be used in conjunction with a performance camshaft (see *Camshaft* section).

With either of these kits, care should be taken to run only the finest premium gas — one which does not have "clean-burning" additives

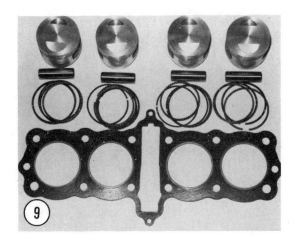

which cause the gas to burn measurably hotter than other brands.

A high-compression-only kit, intended for racing use, is also available from Yoshimura R&D. Like the other kits, it is intended for use with a performance cam.

Big Bore Kit-CB550

As with the 500, two big bore kits are available for the 550 Four. One, from Yoshimura, consists of 10:1 cast pistons which increase displacement to 592cc's; the second, from Action Fours, is a set of 11:1 cast pistons that put displacement to 590cc's.

Due to the CB550's cylinder liner, which is thinner than that used on the CB500, it is impossible to increase bore diameter more than 2.5mm over stock.

These kits, consisting of pistons, rings, wrist pins, clips and head gaskets, are meant to be installed in the overbored stock cylinder, and must be used with a high performance camshaft.

Camshaft—All Models

Choosing the correct camshaft for an engine is an area full of pitfalls. Very few people can translate terms like overlap, lift and duration into meaning for their own riding conditions and motorcycle.

Too many riders decide that, if they're spending the money for a cam, they should pick the hottest one available.

So, they go for a flat maximum horsepower rating, without realizing that this horsepower

rating is probably applicable from 10,000 to 10,500 rpm. That may be well and good for the skilled roadracer with an open track in front of him, but it isn't exactly ideal for the street rider who spends 80% of his time below 4,000 rpm dodging trucks.

Fortunately most reputable camshaft manufacturers give excellent, non-technical recommendations to any prospective customer who exactly and honestly specifies his riding conditions and power increase requirements.

It is strongly suggested that the camshaft chosen for a Honda multi Four be that recommended by the manufacturer of the big bore kit that you intend to install.

First of all, a good engine designer intends for cam and pistons to work together to produce maximum benefits. Secondly and more importantly, there may well be a problem in clearance if pistons are chosen from one manufacturer and camshaft from another. Unless you are prepared to spend a great deal of time checking valve-piston clearance before the engine is run, and very probably having to deck the pistons, go with the same manufacturer for the cam as you purchased your bore kit from.

Once a camshaft is chosen, it should be installed *exactly* as the manufacturer specifies. Use the specified valve springs, set up exactly to the instructions. Backyard ''trick tips'' that involve, say, triple shimming of valve springs, use of another brand of springs or installing the cam with ten or fifteen degrees further advance than specified may, at the least, result in severely decreased power, but could result in major engine damage.

Some of the camshafts mentioned below may be installed with stock springs. However, it is strongly suggested that heavy-duty springs specified by the manufacturer be used. Performance camshafts are almost without exception designed to permit more rpm than stock shafts. Use of stock springs with such a cam won't allow the engine to realize full benefits, since stock Honda springs allow valve float at about 9,000 rpm.

Camshaft—CB400

High performance camshafts for the CB400 are available from both Yoshima and Yoshimura R&D.

The Yoshimura cam, the "Road Special," may be installed with no head modification, and stock springs may be used (although use of the Yoshimura/S&W springs is highly recommended). Although this cam begins developing power from about 5,000 rpm, a big-bore-high-compression-kitted CB400 will still have far greater than stock power in the low rpm range, and scream in the upper rpm ranges.

A higher-performance (yet still streetable) camshaft is available from Yoshima Racing. An equivalent cam, the "Ontario Special," is also available from Yoshimura (**Figure 10**). This increases valve lift 1mm, and intake/exhaust opening/closing to 15/45 degrees.

It *must* be used with heavy-duty valve springs, since the new redline will be 11,000 rpm, and the stock springs permit valve float far below that figure. Yoshima uses S&W 550 Honda heavy-duty springs, with the stock Honda lower spring retainer.

In addition, the head must be modified before this camshaft will fit.

The head must be ground down slightly on either side to permit cam lobe clearance (**Figure 11**) and the valve throughshaft springs must be removed (**Figure 12**).

To prevent the valves from sliding on the shaft, an equivalently-sized washer should be installed on the throughshaft in place of the springs. These springs exist only to position the valves and, obviously, the valve springs will permit proper functioning of the valves when the engine is running.

Camshaft—CB500, CB550

Both Yoshimura and Action Fours offer two different camshafts for the 500/550 Four. Two of them, the Action Fours' DE grind and the Yoshimura TT Special (called the "Isle of Man" in Europe, **Figure 13**), are intended for competition use.

Far better suited to the street are either the Action Fours' DS grind (all Action Fours' camshafts are new billet grinds, made by longtime expert cam grinder Kenny Harmon), and Yoshimura's Street Special Grind.

Both fit into the stock head with no modifications required, and may be used with stock springs (although it is strongly suggested that either Action Fours' super-quality spring kit be used with the DS grind, or the S&W spring kit with the Yoshimura cam, since both cams permit redline increase to over 10,000 rpm).

Both of these cams offer small power increases at low rpm, with increasing benefits being realized as rpm's mount.

Oil Pump Modification—CB400

The CB400, when fitted with big bore high compression pistons and camshaft, and being ridden harder than normal, will run quite hot, even with an oil cooler.

A necessity for competition bikes, and one highly recommended for any modified 400, is the Yoshima oil pump.

⑩

11

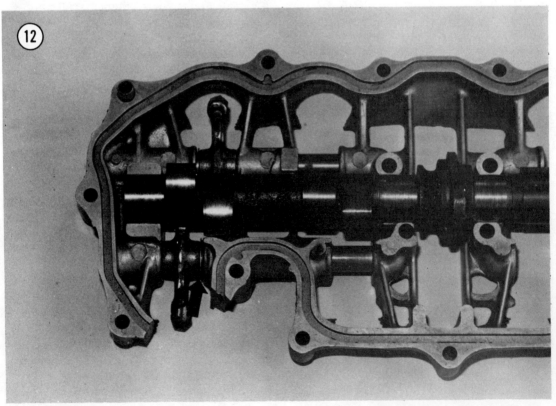

Installation of this 70mm part **(Figure 14)** requires removal of the oil pump cover, and machining the pump mount shaft base to match the shaft itself **(Figure 15)**. The new pump is then dropped into place and the pump cover reinstalled.

Exhaust Systems—All Models

Most performance-oriented cyclists begin engine power modifications by replacing the stock exhaust system with an accessory, "high performance" set of pipes.

However, this is not recommended on any of the small Honda Fours, except for full competition purposes.

There are many four-into-one or four-into-two exhausts available for these machines. However, most of them offer only two advantages: reduced weight and (sometimes) increased longevity over the stock set of pipes. Quite a few of them actually are more restrictive and therefore power-robbing than the supposedly low-power stock pipes. These generally offer only the illusion of increased performance by increasing the noise level.

The few that actually do increase power are also very noisy. A mild increase in noise level will generally make a bike neither obnoxious to other riders, motorists, and neighbors, nor will it become a ticket-getter.

All of the actual increased-performance exhausts available for the small Fours run not only at the borderline of being a major annoyance, but are quite illegal as well.

This is especially problematical with a built-up multi, since redline is generally raised well above stock. At full throttle such a built machine, running with a performance pipe is

11

almost guaranteed to get a ticket from the first cop who hears it.

Exhaust noise level should be of primary concern to all motorcyclists. Every loud bike that is ridden on the street puts cycling one step closer to being legislated out of existence. Under no circumstances should a builder/rider run a modified or open exhaust except under track competition conditions.

Connecting Rods—All Models

If the built-as-outlined Four will still see competition use, or if the CB400 will see another increase in bore size, the stock connecting rods should be replaced.

Heavy-duty connecting rods, available for the 400 from Yoshimura and Yoshima (**Figure 16**), and for the 500/550 from Yoshimura R&D, should be installed. These rods are all at least twice as strong as the stock parts, and are strongly recommended for any hard-ridden engine.

The super-cautious street builder may also wish to add these rods at this point in the modification of his machine, although the expense for many riders may well be prohibitive (cost of teardown/rebuild, plus well over $300 for the new rods).

Cam Chain—All models

A multi that will see prolonged high rpm use, or sudden drag-race-style shifting should have the stock cam chain replaced with a heavy-duty chain from Yoshimura R&D (**Figure 17**).

It is also very important that this chain be adjusted carefully. Do no depend on the spring

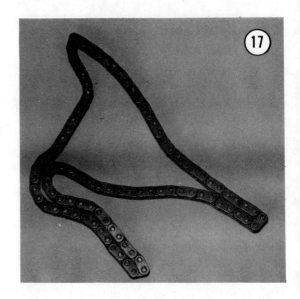

tensioner to automatically take up the slack when the locking bolt is loosened — the spring frequently hangs up. When loose, the locking bolt should be gently tapped with a wrench, or pushed with a finger, to make sure that the spring frees itself. Then tighten the lockbolt as normally specified.

Big Bore Kit—CB400

With heavy-duty rods installed in the engine, it is possible to make one more increase to the CB400's engine size. This kit (**Figure 18**), available from Yoshima or Yoshimura, increases displacement to 492cc's, and retains the 10.5:1 compression ratio used in the smaller big bore kit.

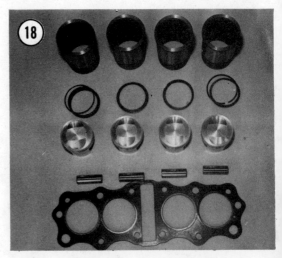

This modification requires removal of the stock liners, boring the cylinders to a larger diameter, and installation of new sleeves.

While serious horsepower increases will be made, for many riders the cost of this kit (kit plus labor plus connecting rods) renders the modification prohibitively expensive.

Ignition—All Models

The stock ignition system on the small Fours is acceptable for normal street riding conditions.

However, under consistent high rpm or competition use, it may well prove to be somewhat inadequate.

The weak point in the ignition system is the stock coils, which put out around 10,000 volts (high pressure firing may require around 18,000 volts to completely fire the mixture). The stock coils should be removed and replaced with two dual-wire high-output Andrews Products coils, which are rated at 30,000 volts.

Attempts to replace the stock coils with four inexpensive single automotive type coils, a modification which is recommended for some motorcycles, have not proven successful on four-cylinder machines, and this modification should be avoided.

For high rpm riding, the ignition points may be double-sprung — an additional set of springs should be installed on each set of points. This will reduce the possibility of points bounce at high rpm, although it will be at the expense of increased points and points cam wear.

For those CB500/CB550 owners interested in reliability, the set-and-forget Martek CDI ignition system from Action Fours may be installed. Since there is no metal-metal contact (firing being triggered by a small light beam), there will be no points wear. No power increases, however, will be made.

Competition-only riders may wish to install Yoshimura's magneto ignition system. This should not be done on any street machine, since there is no provision for the legally-required battery or lighting circuitry with this kit.

Head Porting—All Models

Head porting (**Figure 19**) is an area of performance modification which is simple in

theory, but exceedingly complex in practice. Since no special tools are required other than a dremel-type high speed minigrinder and an assortment of tips, many rider/builders feel that they can get in and root around, and get free (except for the labor) horsepower.

However, amateur headwork is almost certainly going to result in decreased performance, and may well produce a ruined head.

Head porting should only be done by a reputable, experienced motorcycle head porting service such as Yoshimura, Yoshima, Action Fours (who uses Branch Flowmetrics) or any other competition-known service.

Since all of the small Fours have fairly decent intake and exhaust ports in stock configuration, most of the benefits gained by porting these bikes will be on the top end.

Interestingly enough, porting is one of the few horsepower modifications that actually increase economy — the work of improving intake/exhaust flow means that the engine will be running with significantly greater efficiency.

Normally, porting on these machines is rather mild, consisting of little more than smoothing and slight recontouring of the ports. However, a competition job of porting on the CB400 will include sinking the valves 1mm into the head, to prevent possible valve-piston intersection at high rpm.

Trick Valves—All Models

It is possible to have slightly oversize, lightened or stainless steel valves installed in any of the small Four heads. This should most economically be done when the porting job is ordered.

These modifications, though, will be mainly of benefit to racers only, and are of little use to the street or street-track oriented owner-builder.

Carburetor Change—CB400

For competition only, the CB400 may be fitted with Keihin CR carburetors (**Figure 20**). These carburetors give vastly improved flow rates and, at high rpm, allow the engine to develop still more power than one equipped with the stock mixers.

However, due to their complete lack of a choke assembly and rather poor low speed metering, the CR's have proven themselves rather unsatisfactory for street use, and should be avoided by the non-competition builder.

Carburetor Change—CB500, CB550

Keihin CR carburetors are also available for the 500 and 550 Fours from Yoshimura, but the same objection to their use for anything other than competition applies here as it does to the CB400.

A better modification to the completely-built yet still street-ridden 500 or 550 is to replace the stock carburetors with a set of 28mm slide-needle Keihin carburetors used stock on the Honda 750 Four.

These will mate to the existing spigot mounts on the smaller Four, although it will be necessary to slightly ding the gas tank to permit the carburetor linkage the proper clearance on No. 2 and No. 3 cylinders.

Jetting should begin with a 120 main jet, the needle clip in the second position from the top, and one size leaner-than-stock pilot jet installed.

This is a baseline suggestion only, and it is strongly recommended that setting up these carburetors be done either by an experienced owner or by a qualified motorcycle performance shop.

Gearing—All Models

With a completely built engine, it is possible to modify the gearing more extensively. Any four modified to the level outlined in this chapter is capable of pulling more than the stock redline in high gear.

Obviously these recommendations are general, and the rider must make his own changes to meet his personal riding desires and needs.

The CB500's gearing may be changed to a 17 tooth countershaft sprocket, 34 tooth rear sprocket; the CB550 to a 17 tooth countershaft and 37 tooth rear sprocket. These sprockets are available from Action Fours (**Figure 21**). Other sprocket sizes are also available. If the 500 or 550 has been fitted with an oversize tire, two more teeth should be added to the rear sprocket to compensate for the increased drag.

The CB400's gearing may be changed to a 40-42 tooth rear sprocket, depending again on riding conditions. This sprocket may be ordered from Yoshima Racing (**Figure 22**).

HANDLING

Front Forks—All Models

To further improve handling, the CB400 should have the stock fork springs replaced with 70-100 dual-rate S&W springs (**Figure 23**).

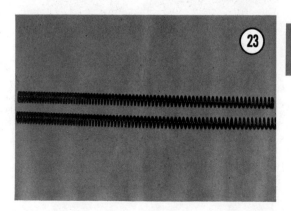

No heavy-duty fork springs are available for either the CB500 or CB550. However, it is possible to slightly preload the springs by installing a 2mm spacer above the fork springs, under the fork caps **(Figure 24)**.

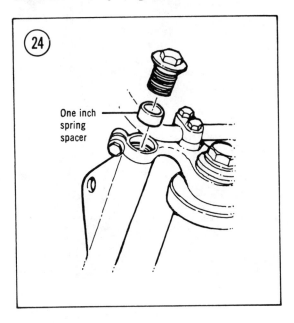

All model Fours should have the stock fork oil replaced with Torco 20-weight fork oil, for slightly improved damping action.

Wheels—All Models

Some reduction in unsprung weight may be made by replacing the stock rims with lightweight Akront or Borrani rims.

However, a better, if more expensive, improvement is to install a set of cast alloy wheels. These will offer slightly reduced wheel weight, vastly increased wheel rigidity (and therefore improved handling) and lessened maintenance time.

Two different wheels are readily available — either the cast wheels from Lester Tire & Wheel, or wheels from Morris Industries.

The Lester Wheel is a bolt-up installation, using both the stock front disc brake and the rear drum brake.

The Morris Wheel uses the stock front disc, but the rear drum must be replaced with an accessory rear disc assembly. Most recommended for street riders is the Grimeca system, available from Morris.

It will be necessary to have a caliper mounting bracket, master cylinder mounting bracket and pedal linkage custom fabricated for your bike after the Grimeca system is purchased, however.

Disc Brakes—All Models

While the stock front disc brake on the Honda multi-cylinders provides excellent stopping power with good control under normal conditions, the stock brakes are fairly close to useless in the rain.

The problem is water buildup on the discs. When the brake is actuated, the puck skates on this film of water. The rider then generally exerts more force on the level — just as the puck scrubs the film from the disc and hooks up with too much force, causing, at the least, a skid and at the most a serious catastrophe.

A common solution in Europe is to replace the stock stainless discs with cast iron discs, available from a number of makers. This will, indeed, solve the problem — but at the expense of looks. Cast iron will rust instantly, and it requires constant and time-consuming maintenance to keep it even slightly decent-looking.

A far better solution is to drill the discs **(Figure 25)**. This modification consists of drilling holes up to ½ inch in diameter laterally through the disc. In the rain, water is then quickly squeezed from between the puck/disc contact area and braking stays approximately the same in wet or dry conditions.

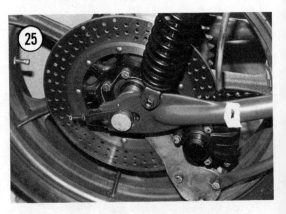

This modification should only be done by an experienced shop. It is possible to drill too many holes, and weaken the disc. If a disc breaks, instant wheel lockup and a crash are guaranteed. In addition, the stainless steel discs require some expertise in drilling to prevent ruining the surface. After drilling, the holes should be slightly countersunk on either size to keep the disc from having a cheesegrater effect on the puck.

This modification may be done inexpensively (around $30) by mail from Bill Bowman, Inc.

Dual Front Disc Brakes—All Models

European owners of 500/550 Hondas have an advantage when building their machines for competition or enthusiastic street riding — the stock left front fork leg is equipped with a mounting bracket for a second disc brake. A complete dual disc kit, from Yoshimura, may be ordered through David Dixon and quickly mounted to the bike.

American-marketed Fours may also have a dual disc added, but at hellish expense. It will be necessary to have a mounting bracket made and heliarced to the lower fork leg (**Figure 26**). Since there is a good possibility that the leg may be weakened by bad welding, the modification must be done by an extremely experienced welder.

When the bracket is mounted, a complete disc, caliper, and bracket may be purchased from a Honda dealer and mounted on the bike. Dual stainless steel brake lines may be custom-ordered from Earl's Supply.

OVERALL

The Honda 350-400-500-550 series motor-cyles have not only proven their reliability and performance in stock trim, but in highly modified form as everything from stoplight-to-stoplight street power bikes to full-on roadracers.

It is a tribute to the engineering excellence of Honda that these modified machines, produc-ing up to 50%-greater-than-stock power, are ridden with no loss in rideability or reliability. In spite of their discontinuation, it's obvious that the Honda small Fours will be around for a good many years to come.

11

Table 1   MANUFACTURERS AND SERVICES

Manufacturer	Service
Action Fours 1517 E. McFadden Santa Ana, Calif. 97205	All high performance parts and engine building
Andrews Products 9872 Farragut St. Rosemont, Ill. 60018	Coils
Barnett Tool & Engrg. 4915 Pacific Vernon, Calif. 90058	Clutch kits, clutch springs, cables
Bill Bowman, Inc. 2546 Manhattan Ave. Montrose, Calif. 91020	Disc brake drilling
Branch Flowmetrics 2625 Lime St. Long Beach, Calif.	Porting
David Dixon 1 High St. Godalming, Surrey, England GU7-1AZ	European Yoshimura R&D distributor
Earl's Supply 14611 S. Hawthorne Blvd. Lawndale, Calif. 90260	Braided steel line
The Lester Tire & Wheel Co. 26118 Cannon Road Bedford Heights, Ohio 44146	Cast alloy wheels
Morris Industries 2901 W. Garry Ave. Santa Ana, Calif. 92704	Cast alloy wheels, disc brake components
S&W Engineered Products 2617 W. Woodland Dr. Anaheim, Calif. 92801	Shocks, fork springs, valve springs
Yoshima Racing 1079 Burbank Blvd. North Hollywood, Calif. 91601	All high performance products, engine building
Yoshimura R&D of America 5517 Cleon Ave. North Hollywood, Calif. 91601	All high performance products, engine building

APPENDIX

GENERAL SPECIFICATIONS

This section contains specifications and performance figures for the various Honda models covered by this book. The tables are arranged in order of increasing engine size.

GENERAL SPECIFICATIONS, CB350

Dimensions	Overall length	81.1 in. (2,060mm)
	Overall width	30.7 in. (780mm)
	Overall height	42.9 in. (1,090mm)
	Wheelbase	53.3 in. (1,355mm)
	Seat height	30.7 in. (780mm)
	Foot peg height	11.8 in. (300mm)
	Ground clearance	6.1 in. (155mm)
	Dry weight	373 lbs. (170 kg)
Frame	Type	Semi-double cradle
	Front syspension, travel	Telescopic fork, travel 4.5 in. (114.6mm)
	Rear suspension, travel	Swing arm, travel 3.6 in. (91.0mm)
	Front tire size, pressure	3.00-18 (4PR), 26 psi (1.8 kg/cm^2)
	Rear tire size, pressure	3.50-18 (4PR), 28 psi (2.0 kg/cm^2)
	Front brake, lining area	Disc brake lining swept area 44.8 sq. in. (288 cm^2)
	Rear brake, lining area	Internal expanding shoes, lining swept area 23 sq. in. (150 cm^2)
	Fuel capacity	3.2 U.S. gal., 2.6 Imp. gal. (12 lit.)
	Fuel reserve capacity	0.5 U.S. gal., 0.4 Imp gal. (2 lit.)
	Caster angle	63° 40′
	Trail length	3.3 in. (85mm)
	Front fork oil capacity	4.2 ozs. (125cc)
Engine	Type	Air cooled, 4-stroke OHC engine
	Cylinder arrangement	Vertical four, parallel
	Bore and stroke	1.850×1.969 in. (47.0×50.0mm)
	Displacement	21.1 cu. in. (347cc)
	Compression ratio	9.3:1
	Valve train	Chain driven overhead camshaft
	Maximum horsepower	32 HP/9,500 rpm (SAE J245 at transmission shaft output)
	Maximum torque	19.5 ft.-lb./8,000 rpm (2.7 kg-m/8,000 rpm)
	Oil capacity	3.7 U.S. qt., 3.1 Imp. qt. (3.5 lit.)
	Lubrication system	Forced-feed and wet sump
	Cylinder head compression pressure	170.7 psi (12 kg-cm^2)
	Intake valve Opens	At 5° (before top dead center)
	Closes	At 35° (after bottom dead center)
	Exhaust valve Opens	At 35° (before bottom dead center)
	Closes	At 5° (after top dead center)
	Valve tappet clearance	Intake & exhaust 0.002 in. (0.05mm)
	Idle speed	1,200 rpm
Carburetor	Type	Piston valve
	Setting mark	656 c
	Main jet	#75
	Slow jet	#35
	Air screw opening	$\frac{7}{8} \pm \frac{3}{8}$
	Float height	0.827 in. (21mm)

(continued)

GENERAL SPECIFICATIONS, CB350 (continued)

Drive train	Clutch	Wet, multi-plate type
	Transmission	5-speed, constant mesh
	Primary reduction	3.423
	Gear ratio, 1st	2.733
	Gear ratio, 2nd	1.850
	Gear ratio, 3rd	1.416
	Gear ratio, 4th	1.148
	Gear ratio, 5th	0.965
	Final reduction	2.235
	Gearshift pattern	Left foot operated return system
Electrical	Ignition	Battery and ignition coil
	Starting system	Starting motor and kickstarter
	Alternator	A.C. generator 5,000 rpm/0.156 kW
	Battery capacity	12V-12AH
	Spark plug	NGK D8ESL ND X24ES
	Headlight	Low/high beam 12V-35W/50W
	Tail/stoplight	A4828
	Turn signal light	A4527
	Indicator lights	A72

12

GENERAL SPECIFICATIONS, CB400

Dimension	Overall length	80.3 in. (2,040mm)
	Overall width	27.8 in. (705mm)
	Overall height	40.9 in. (1,040mm)
	Wheelbase	53.3 in. (1,355mm)
	Seat height	31.1 in. (790mm)
	Foot peg height	13.0 in. (330mm)
	Ground clearance	5.9 in. (150mm)
	Dry weight	375 lb. (170 kg)
Frame	Type	Semi-double cradle
	Front suspension, travel	Telescopic fork, travel 4.5 in. (114.5mm)
	Rear suspension, travel	Swing arm, travel 3.1 in. (79.0mm)
	Front tire size, pressure	3.00S-18 (4PR), air pressure 26 psi (1.8 kg/cm²)
	Rear tire size, pressure	3.50S-18 (4PR), air pressure 28/36 psi (2.0/25 kg/cm²)
	Front brake, lining area	Disc brake, lining swept areas 5.9 sq. in. (38 cm²)
	Rear brake, lining area	Internal expanding shoes, lining swept areas 10.9 sq. in. (70 cm²)
	Fuel capacity	3.7 U.S. gal., 3.1 Imp. gal. (14 lit.)
	Fuel reserve capacity	0.8 U.S. gal., 0.7 Imp. gal. (3 lit.)
	Caster angle	63° 30′
	Trail length	3.3 in. (85mm)
	Front fork oil capacity	5.6-5.8 ozs. (160-165cc) to fill if dry
	Front fork oil capacity	4.8-4.9 ozs. (145-150cc) refill after draining
Engine	Type	Air cooled, 4-stroke OHC engine
	Cylinder arrangement	Vertical four, parallel
	Bore and stroke	2.008 × 1.969 in. (51.0 × 50.0mm)
	Displacement	24.9 cu. in. (408cc)
	Compression ratio	9.4:1
	Valve train	Chain driven overhead camshaft
	Oil capacity	3.7 U.S. qt., 3.1 Imp. qt. (3.5 lit.)
	Lubrication system	Forced and wet sump
	Cylinder head compression pressure	170.7 psi (12 kg/cm²)
	Intake valve Opens	5° before top dead center
	Intake valve Closes	35° after bottom dead center
	Exhaust valve Opens	35° before bottom dead center
	Exhaust valve Closes	5° after top dead center
	Valve tappet clearance	Intake & exhaust 0.002 in. (0.05mm)
	Idle speed	1,200 rpm
Carburetor	Type	Piston valve
	Setting mark	054-A
	Main jet	No. 75
	Slow jet	No. 40
	Air screw opening	2 ± ½ turns
	Float height	0.827 in. (21mm)

(continued)

GENERAL SPECIFICATIONS, CB400 (continued)

Drive train	Clutch	Wet, multi-plate type
	Transmission	6-speed, constant mesh
	Primary reduction	3.423:1
	Gear ratio, 1st	2.733:1
	Gear ratio, 2nd	1.800:1
	Gear ratio, 3rd	1.375:1
	Gear ratio, 4th	1.111:1
	Gear ratio, 5th	0.965:1
	Gear ratio, 6th	0.866:1
	Final reduction	2.235:1
	Gearshift pattern	Left foot operated return system
Electrical	Ignition	Battery and ignition coil
	Starting system	Starting motor and kickstarter
	Alternator	Alternator 5,000 rpm/0.156 kw
	Battery capacity	12V-12AH
	Spark plug	NGK D8ESL, ND X24ES
	Headlight	Low/high beam 12V-35W/50W
	Tail/stoplight	A4828
	Turn signal light	A4527
	Indicator lights	A72

12

GENERAL SPECIFICATIONS, CB500

Dimensions	Overall length	83.0 in. (2,105mm)
	Overall width	32.5 in. (825mm)
	Overall height	44.0 in. (1,115mm)
	Wheelbase	55.5 in. (1,405mm)
	Seat height	31.7 in. (805mm)
	Foot peg height	12.4 in. (315mm)
	Ground clearance	6.5 in. (165mm)
	Dry weight	403.5 lb. (183 kg)
Frame	Type	Double cradle tubular steel
	Front suspension, travel	Telescopic fork, travel 4.8 in. (121mm)
	Rear suspension, travel	Swing arm, travel 3.1 in. (78.5mm)
	Front tire size, type	3.25-19 (4 PR)
		25.6 psi (1.8 kg-cm^2)
	Rear tire size, type	3.50-18 (4 PR)
		28.5 psi (2.0 kg-cm^2)
	Front brake, lining area	Disc brake, lining area
		32.36 in.$^2 \times 2$ (288.8 cm$^2 \times 2$)
	Rear brake, lining area	Internal expanding shoe, lining area
		26.28 in.$^2 \times 2$ (169.6 cm$^2 \times 2$)
	Fuel capacity	3.7 U.S. gal., 3.1 Imp. gal. (14.0 lit.)
	Fuel reserve capacity	1.1 U.S. gal.,0.9 Imp. gal. (4.0 lit.)
	Caster angle	64°
	Trail length	4.1 in. (105mm)
	Front fork oil capacity	5.4 ozs. (160cc)
Engine	Type	Air-cooled, 4-stroke, OHC engine
	Cylinder arrangement	4-cylinders in line
	Bore and stroke	2.205 $\times$ 1.992 in. (56.0 $\times$ 50.6mm)
	Displacement	30.38 cu. in. (498cc)
	Compression ratio	9.0:1
	Carburetor, venturi dia.	Four, piston valve; 22mm dia.
	Valve train	Chain drive overhead camshaft
	Maximum horsepower	50 BHP (SAE)/9,000 rpm
	Maximum torque	30.4 ft.-lb./7,500 rpm
		(4.2 kg-m/7,500 rpm)
	Oil capacity	3.2 U.S. qt., 2.6 Imp. qt. (3.0 lit.)
	Lubrication system	Forced pressure and wet sump
	Air filtration	Paper element
	Valve tappet clearance	Intake: 0.002 in., Exhaust: 0.003 in.
		(Intake: 0.05mm, Exhaust: 0.08mm)
	Engine weight	152 lb. (69 kg)
	Air screw opening	1 $\pm$ 1/8 turns
	Idle speed	1,000 rpm
Drive train	Clutch	Wet, multi-plate
	Transmission	5-speed, constant mesh
	Primary reduction	3.063
	Gear ratio, 1st	2.353
	Gear ratio, 2nd	1.636
	Gear ratio, 3rd	1.269
	Gear ratio, 4th	1.036
	Gear ratio, 5th	0.900
	Final reduction	2.000, drive sprocket 17 teeth,
		driven sprocket 34 teeth
	Gearshift pattern	Left foot return type

(continued)

GENERAL SPECIFICATIONS, CB500 (continued)

Electrical	Ignition	Battery and ignition coil
	Starting system	Starting motor and kickstarter
	Alternator	Three phase A.C. 12V-0.2 KW/5,000 rpm
	Battery capacity	12V-12AH
	Spark plug	NGK D-7 ES, DENSO X-22 ES
	Headlight	Low/high, 12V-40W/50W
	Tail/stoplight	A4828
	Turn signal light	A4527
	Indicator lights	A72

12

GENERAL SPECIFICATIONS, CB550

Dimensions	Overall length	83.5 in. (2,120mm)
	Overall width	32.5 in. (825mm)
	Overall height	43.9 in. (1,115mm)
	Wheelbase	55.3 in. (1,405mm)
	Seat height	31.7 in. (805mm)
	Foot peg height	12.4 in. (315mm)
	Ground clearance	6.5 in. (165mm)
	Dry weight	423.0 lb. (192 kg)
Frame	Type	Double cradle tubular steel
	Front suspension, travel	Telescopic fork, travel 4.8 in. (121mm)
	Rear suspension, travel	Swing arm, travel 3.0 in. (77.3mm)
	Front tire size, type	3.25-19 (4 PR) rib 28.0 psi (2.0 kg-cm^2)
	Rear tire size, type	3.75-18 (4 PR) block 34.0 psi (2.4 kg-cm^2)
	Front brake, lining area	Disc brake, lining area 32.36 in.$^2 \times 2$ (288.8 cm$^2 \times 2$)
	Rear brake, lining area	Internal expanding shoe, lining area 26.28 in.$^2 \times 2$ (169.6 cm$^2 \times 2$)
	Fuel capacity	3.7 U.S. gal., 3.1 Imp. gal. (14.0 lit.)
	Fuel reserve capacity	1.1 U.S. gal., 0.9 Imp. gal. (4.0 lit.)
	Caster angle	64°
	Trail length	4.1 in. (105mm)
	Front fork oil capacity	6.5 ozs. (190cc)
Engine	Type	Air-cooled, 4-stroke, OHC engine
	Cylinder arrangement	4-cylinders in line
	Bore and stroke	2.303 × 1.992 in. (58.5 × 50.6mm)
	Displacement	33.19 cu. in. (544cc)
	Compression ratio	9.0 : 1
	Carburetor, venturi dia.	Four, piston valve; 22mm dia.
	Valve train	Chain drive overhead camshaft
	Maximum horsepower	50 BHP (SAE)/8,500 rpm
	Maximum torque	30.4 ft.-lb./7,500 rpm (4.2 mkg/7,500 rpm)
	Oil capacity	3.2 U.S. qt., 2.6 Imp. qt. (3.0 lit.)
	Lubrication system	Forced pressure and wet sump
	Air filtration	Paper element
	Valve tappet clearance	Intake: 0.002 in., Exhaust: 0.003 in. (Intake: 0.05mm, Exhaust: 0.08mm)
	Engine weight	159 lb. (72 kg)
	Air screw opening	1½ ± ⅜ turns
	Idle speed	1,000 rpm
Drive train	Clutch	Wet, multi-plate
	Transmission	5-speed, constant mesh
	Primary reduction	3.063
	Gear ratio, 1st	2.353
	Gear ratio, 2nd	1.636
	Gear ratio, 3rd	1.269
	Gear ratio, 4th	1.036
	Gear ratio, 5th	0.900
	Final reduction	2.176, drive sprocket 17 teeth, driven sprocket 37 teeth
	Gearshift pattern	Left foot return type

(continued)

GENERAL SPECIFICATIONS, CB550 (continued)

Electrical	Ignition	Battery and ignition coil
	Starting system	Starting motor and kickstarter
	Alternator	Three phase A.C. 12V-0.11 KW/2,000 rpm
	Battery capacity	12V-12AH
	Spark plug	NGK D-7 ES, DENSO X-22 ES
	Headlight	Low/high, 12V-40W/50W
	Tail/stoplight	A4828
	Turn signal light	A4527
	Indicator lights	A72

12

TORQUE SPECIFICATIONS — ALL MODELS

ENGINE		
	Torque	
Tightening Point	**ft.-lb.**	**kg-cm**
Crankcase and crankcase covers	5-8	70-110
Cylinder head	15 Apply oil to the nuts before tightening	200 (Apply oil to the nuts before tightening)
Carburetor insulator-to-cylinder head	5-8	70-110
Cam sprocket	12-15	160-200
Alternator rotor	22-29	300-400
Primary drive gear	22-29	300-400
Tappet adjusting nut	5-8	70-110
Upper and lower crankcases	15-19	220-260
Cylinder head cover	5-8	70-110
Clutch center	29-33	400-450
Connecting rod	14-15	200-220

FRAME		
	Torque	
Tightening Point	**ft.-lb.**	**kg-cm**
Steering stem nut	58-87	800-1,200
Fork top bridge to front forks	13-17	180-230
Handlebar holder	13-17	180-230
Front fork bottom bridge to front forks	13-17	180-230
Spokes		
Front wheel	1.9-2.2	25-30
Rear wheel	1.5-1.9	20-25
Swing arm pivot bolt	40-50	550-700
Front axle nut	33-40	450-550
Front fork axle holder	13-17	180-230
Engine hanger bolt	22-29	300-400
Rear axle nut	58-72	800-1,000
Final driven sprocket	29-36	400-500
Brake arm	6-7	80-100
Front and rear brake torque links	13-17	180-230
Rear shocks	22-29	300-400
Foot peg	33-40	450-550
Gear change pedal and kick arm	6-7	80-100

INDEX

13

13

Do-It-Yourself Boat Maintenance

The world's largest publisher of automotive and motorcycle manuals now offers a complete line of maintenance and tune-up handbooks for owners of sailboats, powerboats, outboard motors, stern drive units, and small inboard engines.

Each title features step-by-step procedures for maintaining and repairing the hull, fittings, interior, electrical systems, plumbing, galley equipment, and the countless other items that keep boat owners busy.

As in all Clymer handbooks, the expert text and detailed photos and illustrations will put money-saving maintenance well within the reach of anyone reasonably handy with tools.

The titles listed below are available through your local bookstore, marine outlet, or postpaid direct from Clymer Publications.

SAILBOAT MAINTENANCE . . . . (B600) $9.00

POWERBOAT MAINTENANCE . . . . (B620) $9.00

BRITISH SEAGULL OUTBOARDS, 1.5 TO 6 HP . . . . (B660) $8.00

CHRYSLER OUTBOARDS, 3.5 TO 20 HP, 1966-1977 . . . (B655) $8.00

CHRYSLER OUTBOARDS, 25 TO 135 HP, 1966-1977 . . . (B657) $8.00

EVINRUDE OUTBOARDS, 1.5 TO 33 HP, 1965-1977 . . . (B644) $8.00

EVINRUDE OUTBOARDS, 40 TO 140 HP, 1965-1977 . . (B647) $8.00

JOHNSON OUTBOARDS, 1.5 TO 33 HP, 1965-1977 . . . (B663) $8.00

JOHNSON OUTBOARDS, 40 TO 140 HP, 1965-1977 . . . (B665) $8.00

MERCURY OUTBOARDS, 4 TO 40 HP, 1964-1977 . . . . (B650) $8.00

MERCURY OUTBOARDS, 50 TO 150 HP, 1964-1977 . . . (B653) $8.00

SAILBOAT AUXILIARY ENGINES (Atomic, Chrysler,
   Ford, Perkins, Pisces, Volvo-Penta,
   Westerbeke, and Yanmar) . . . . (B610) $9.00

STERN DRIVE UNITS (OMC, MerCruiser, Volvo,
   Stern-Powr, Berkeley, and Jacuzzi) . . . . (B641) $9.00

CLYMER PUBLICATIONS

12860 MUSCATINE STREET • P.O. BOX 20 • ARLETA, CALIFORNIA 91331